SATURDAY NIGHT FOREVER

To Mike Childs, my oldest friend in
the world, and his wonderful wife
Sharon Kent
ALAN JONES

To my wife Tuija
JUSSI KANTONEN

Saturday
Night
Forever

The Story of Disco

Alan Jones and **Jussi Kantonen**

EDINBURGH AND LONDON

Revised and Updated, 2005

First published in Great Britain in 1999 by
MAINSTREAM PUBLISHING COMPANY
(EDINBURGH) LTD
7 Albany Street
Edinburgh EH1 3UG

ISBN 1 84596 067 X

A catalogue record for this book is available from
the British Library

Typeset in Allise, Apollo and Gill Sans
Printed and bound in Great Britain by
Cox & Wyman Ltd

Acknowledgements

The authors would like to thank Greg Day, as well as Lysette Anthony, Asia Argento, Mark Asworth, Steve Barlow, Paul Brown, Grant Burnside, Frederick S. Clarke, Ben Cobb, David Cox, Nigel Diamond, Fernando Dos Reis Prazeres, Tim Harvey, Jarmo Hepo-oja, Stefan Jaworzyn, Reijo Lammasniemi, Matthew Eugene Lemcio, Liisa Lankia, Annukka Leppänen, Frederic Albert Levy, Bernard E Lopez, Frances Lynn, David McGillivray, Maitland McDonagh, Paul McStravick, Aicha Mahjoubi, Minna Maunula, Michelle of Discostyle.com, Sami Montell, Russell Mulcahy, Rel Pinto, David Price, Jonathan Rutter, Geoffrey Robert Simm, Whit Stillman, Steve Swindells, Yuval Taylor, Anthony and Marguerite Timpone, Keith Williams and Kjell Wirum.

Acknowledgements are due to Whit Stillman and Castle Rock Entertainment for permission to reprint the dialogue from *The Last Days Of Disco*, and to A&M, Ariola, Atlantic, Barclay, Capitol, Casablanca, CBS, Columbia, Elektra, Prelude, Polydor, Polygram, RSO, Salsoul, TK and Warner Bros record labels.

Every effort has been made to acknowledge copyright holders in this book. The authors and publisher apologise if anyone has inadvertently been omitted.

Contents

'Disco will . . . never be over. It will always live in our minds and hearts. Something like this, that was this big and this important, and this great, will never die. Oh, for a few years, maybe for many years, it will be considered passé, and ridiculous. It will be misrepresented and caricatured and sneered at – or worse, completely ignored. People will laugh about John Travolta, Olivia Newton-John, white polyester suits and platform shoes, and going like this. [*Imitates Travolta dance pose*] Though we had nothing to do with those things and still loved disco. Those who didn't understand will never understand. Disco was much more and much better than all that. [*Pauses, looks around*] Disco was . . . too great and too much fun to be gone forever. It's got to come back, someday. I just hope that will be in our own lifetimes.'

Climactic dialogue as spoken by Josh, played by actor Matt Keeslar, in director Whit Stillman's *The Last Days Of Disco* (1998)

Preface

Disco is D – Delightful, I – Incredible, S – Supersexy, C – such a Comfort, it is Oh, oh, oh . . .

We believe in mirror balls.

If all disco means to you is records like 'I Will Survive' by Gloria Gaynor and 'YMCA' by the Village People, or recent CD compilations filled with early-'80s electro tracks plus tacky glitter '70s fashions and impossible-to-get-into nightclubs of the Studio 54 variety, this book should be a real eyeopener. Sure, the above description sums up disco on the mainstream surface and to the casual Saturday-night clubber. But it really was so very much more than a just camp footnote in pop history.

For every chart hit that pounded into the public's consciousness, there were fifty far superior tracks from all over the world created by talented producers being played at some hard-to-find basement club. Some of these cuts would enter the lower regions of the Top 100 six months later. Others would remain deliciously obscure and cause an ethereal trance-like beauty to envelop the disco fanatic whenever they were obsessively discussed in terms of the hair-raising highs they engendered on the dance floor.

This book is for those who loved disco so much it became a necessary soundtrack to their lifestyles as much as it is for the curious who have been fascinated by the recent massive interest in everything retro-'70s, from *Saturday Night Fever* to *Boogie Nights*.

Disco was a glamour-packed reaction against the plodding and self-indulgent rock music of the late-'60s overspill into the excitement-parched early-'70s. Created by people marginalised by their colour (black), class (working), race (Hispanic) or sexuality (gay), it was adopted by suburban trendies once the media gave it their signed, sealed and delivered approval. Yet, The Bee Gees and 'Stayin' Alive' were never disco and this book reveals why as it uncovers the multilayered genre in all its shining, strobe-lit glory.

The popularity of disco came about mainly because it was *Star Wars*, *Fantasia* and *Close Encounters* of the wildest kind all at once, all in one place and all to the hypnotic 'thump, thump, thump' of the latest cool sounds. Significantly, it was something you could enjoy entirely on your own. You didn't need a date. You didn't need a dance partner. You didn't have to touch anybody while you got lost in music. You didn't even need to make eye contact as you took your place amongst the best free floor show in town. Drugs? Sometimes. Sex? Often. The hustle? I'd love to!

This book came about because of a trip I made to Helsinki in the summer of 1991 with my good friend Greg Day, now head of publicity for Entertainment and Drama at Channel Five. Back then, though, he was the press officer for Entertainment at Channel Four and on the way to becoming the senior press officer for the network. We had both been invited to Finland by one of his childhood friends, Jussi Kantonen, to give lectures at the Jyväskylä Arts Festival. Jyväskylä is the suburban town in central Finland where Jussi is based as one of the area's leading architects. For the record, I was scheduled to give a lecture on the horror film genre, a subject on which I

12

write, broadcast and report extensively all over the world, and Greg delivered a talk on the inner workings of Channel 4.

Although I had met Jussi on previous occasions when he was visiting Greg in London, we were more acquaintances through our shared admiration of Italian horror films than close friends. That all changed one night when we went out to an open-air bar in central Helsinki and the subject of music came up. We both discovered we absolutely adored disco music and spent the rest of the night talking about our favourite albums, artists, dance moves and clubs. Our ravings continued throughout the next day as we drove to Jyväskylä and listened to endless disco mix tapes on the car stereo. We also drove Greg mad because we didn't make any effort to include him in the conversation – he was such a disco virgin. I mean, he thought Kat Mandu was an Asian province. Everyone knows that was the name credited to the brilliant disco galloper 'The Break' in 1979!

Greg and I returned to Jyväskylä twice over the next four years. Each time Jussi and I would have a non-stop disco discussion and go searching for those elusive CD reissues. (For some reason Finland has cornered the market in cheap disco compilations.) It was Greg's idea that we write a book on the subject – mainly, I think, because our enthusiasm rubbed off on him enough to make him go out and buy one of those 'Best Disco Album in the World . . . Ever' series. The diehard Abba fan even confessed to liking the music.

But the more I thought about a disco chronicle, the more it seemed a good idea. Although Jussi and I had had different upbringings, in completely different cultures, we both loved exactly the same songs, instrumental breaks, dances and clubs. He was married; I was not. He was a top disco deejay and the Latin Hustle Dance Champion of Finland in 1979; I was a mere punter in the disco movement and attendant lifestyle. Yet we shared the same experiences in nearly every area. Clearly, there were more people out there who had been touched by the magic of disco and were as desperate as we were to see the much-maligned genre given the respect and respectability it truly deserved. Neither of us has approached this book with rose-tinted glasses or some distorted sense of nostalgia. We've done it because we are part of a proud and defiant subculture and are not ashamed to admit we loved being there and being a part of the disco landscape. And because the music was so powerful and fantastic.

The result of our rabid fan-dom is now in your hands. What you are going to read is very much a personal odyssey through every aspect of disco culture, taking in all the relevant facts along the way. If it's a camp send-up you're expecting, you've got the wrong book. But if you want to gain some insight into the defining disco era and understand why those of us who danced through it will never forget the atmosphere, the fun or the thrill of the music, then the velvet ropes are being unhooked especially for you.

Come on, dance, dance.

Alan Jones

Introduction

It's two o'clock in the morning and I'm dripping with sweat in Glades (soon to be transformed into Heaven), a gay disco underneath the Arches at Villiers Street in London's West End. I'm coming down from my usual Wednesday night ritual (Glades was only operational on that night during the last years of the '70s) with the oh-so-predictable routine starting at my flat in Little Venice, Maida Vale, around seven o'clock in the evening.

What to wear was always the problem for clubbing in the just-happening Village People days. Leather was too hot if you were going to dance and I didn't intend merely to strike macho poses in the cramped confines of the club. Levi 501s didn't quite have the clone cachet they would eventually achieve either. Punk gear was out, too. I was working for Vivienne Westwood at the time in Sex, her Worlds End boutique, and practically lived in her de rigueur Sex Pistols outfits. But they were hopeless cruise wear. So many men seemed put off by fake track marks applied with a syringe full of stage blood to show up under a see-through tight black nylon top and bondage trousers. The outfit I'd invariably end up wearing would be army trousers (from Lawrence Corner, Euston) and a check shirt with the sleeves cut off and frayed at the edges. Simple, loose – yet tight in the right places – and perfect for throwing yourself around the disco floor, which, in the case of Glades, was quite a limited area. You'd have to cross it, too, to get from one end of the bar to the other, which could be so annoying.

Next step: meet everybody at Geoff's place off Tottenham Court Road. Who'll turn up tonight? More people if Art deigns to come. He always has the best drugs. Shall I drop some acid or swallow some dope? I can't smoke it – I hate people who smoke! No, I want to really dance the night away. So many fabulous new records have come out this week and I want to get lost in the music, especially 'Deliverance' by Space. I know deejay Chris, from the Catacombs in Earl's Court, will play it. He seems to have an instinctive ear for what I love to hear. Half an acid blotter it is.

Geoff, as usual, takes ages getting ready. His boyfriend Tom is bitching about the lime-green PVC biking trousers Geoff thinks he might like to wear. I tell him it doesn't matter in his case because he doesn't have to score, so he can look as much like a human lava lamp as he wants. Tom, of course, wants his friends (I can't believe he has any) at the club to be impressed by his main squeeze and is trying to charm the pants off him. Again! This from the guy who shoved large ball-bearings up Geoff's arse – he'd read about it improving one's sex life in the American magazine *Blueboy* – and when Geoff tried to get them out, he farted, and shattered the toilet he was sitting on at the time. The plumber just couldn't understand how the damage had occurred.

Art dithers in time-honoured fashion. Should he leave the cocaine behind in Geoff's flat? There's a chance it might liquidise in his pocket in the heat otherwise. But then he may need another line or two, or three, or four, later on in the evening. A chorus line shouts, 'Take it with you, Art', and we set off at 10.45 p.m. in order to get to the club by eleven – just before the pub-closing-time rush. Walking down Tottenham Court Road and Charing Cross Road, to the beginning of the Strand and the top of Villiers Street, we ignore all shouts from speeding cars of 'Poofs', 'Queers' and 'Pansies'. I kind of wish Geoff hadn't worn those lime-green trousers.

16

Glades is packed as always. Oh-oh, there's a Barbra Streisand drag act on tonight. I pray for the day when the powers-that-be stop thinking we need any entertainment other than the music. I hate it when the disco stops for some talentless queen to strut her junky stuff. We head up the staircase for the first-floor area (the ground floor of the one-time Global Village complex is closed off) and immediately get swept up in the ever-growing beat as we near the dance floor. I timed the acid drop perfectly. The sounds begin to wrap their notes around me; everything is sparkling, the lights look dazzling, there are some sexy guys lurking around and people are gyrating like demons to 'Lovin' Is Really My Game' by Brainstorm on the dance floor.

Home at last!

How does one describe disco to people who didn't experience it? Things aren't the same today, not by a long chalk. The drugs may be more 'designer', the venues open all night – and all day in some cases – and the people more image-conscious. But the music fuelled the lifestyle then, not vice versa. I can't think of any time, event, action or sexual encounter from the era without an appropriate disco track to accompany it. The day my first film feature was published in an American magazine I danced to Meco's 'Star Wars'. The roller-disco trip to Brighton we spent listening to 'Beautiful Bend' non-stop on the car's cassette deck. The night we took Keith from Heaven to the casualty ward after he broke his ankle dancing to Boys Town Gang's 'Can't Take My Eyes Off You'. The time I bought *Hunchback Of Notre Dame* by Alec R. Costandinos on import for £1.99 from Our Price Records, Queensway, when I was absolutely flat broke, because I couldn't wait to hear it. I wouldn't trade those musical memories for the world.

Those were the days when *Record Mirror* published disco charts and reviews by the sorely missed columnist/deejay James Hamilton. Likeminded fans would head to Track Records in Soho's Greek Street to hear all his recommendations for possible purchase. Knowing the words to the latest import sensations and singing along at the disco always earned jealous respect. I still have favourite cuts from the era I play each and every day, as there was an epic emotional richness to disco before the tyranny of the electronic keyboard set in that still catches in my throat and touches my heart. And anyone who always wondered why Patrick Juvet's 'Lady Night' faded out far too soon on one of the best disco violin breaks ever will know exactly what I mean.

Alan Jones

It's 1977 and the disco underground has yet to go global with *Saturday Night Fever*. Your record box is filled with diverse delights, hot new 12-inchers and albums straight from New York bound to lift everybody off the floor. You can throw down a scorching Latin set and watch the girls launch themselves into sinuous displays of hipswaying and fancy footwork. Or you can plunge deep into the roots of jazz and pump the crowd with 'Could Heaven Ever Be Like This' by Idris Muhammad. You know that will thrill the soul boys standing by the wall, solemnly nodding their heads to the beat.

Next you boost the bass and slip into the totally bizarre 'Heaven Is A Disco', the latest USA sensation which is causing Bible Belt controversy. The notorious Paul Jabara-penned mini-musical gets under way with thudding drums and the prologue 'Shut Out'. As sung by Jabara himself, the main character of this disco fantasy is a young man on a night out who is refused entrance to the hottest club in the town for not carrying an ID card. To his dismay, his friends are allowed in and so the victim of circumstance can only go back home and dance alone to his collection of Donna Summer records. The depressed guy sings a plea to his favourite *chanteuse,* who miraculously answers his prayers through the speakers and promises to take the boy out for a spin. Completely confused, the lonely dancer loses his grip on reality and commits suicide.

Miss Summer herself is on guard at the Pearly Gates to meet the recently deceased and asks him some hard and revealing questions. Subsequently chastised, the boy is forgiven for his sins and sent forward as the rejoicing chorus breaks into a triumphant hymn. The music twirls and gallops madly as we fly through the air and he makes his entrance on roller-skates. This is Heaven. The ultimate disco where the Lord is the deejay, the angels are the waiters and it's hotter than Hell! The ultimate party begins. Angel Dust is thrown around. The orchestra goes into overdrive. The exhorting chorus screams itself into a frenzy with 'Amens' and 'Hallelujahs'. The urgent command, 'Dance!', is screamed out as everybody prepares for an eternity lost in a swooning spiral of lush sounds and beats per minute.

Paul Jabara's classic disco passion play says it all. This is what disco meant for those who were there sweating and gyrating from early1973. Disco was life. Disco was *bigger* than life. The Jabara record is a perfect example of the cinematic versatility of music, where beloved genres are rendered so that it is the dancer, not the deejay, who gets to be the entertainer and the star. While some get completely lost in music and spend the night in a weird state of alert stupor, other more expressive dancers adapt themselves instantly to every mood change. Musical scenarios are acted out on the floor — bodies freeze at appropriate moments, the strobe lights shimmer off vast expanses of glistening skin, hands fly in the air as the melodic chorus breaks through.

This is why you love disco. You love its total hedonistic excess. You love it for its drive, punch and sweet, catchy melodies. Unlike the popular misconception of the day, this music does not all sound the same. It is more than just a synthesised engine repeating a musical formula *ad nauseam*. There was nothing greater for a deejay than to be rewarded with satisfied yelps and sighs from the flashing floor as one record segued seamlessly into another, meaning the committed dancer didn't have to move a muscle out of synch.

Deejays of the '70s were pioneers in what is now seen as being an art form in its own right: creating kaleidoscopic sonic textures by playing records. In its infancy, this meant little more than segueing together rhythmically matching songs within the same bpm range, or getting narrative ideas across with songs. The science of mixing was gradually learned by constant experimentation and countless pre-opening hours at the club trying out records and counting the beats with a metronome. And you had to travel.

Being a self-respecting deejay during the early disco years meant going on pilgrimages to such hallowed places as 12 West and Paradise Garage in New York or The City in San Francisco. You talked to the specialist dance store assistants, like the guys behind the counter at New York's Downstairs Records, to find out who was playing what, when and where. You hung around the counter for hours listening to the guys inspect the latest arrivals and spying at the labels. You scribbled down titles on little notes. At the clubs you memorised particularly thrilling segues and tried to recreate those dazzling displays of turntable virtuosity back on your home disco turf.

You had to develop your own style and your own sound that the dancers would come back for. All the latest imports mixed with Latin percussion breaks and lots of Euro instrumentation, for example. But you were there not to impress visiting deejays with your esoteric collection of French obscurities. You were there solely to make people dance, dance, dance . . . and maybe educate them a little in the process. Not necessarily with ritual drumming from Tibet, but by playing them only the best music to make them move like they never knew they could.

That's the rush. And the one I still get today whenever I play disco.

Jussi Kantonen

Let the Music Play

MAKING AN ENTRANCE WITH ARTHUR, REGINE AND BARRY WHITE

In the beginning there was a little Parisian bar called La Discothèque in the Rue Huchette where you could order your favourite *le jazz hot* 45 along with your Pernod. Formed by analogy with the French word *bibliothèque*, meaning 'library', the term 'discothèque' was born, implying not only a record library but a place in which to dance. With one stroke of genius, a whole hedonistic lifestyle began.

Up until this seismic turning point, the generally accepted idea of a night out dancing was dinner at the Copacabana or the Café de Paris and then a quick quick-step to an on-stage band. Replacing live entertainment with records merely being played in succession was seen as perplexing, and seemed about as likely to contemporary movers and shakers as sound movies replacing silent pictures did back in the early-1920s.

The revolution came about because the middle classes wanted to join inexpensively in the high life they saw depicted by Hollywood, and because of the joy-riding demands of an emerging teenage generation. For every rebel with a cause, café society was just that: rockers, wannabe juvenile delinquents and beat girls hanging out at the local coffee bar feeding coins into the hungry jukebox and trying to jive between the cramped formica-topped tables.

But the paparazzi scenes and front-page scandals at such internationally famous clubs as Chez Regine in Paris, Arthur in New York, (owned by Sybil Burton, ex-wife of Richard) and the Whisky A Go Go in London started giving these fêted establishments an alluring mystique. Le Club was the first disco on the New York scene in 1960 but Arthur (or 'Arfer' as the expatriate Glamour Set called it) was the Big Apple's first really chic disco, and opened on Manhattan's East Side in 1965. Its reputation was quickly established when it turned away Hollywood hunk Rock Hudson at the door.

Soon everyone was following the Arthur Beautiful People and the jet-setters of St Tropez, who were deserting their usual glamorous watering-holes in the glittering playgrounds of the *monde* and the *demi-monde*, to join the in-crowd at such hip Euro haunts as The VoomVoom Club. She was frugging wildly in her hip-hugging yellow capri pants, matching chain belt and knee-length white vinyl go-go boots. He was the epitome of cool in his sharp Italian suit, Cuban heels and shades, snapping his fingers along to the bossa nova beat.

Soon it was all happening at the discothèque. It became the place where you went to see and be seen. And Chubby Checker's early-'60s anthem 'At The Discotheque' did much to put the new word on everybody's lips. The wild, the cool and the crazy were drinking warm white wine and twisting along to Little Eva's 'The Locomotion' or doing the pony to The Four Tops singing 'I Can't Help Myself' as the '60s geared up to full swing, spurred on by Twiggy, Alfie and James Bond. Now the Beautiful People had found their feet, however, it became crystal clear that an appropriate soundtrack was needed. Top 40 chart hits weren't enough, especially as most were rhythmically inadequate and didn't provide the conducive backdrop to the easy promise of *la dolce vita*.

In America, where society was being fractured by the Vietnam War, *Easy Rider*, the Love Generation and the dawning of the Age of Aquarius, the airwaves of the urban inner-cities were ruled by James Brown, Aretha Franklin and the stars of the Tamla Motown and Stax labels. Then, suddenly, in 1971 the radio boomed out the funky question: 'Who's the black private dick who's a sex machine to all the chicks?' And the backing girls in silver hot-pants orgasmically screeched the answer: 'Shaft!' Isaac Hayes bellowed the theme song to the breakthrough 'blaxploitation' classic *Shaft*, surprisingly won an Oscar for it, and set the style for every hopeful ghetto pimp and badass for the next decade. For, as *Shaft* redefined the action movie for an Afro-American generation, with its fast and furious gunplay and streetwise attitude, it would also prove to be musically directional and stylistically aspirational.

In the ghetto the look was Pimp. You wore a purple flared velveteen suit, a white frilly shirt with hang-glider collars, leopardskin platform shoes, a wide-brimmed fur-lined hat, and topped the whole ensemble off with masses of gold rings, medallions and shiny teeth. Other expensive accessories included a foxy lady on each arm, a customised Cadillac, heavy artillery and lines of coke. You were tired of grimy funk, papa's brand new bags and bumping with big fat women. You wanted Hollywood-style glamour. You wanted everything in widescreen, Technicolor, bigger, better and with a lush orchestral accompaniment.

Enter Barry White and his Love Unlimited Orchestra. This legendary recording artist, composer and arranger was not just flashier, larger than life and more entertaining than any of the smoochier soul singers of 1972, he was also of seminal influence to the development of dance culture. However, his first releases by the girl group Love Unlimited were not designed to encourage people to get up and dance in the upright position. Early hits such as 'Walking In The Rain With The One I Love' encapsulated young lovers in an acoustically carpeted love nest, with soaring strings and swooningly romantic melodies. It was when the Maestro himself decided to introduce his instantly recognisable bass voice to the productions that the

23

Barry White formula was born. Eagerly anticipating an evening of musical seduction, women all over the world shut themselves in the intimacy of their bedrooms, poured a glass of wine and dropped the *I've Got So Much To Give* album on the turntable. Always the perfect gentleman, White would commence his verbal foreplay slowly, accompanied by a relaxed, yearning groove and a voluptuous wash of violins, harpsichords, French horns and flutes from the almost classical-sounding orchestra. As the lady slowly but surely began to surrender, his caressing voice would become more commanding, telling her gently but firmly to remove her brassiere – and he would not want to see any baby-blue panties, either . . .

The instrumental 'Love's Theme' arrived in grand style in 1974, spiralling up the American pop charts to number one and setting the tone for the emergent disco culture, where all were eager to be lost in an all-encompassing universe of romance and rapture, denying the sometimes grim reality. Numerous satin soul hits followed, and many a child of the '70s began living within the silky deep-voiced dramas of 'You're The First, The Last, My Everything' or the *I've Got So Much To Give* album. Moreover, as described in the cult novel *Dancer From The Dance* by Andrew Holleran in 1974, 'Love's Theme' connected to an entirely different dancer altogether. Around the world, young men in tight jeans were responding to the luxurious symphonic sex of White's grooves, part amused by the overblown scenarios of the records, part turned on by the power of their beats. The gay bar had come into its own ever since the infamous Stonewall riots in New York's Greenwich Village in June 1969, when homosexuals and drag queens, enraged by police harassment, stood up for their love rights.

This defiance spawned not only the Gay Liberation movement but the whole ethos of cutting-edge flamboyance, outrageous fashion statements and trend-setting ideals that would later be copied by the mainstream. Many disco

24

celebrities and their pioneering artistry were first embraced by these terminally hip scene-makers. Deejays catering to this ever-demanding crowd would seek out exotic imports from unusual world music sources, as in the case of the ground-breaking 1973 French release 'Soul Makossa' by the African percussionist Manu Dibango.

The cognoscenti consider this Afro-lounge milestone to be the very first true disco record. Its primal African rhythm had been played against a modern urban feeling before – as in the popular 'Sultana' and 'Rain 2000' by the rock group Titanic – but this time the syncopated drumming was recorded much more upfront. The groove was now truly in the heart, and the amorphous swirls of piano arpeggios, sax solos and romantic melodies would all be set to this solid new-found structure.

DISCO FACT!
'I Will Survive' by Gloria Gaynor is Prince Charles's favourite ever record.

DISCO FACT!
The Food and Drug Administration of America alerted dancers to the disco hazard of possible skin burns and eye damage through constant exposure to lasers in light shows in 1977.

Ain't No Stopping Us Now

ON THE LOVE TRAIN WITH
GEORGE McCRAE AND GLORIA GAYNOR

The more Bohemian white kids on American college campuses grooving to James Brown or The Temptations during the late-'60s found it liberating to articulate anxieties through popular music, in much the same way that rap is favoured by the trendier contingent today. The '60s were riddled with racial tension, and the majority of white record-buyers shunned black dance rhythms in favour of psychedelic head music or pompous progressive rock operas.

Although black and Latin influences had been apparent in dance band repertoires all through the '60s, still the best known – and by far the best paid – blues and soul singers throughout the era had been white rock artists. Janis Joplin and Mick Jagger had adopted Afro-American vocal styles and were able to get their black-sounding (but still, in theory, white) product played by suspicious and often openly prejudiced radio programmers. 'Race Music' meant trouble but what Jagger was singing was considered rock. Therefore it was acceptable.

Erratic record sales during the early-to-mid-'70s worldwide recession made music industry executives take notice of what the minorities in the inner-city areas were getting up to.

Suddenly blacks and Hispanics were spending more of their income on records, car radios and hi-fi equipment than whites were. This meant more specific advertising and more rhythmically accented sounds had to emanate from that shiny new equipment. The rapid increase in the number of black radio stations and more liberal programming during the early-'70s brought some of the fledgling boogie even as far as the Bible Belt states, often in the guise of an accepted protest song like 'Cloud Nine' by The Temptations.

Along with ethnic minorities, white women were starting to purchase more physical soul-based music, challenging the view of women in general as being passive consumers manipulated into buying whatever the industries or cultural guidelines dictated. A single woman could now go out bar-hopping and nightclubbing without the fear of being labelled 'easy' or, worse, a prostitute. For white women, independence meant also freedom from the traditional male-centred world of rock music that their dates had expected them to enjoy. Many men could go for hours on end without dancing at gigs but women did dance. Single and career women could spend all their money on themselves, and their musical tastes were becoming apparent. They dug Barry White and 'Love's Theme' too.

The early-'70s were awash with peculiar crazes like Touch Therapy and EST. *The Naked Ape*, the pseudo-scientific body-conscious opus by Desmond Morris, was right up there with *Jonathan Livingston Seagull* by Richard Bach and *The Exorcist* by William Peter Blatty at the top of the bestseller lists. Streaking – sudden and surprising spurts of nude running in public places – was, if not practised by everyone, part of most people's party small-talk. Films and posters depicting the bulging, shirtless torso of *Enter The Dragon* star Bruce Lee popularised the disciplined physicality of martial arts. Queues were forming in front of cinemas showing the latest chic porno hits such as *The Devil In Miss Jones* and *Behind The*

Green Door. And it wasn't just men in raincoats waiting to get in either. The age was ripe with rampant media sexuality and everyone was supposed to be 'doing it'. One had to participate to belong.

Passive music, therefore, was out. Such listening habits were clearly not in tune with the changing times. A whole new generation of funseekers was abandoning traditional funk and rock for good-time party sounds, which at this time were still known as 'soul' records. Too lightweight to be called soul yet nevertheless heavy on drum and basslines, these disco prototypes were favoured by top-rated radio stations and sold enormous quantities as a result. Sly and the Family Stone's 'Dance to the Music' and 'Everyday People', Stevie Wonder's 'Yester-Me, Yester-You, Yesterday' and 'Superstition', The Incredible Bongo Band's 'Bongo Rock' and the Average White Band's 'Pick Up The Pieces' and 'Cut The Cake' were moulds for early disco demos. As the bright city lights became alluring to more and more suburbanites, John Denver's vapid 'Annie's Song' was quickly replaced on the airwaves by the raunchier Stevie Wonder hit 'Boogie On Reggae Woman'.

The stage was set for an impending musical and social explosion. Although records were not yet being specifically tailor-made for the fast-spreading discothèque market, the first distinctive disco beat was the Sound of Philadelphia. Musically, the Philly Sound smoothed out the poppy high tone 'It's my party and I dance if I want to!' frequencies of Motown and introduced a more sophisticated, structurally advanced and orchestrated palette. Played to perfection by seasoned session musicians, the arrangements for strings, R&B-rooted rhythm sections and rolling bass-lines were complemented by urgent, gospel-influenced vocal styling by the likes of Teddy Pendergrass of Harold Melvin and the Blue Notes, singers of the original 'Don't Leave Me This Way'. The sound also captured the post-Watergate feeling of optimism about the possibility of social change, while addressing issues such as inner-city heathcare problems, illiteracy and political corruption.

The biggest hits from the city of Brotherly Love ran the gamut of tuneful emotion from 'When Will I See You Again' by The Three Degrees to 'I'll Always Love My Mama' by The Intruders. Floors around the world were filled by the commanding voice of Eddie Levert of The O'Jays booming out the million-selling 'I Love Music' along with the new black national anthem 'TSOP (The Sound of Philadelphia)' by the company house orchestra MFSB ('Mothers, Fathers, Sisters and Brothers'- or, allegedly, 'Mother Fucking Sons of Bitches') which became the theme tune to the highly influential American television pop show *Soul Train.*

Songwriters Kenny Gamble and Leon Huff were the artistic backbone of the Philadelphia International phenomenon because their heartfelt pleas for tolerance, justice and community values touched the collective nerve of the time and filled the often seedy basements-turned-dance clubs with uplifting vibes. They provided The O'Jays with the global peace and harmony message 'Love Train', the hard-edged 'Back Stabbers', the energy rush 'Livin' For The Weekend' and the searing 'For The Love Of Money'.

While other record labels were slow to catch on to the vibrant new sound of young black America, content to churn out rehashes of exhausted R&B formulas, Philadelphia International made music-business headlines by grossing in excess of $25 million annually to become the fifth-largest black corporation by the mid-'70s.

But it wasn't just happening in Philadelphia. In Miami, Henry Stone was lighting his own fuse to the disco explosion. Stone had changed the name of his tiny record label, Alston, having had a US Top 10 hit with Betty Wright's 'Clean Up Woman', to the now legendary TK. Wright's touring band line-up had included Harry Casey, who would soon find success with 'Get Down Tonight' and enormous fame with 'That's The Way (I Like It)' as KC and The Sunshine Band. 'Get Down Tonight' is notable for creating its electronic-sounding intro by using speeded-up guitars instead of synthesised effects, and in the string of popular house-party hits to follow, the warm atmosphere the band strived for was maintained by the use of acoustic instruments only. It was an earlier, lesser-known KC recording, 'Blow Your Whistle', which would play a pivotal part in changing the disco landscape forever. Singing backing vocals on that track were Betty Wright and the husband-and-wife session team of George and Gwen McCrae. Stone felt that George would be perfect to sing 'Rock Your Baby', a song composed by Casey and Rick Finch, an engineer whom Casey had met in the TK offices.

Released in the summer of 1974, the instantly recognisable 'Rock Your Baby' was a cataclysmic hit around the world and achieved platinum status in most world markets. Unobtrusive enough to appeal to the widest tastes, this three-minute wonder slowed down the drum machine throb of Hot Butter's 'Popcorn' for a sunny and relaxed summer-time groove, and topped that with falsetto vocals by McCrae. The critics were not amused. Other than the simple hooks and the clear and sparse clip-clop of the synth, there was little on offer musically. 'Rock Your Baby' was certainly far too light to be considered R&B, nor was it really black or funky or bluesy, attributes that objectified anything fitting under the umbrella of 'soul' music. But when this bastard child of a record began to bop through radios, people worldwide snatched a few dance steps and felt here was an undemanding yet hip sound they could relate to in physical terms. Lightly Latin, somewhat soulful, and not too downright funky, 'Rock Your Baby' later came to be known in global vocabularies as *disco*.

Racing up the charts hot on the heels of the McCrae monster was another defining disco milestone. 'Rock The

30

Boat' by The Hues Corporation, a bouncy, up-beat pop ditty, elbowed McCrae out of the No. 1 chart spot and this disco double-whammy made the usually complacent music business wonder what was happening. Then, in early-1975, Labelle shrieked, '*Voulez-vous coucher avec moi?*' in 'Lady Marmalade', considered risqué by contemporary standards, and every label executive sat up and took serious notice. Each of these dancefloor favourites had one basic limitation, however: they were no more than the standard three minutes long. The magical momentum created by each tune was hard for the deejay to develop, sustain and effectively build to a euphoric crescendo. Everyone wanted more, more, more.

Gloria Gaynor, the First Lady of disco, was waiting in the wings to provide just that. Her debut album was the first ever to put a disco mix of songs together as a seamless medley 'Honeybee' slid effortlessly into 'Never Can Say Goodbye' and then segued into 'Reach Out, I'll Be There' to bring the whole glorious twenty minutes to a frenzied climax.

Born and raised in Newark, New Jersey, in 1947, Gaynor realised at the age of thirteen that singing was in her blood. Learning diction from listening to Nat King Cole's delivery and vocal styling from Sarah Vaughan, it was a friend who suggested she should be singing at a local club and then with the group The Soul Satisfiers. Gaynor made such an impact that she soon found herself in a studio recording the ornate and totally arresting *Never Can Say Goodbye* album with producers Meco Monardo, and Tony Bongiovi.

The A-side medley swept the airwaves across the globe and was never far from any deejay's turntable throughout 1975. Musically, the three-track breakthrough for the fledgling disco market was a refined, revved-up approximation of the Philly Sound with several instrumental breaks placed at strategic points between the melodic passages allowing for shifts of mood and pace. Despite being initially treated as a one-off fad, and being criticised as indulgent for 'forcing' dancers to carry on solidly for an unheard-of period of time, Gaynor's landmark release created the soon-to-be standard disco formula.

DISCO FACT!
42,000 spectators jammed into Philadelphia's Veteran Stadium on 5 May 1977 to cheer on contestants in the disco fever competition organised by the *Philadelphia Daily News.*

DISCO FACT!
Television jumped on the disco bandwagon with *American Bandstand* host Dick Clark ('the oldest teenager in the world') introducing *Le Disco*, a 90-minute pilot shown on the NBC network on 19 August 1977. Other TV specials included *Disco Magic* and *Hot City.*

You're Just the Right Size

12-INCHERS, BREAKS AND BAMBOO LOGOS

Albums were one thing, single recordings were another. At the dawning of disco many single releases were divided into Parts 1 and 2 on the A and B sides. Part 1 was always the main body of the melody and Part 2 was additional instrumental material. Examples of this split format include 'Express' by BT Express and 'Hollywood Hot' by Eleventh Hour. Deejays would be mixing between two discs on separate turntables to extend the length of the popular tracks. Also, 45s tended to sound tinny when turned up to the maximum volumes needed to create the proper disco ambience and often highlighted many of the imperfections inherent in the vinyl pressing. Clearly a new format was necessary to eradicate these problems and lighten the deejay's workload.

American labels soon cottoned on to this deficiency and started manufacturing 12-inch singles for use as promotional tools, although in the very beginning only the short 45rpm versions of the song in question were transferred for sound-quality purposes. While extended mixes were to come, Tamla Motown set up the Eye Cue label specifically to market the 12-inch single to the clamouring deejays. They knew how important it was to get their product played in the disco environment to ensure maximum sales interest.

The first company to produce a 12-inch extended version disco 45 was Scepter/Wand and it would also be the last ever record to sport the logo of the famous New York independent hit-making concern which had done so much to launch the career of *chanteuse* Dionne Warwick. Their doubling up of Jesse Green's 'Nice And Slow' with Sweet Music's cover version of the KC and The Sunshine Band track 'I Get Lifted' was quickly noted by CBS/Epic, who followed suit with 'I Found Love (On A Disco Floor)' by The Temprees. Another very early 12-inch was 'Dance Dance Dance' by Calhoun.

Atlantic were the first label to release virtually all their disco product in the 12-inch promo format and they hit pay-dirt with The Trammps' anthem 'That's Where The Happy People Go', The Spinners' 'Love Or Leave' and The Detroit Emeralds' 'Feel The Need In Me '76'.

Other promo records out on the new format included William DeVaughan's 'Be Thankful For What You've Got', Timmy Thomas's 'Why Can't We Live Together?', Silver Convention's 'Fly Robin Fly', Barrabas's 'Mellow Blow' and Frankie Valli's 'Swearin' to God'.

But it wasn't until the first crossover hit from the now legendary Salsoul label, 'Ten Per Cent' by Double Exposure in 1976, that these discs became commercially available, as public demand became a market force that could no longer be ignored. Other 12-inchers, or 'twelves' as they got named, quickly followed, among them Four Below Zero's 'My Baby's Got ESP' on Roulette and T-Connection's 'Do What You Wanna Do' on TK. All these early releases came in collectable picture sleeves, which was an innovation at that time. TK's, for example, was a tropical island with their logo drawn as pieces of bamboo.

The Jesse Green/Sweet Music 12-inch was engineered by Tom Moulton, and the eminent studio presence (and *Billboard* magazine contributor who instigated a regular dance chart column) is considered the pioneer of the long disco mix. He was responsible for putting Gloria Gaynor on the map and he also reshaped Al Dowling's early-1975 dance hit 'I'll Be Holding On' – by popular consensus the first track ever to be remixed to cater to club preferences. If any recording had 'A Tom Moulton Mix' printed on the label, it was a sure sign of quality and a floor-filling guarantee. Longer mixes gave each artist additional playing time in the clubs and were soon considered an essential tool in breaking any new act.

Moulton and his contemporary luminaries Larry Levan, Walter Gibbons, Rick Gianatos and Jim Burgess were required to create longer intros and break sequences in the middle of songs for mixing purposes to stretch a track's dance-floor-filling properties to the max. These breaks would also provide a window for the remixers and deejays alike to stamp their own personality and interpretations on the cut by integrating other music with a matching beat and shuffling segments of the same song.

Walter Gibbons completely transformed Double Exposure's 'Ten Percent' from a three-minute album track into an eleven-minute break-feast, building the momentum up with extended percussion elements and finally bringing back the surging vocals. This reconstructed song single-handedly revolutionised the underground club scene in New York, woke deejays up to the true possibilities of the 12-inch 'gimmick' and began to promote its use worldwide. Gibbons' trademark was to concentrate on the percussive elements of the song and on the singer. While many of the contemporary Salsoul releases were heavily orchestrated, he stripped down to the very essence each track he remixed to the 12-inch format. Two Salsoul albums, *Disco Boogie Volumes 1 and 2* (the first ever disco party album) and *Disco Madness*, feature Gibbons at the height of his remixing powers. The latter even had him singing the vocal lead on 'It's Good For The Soul'.

For his part, Tom Moulton offered two volumes of *Disco Gold* in late-1975, revisiting and remixing many of the greatest dance moments in the Scepter/Wand catalogue, such as

'Undecided Love' by The Chequers and 'Chinese Kung Fu' by Banzaii, and he would later prove a hugely influential force on the career of disco diva *extraordinaire* Grace Jones and her camp epics 'I Need A Man' and *'La Vie En Rose'*. But it was another deejay, David Mancuso, owner of the famous, seminal New York club The Loft, who saw the sense of forming a subscription-only disco pool – an organised union for deejays to receive all the new 12-inch releases from the record labels on a regular basis.

Yet while the most obvious effect the stretched-out 12-inch singles had on club culture was to extend the groove and keep dancers in a perpetual state of excitement, they were soon to have even greater importance. Pop composers would use all the available time now provided by the new format to tailor their songs to the product. Many songs written before the advent of the disco mix faded abruptly at the end, leaving the listener begging for more. Now they could be transformed into glissando poperettas, highlighting elements of chiaroscuro symphonic drama, sweeping vocal interpretation and pounding rhythmic structure. Many songwriters were eager to take up the challenge and explore this uncharted musical panorama.

DISCO FACT!
When Farrah Fawcett-Majors, star of *Charlie's Angels* held her birthday party at New York New York, she insisted on having the fog machine turned off because she was against smoking.

DISCO FACT!
Lighting pioneer Larry Silverman, consultant on *Saturday Night Fever* and *Thank God It's Friday* said, 'The integrated circuits used in discos were developed for the space programs. If it weren't for NASA, you wouldn't have Studio 54.'

Salsoul Rainbows

FROM LOLEATTA HOLLOWAY TO CHARO

Hot nights. Summer in the city. You found more than a rose in Spanish Harlem in New York *circa* 1975. The streets were pulsating with music throbbing from the eight-track car stereos, the bodegas and the open-windowed apartments. *I like to be in America* . . . if only I could have this urban gringo music spiced up with Afro-Cuban jungle fever.

Informed by the big-band sound of Xavier Cugat, the percussive power of Latin American greats like Tito Puente and other Mambo Kings, and a disco-savvy street sense, a new urban sound emerged with Joe Bataan's instrumental cover version of Gil Scott-Heron's 'The Bottle'. Its dirty sax and razor-sharp horn section overlaying a grinding salsa beat (incredibly, recorded live on the first take), hit the D-spot and launched a major force in the disco music industry. The track did so well commercially that Mericana Records, an old-established Latin label, decided the time was right to put into operation an exclusively disco-orientated releasing arm. They called it Salsoul Records.

Defined by a multi-coloured neon rainbow logo, Salsoul offered Philadelphia style, highly orchestrated music with massive string sections and soulful vocals. Modelled after Philadelphia's MFSB, and often employing the same session musicians heard on the Philly classics, The Salsoul Orchestra was put together by producer Vincent Montana Jr who also wrote and arranged their most popular tracks: 'Nice 'N' Naasty', 'You're just The Right Size' and 'Chicago Bus Stop (Ooh, I Love It)'. The Salsoul Orchestra would also please the crowds with their cult tracks 'Salsoul 3001' (Richard Strauss's *Also Sprach Zarathustra* discofied), 'Tangerine' (a campy update of the Johnny Mercer standard), 'Street Sense' and even a medley of show tunes from the blockbuster Broadway musicals *Fiddler On The Roof* and *West Side Story*.

Scoffed at by the funkier chapter of the burgeoning disco brigade, these slices of exotic quirkiness endeared themselves to hardcore fans. The Salsoul Orchestra's kitsch apotheosis was reached by their two wonderfully vulgar *Christmas Jollies* albums which strung together festive favourites ('Rudolph The Red-Nosed Reindeer'), church carols ('Silent Night') and specially composed holiday material ('Merry Christmas All') sung by Montana's daughter Denise, whereas usually all background vocals were harmonised by Carla Benson, Yvette Benton and Barbara Ingram. Collectively known as The Sweethearts of Sigma, named after Sigma Sound Studios in Philadelphia, this girl group trio were the heart and soul of most Salsoul releases.

The Philly girl group First Choice had recorded such rough-and-ready tracks for the company as 'Armed And Extremely Dangerous' and 'Smarty Pants', but they also found increased fame under the guidance of Salsoul, with the ageless and still endlessly remixed songs 'Dr Love' and 'Let No Man Put Asunder'.

The undisputed queen of the Salsoul sound was Loleatta Holloway. While the majority of disco divas displayed dizzy style over vocal content, Loleatta Holloway's colossal vocal chords have shaken the structures of dance halls from mid-'70s New York to the superclubs of Ibiza today with a power that has made her an integral part of club culture's soul psyche. These vocal skills were developed while singing with her mother through the churches and community halls of Chicago, where

Loleatta also got her first taste of showbiz when she was signed to the cast of the musical *Don't Bother Me, I Can't Cope*. She toured, travelled and scored a number of hit-ettes with her future producer and husband, Floyd Smith, before stumbling to the attention of famed Philly producer Norman Harris in 1976.

With the more sophisticated recording facilities and studio production staff used by Harris's Gold Mind label, Loleatta's talents could now be properly unleashed. As a tester, she first delivered a ballad, 'Worn Out Broken Heart', vocalising a heart-wrenching plea for better times from a woman burned out by doomed relationships. The Holloway/Harris business relationship blossomed, though, and the urgency and passion in her voice gave the 1977 debut album *Loleatta* an edge that swept her out of the minor leagues into global consciousness via three sweat-ridden club stormers. 'Hit And Run' and 'Ripped Off' rolled with the meatiest guitar riffs, containing gritty female choruses addressing cheating cavaliers and the repossessing of stolen diamond rings. 'Hit And Run' also exists in an extra-percussive eleven-minute Walter Gibbons version, dispensing with the actual song and fully exploring the possibilities of the killer groove, with additional wailing by the clearly enthusiastic Loleatta. The third hit from the album was 'Dreamin''. After a typical Philly-style and fairly laid-back melodic main body, this sound-warning to all adulterers broke down to a long, gospel-influenced shouting match between the ecstatic Loleatta and her back-up singers – the ladies blowing the roof off with vocal fireworks that have to be heard to be believed.

The Vincent Montana Jr-penned 'Run Away', released on the Salsoul Orchestra's 1977 *Magic Journey* album, was another solid-gold club standard with jazzy scat-style singing and a cool Montana vibes solo. The next year's *Queen Of The Night* caused tremors mainly in the club underground, as did the brilliant 'The Greatest Performance Of My Life', cut from the Loleatta Holloway self-titled album of 1979. Later that year, of course, Loleatta made clubland history with a record that has been passed down like folklore in dance palaces, the timeless and endlessly recycled Dan Hartman production 'Love Sensation'.

The complete flipside of the Loleatta Holloway experience came from Charo, Salsoul's flaming Hispanic diva, a cartoon character study in curvaceous figure and an enormous blond hairdo. Originally from Murcia in Spain, Charo first hit the music headlines in the mid-'60s by marrying Xavier Cugat and performing with his band for three years. It was on this cabaret circuit that she gained the experience of how to communicate with an audience and how to turn her lack of English into a charmingly funny asset. She lisped, purred and strangled words into double entendres not only on record but eventually on television in *The Love Boat* and on screen in *The Concorde – Airport '79*.

Because none of the Salsoul releases had really achieved sales chart success – each seemed to just miss making its commercial mark – Salsoul saw in Charo the perfect perpetual promotion vehicle for cross-over potential into the broader-based MOR and gay record-buying public. The camp spitfire's first album, *Cuchi-Cuchi*, showcased such eclectic tracks as hysterical renditions of 'Lets Spend The Night Together' and 'Speedy Gonzalez' alongside Vince Montana-penned club hits, a delightfully shuffling 'Dance A Little Bit Closer' and a fabulously flamenco-flavoured title track. Charo would only release one other Salsoul album. Tracks on this second album included 'The Love Boat Theme', 'Stay With Me' and, because she was an accomplished classical guitarist, an ear-bending ten-minute version of Rodrigo's 'Concerto De Aranjuez'. To top everything off in perfect OTT mink-lined Charo manner, the track 'OIe Ole' was released as a 12-inch single pressed on shocking-pink vinyl.

In addition to the albums, two more melting pots filled with entertaining hilarity arrived from Charo during the late-'70s. The first of the 12-inchers in question was 'La Salsa', a rarely spun yet enthusiastic 1976 dance lesson from the chattering discomedienne, combining mock-Latin rhythms with chugging

40

mid-tempo disco beats. '*Mamacita, Donde Esta Santa Claus*?' presented her as a little girl in a gloriously cheesy yuletide pictorial, redeemed by typically sharp Salsoul instrumentation.

Salsoul decided to explore another avenue in their quest to achieve an elusive chart hit. In 1975, producer Tom Moulton had remixed the European holiday smash hit '*El Bimbo*' by Bimbo Jet for the American market, Taking their cue from Moulton, Salsoul searched the globe for other similar money-makers and came up with the hopeful contenders 'Kings Of Clubs' by The Chocolat's (from Belgium), 'Love Is Still Blue' by Paul Mauriat and his Orchestra (from France), and Bebu Silvetti's 'Spring Rain' (from Spain). This last was the perfect example of a flourishing Eurodisco industry looking to America for bankable inspiration. With its irresistible piano intro, Silvetti's featherlight confection became the first credible global club hit for Salsoul.

Before its demise in 1985, the label would also score with the percussive 'Jingo' by Candido, 'Ain't No Mountain High Enough' by Inner Life, 'This Will Be A Night To Remember' by Eddie Holman, 'I Got My Mind Made Up' by Instant Funk and 'Helplessly' by Moment of Truth. The heritage of the Salsoul phenomenon is kept alive in today's clubland through persistent sampling (Black Box's 'Ride On Time' used huge chunks of 'Love Sensation') and collectable merchandise from the label's heyday like the infamous 'Dance Your Ass Off' T-shirt which commands a hefty price among an ever-growing band of rare groove/nuyorica enthusiasts.

DISCO FACT!
In 1967 American nightclub patrons spent an average of 68 cents per night on their dance entertainment. Ten years later, at the height of the disco craze, it was $3.40.

DISCO FACT!
Club 747 in Buffalo, New York, was the first club to use actual aeroplane accessories for interior decoration.

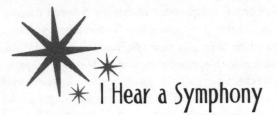

I Hear a Symphony

ORCHESTRAL DISCO

Before the rise of the computer wizard alchemising techno tracks into pure electronic dance textures, music was played on acoustic instruments. Instead of fiddling with the knobs on a synthesiser and a sequencer, you had some forty musicians gathered in a studio ready to play their G-strings off. These seasoned freelance guitarists, drummers, percussionists and so on fronting entire, classically trained orchestras could take one look at any piece of sheet music and deliver the trickiest rhythmic structures, not only with deadly accuracy but with the ability to improvise with skill. Completely at ease with Latin, jazz and disco music, and often allowed to stretch out at will, these Mozart Musketeers could turn recording into hot jam sessions. Many of the classic Salsoul tracks feature long ultra-tight jazz-based solos by ace musicians, like tenor saxophonist Leon Zachery and organ player Lenny Pakula, in perfect balance with the beat.

In New York the fast Latin dance rhythms had only a few years to go before being properly renamed 'salsa'. The word salsa ('spicy sauce') had long been used by Cuban immigrants as something analogous to the term 'swing'. And this fusion of jazz and Cuban salsa was instantly adaptable to the heavily orchestrated disco style of the mid-'70s. The adding of syncopated drumming and masses of strings to the vibrating percussive salsa became synonymous with the New York disco sound, and fast and zippy hi-hat rhythms and extravagant orchestrations became the orchestra custom. In the wake of the success of the Salsoul output and the happening Ritchie Family's 'Brazil' on the hip 20th Century Records label, full disco orchestras were quickly swung into action to mine the trend.

America, of course, led the way, with all the different groove collectives of the Philadelphia sound architects Kenneth Gamble, Leon Huff and Vincent Montana Jr. While the Gamble-Huff collaboration produced more singularly soulful compositions, Montana's output was straightforward, no-frills disco. The vibraphonist/arranger/composer had cut his teeth doing back-up for such luminaries as Sarah Vaughan and Charlie 'Bird' Parker and had recorded with stars like twist tsar Chubby Checker and *Beach Party* teen idol Frankie Avalon. All this musicianship and expertise was evident in his dance-floor concepts, from his own one-off projects like Goody Goody, The Anvil Band and Sounds of the Inner City (who hit it big with the theme from the cult sitcom *Mary Hartman, Mary Hartman*), to the Salsoul Orchestra and his own Montana Orchestra. For the latter he produced the spectacular 'A Dance Fantasy Inspired By The Motion Picture *Close Encounters Of The Third Kind*' (somewhat overshadowed by the poppier Meco-produced version) and the perennial favourite 'Heavy Vibes'. His *Cross-Over* album, featuring The Fania All Stars, from 1979 contained one complete side of fiery salsa with vocals by Ruben Blades and Latina legend Celia Cruz, and a flipside of sophisticated semi-instrumental disco.

On the West Coast, former Detroit session guitarist Dennis Coffey and his long-time arranger partner Mike Theodore unleashed the monster club and chart hit 'Devil's Gun' in 1977, performed by the strongly gospel-influenced vocal group C.J. & Co. This huge production made the emerging Westbound label and especially Mike Theodore names to watch. Theodore's trademark was suspenseful musical intros and dramatic build-ups to peaks of excitement, and they boomed back in the same year, magnified to lush perfection, as heard in 'Cosmic Wind' by his own namesake orchestra. The thrilling science-fiction-influenced track begins with a massive rumbling bassline which is repeated and repeated until chilling female voices warble warnings of the approaching space storm. Weird piano chords and wind effects are added, gigantic bass-line breaks erupt, melodies swirl around like the candy floss at a funfair and the whole galactic fantasia comes to a surging climax with the wailing girls seven tension-filled minutes later.

'The Bull', 'Brazilian Lullaby', 'I Love The Way You Move' and 'Ain't Nothing To It' from the *Cosmic Wind* album proved Theodore's genius at orchestral disco arrangement. His follow-up album, *High On Mad Mountain*, and the track 'Wonder Man' were equally popular in clubs, and Theodore triumphed again the same year with another intricately arranged and produced classic, 'Manhattan Love Song', sung by famed percussionist King Errisson. High on the discognoscenti's list of all-time greats, this ten-minute odyssey swooshes the dancer around the neonlit sidewalks of sleazy Times Square into a vortex of glitz and glamour. The long middle break in this cut is one of the hottest ever, with a blinding piano concerto and wild urban jungle screeches amid the thundering Latin percussion.

Numerous 'disco orchestras' made their mark on the dance charts during the mid-'70s, including the oddly named Rice and Beans Orchestra headed by Pepe Luis Soto from Puerto Rico. 'Rice And Beans Theme' was jazzy Salsoul, but the rest, like 'You've Got The Magic' and especially 'The Blue Danube Hustle', bounced around in merry Ritchie Family style with urgent arrangements and a jolly girlie chorus. Soto was married to Celi Bee who, with her own Buzzy Bunch, hit the disco big time herself with the infectiously poppy 'Superman', 'One Love' and 'Fly Me On The Wings Of Love'.

With his Love Unlimited Orchestra, Barry White would wow the crowds with 'My Sweet Summer Suite', one of the most extravagantly produced records of the era. The full-length 12-inch version first gets a hot Brazilian thing going with a tasty intro complete with shuffling carnival maracas. The scene then shifts unexpectedly to Vienna, as a huge wave of violins transforms the rhythm into something resembling a fabulous Strauss waltz. 'Brazilian Love Song' and 'Theme From King Kong' were similar riots of grandiose orchestral movements, providing incredibly strange yet brilliant mood music for disco-age bachelor pads.

From the producers of the *Ultimate* album came an equally sublime disco lounge project called *Tangerue*. Here soft vocal shadows and distant operatic wailings were cast over four gently throbbing tracks abounding with baroque instrumentations, creating illusory dance zones richly saturated with layers of colourfully kitsch exotica.

John Davis and the Monster Orchestra was another class act that never disappointed even the most demanding dancers. Best known for his punchy 'Ain't That Enough For You' and 'Love Magic' hits and his arrangements for numerous solo acts (such as Charo and Ruth Waters), John Davis employed the ever-reliable Philly session men but with stronger-than-usual participation from the rhythm section. His first Monster Orchestra release, 'Night And Day', comprised a collection of Cole Porter classics speeded up and spiced up with sexy chanting. 'Up Jumped The Devil' from 1977 contained yet another eighteen-minute medley-style composition built around a central theme song, this time the moodily romantic 'The Magic Is You'. After some five minutes or so, this type of song would mutate into a long instrumental passage and then turn into a new tune faintly reminiscent of the original. More breaks and instrumental segments later, there would be a return to the leading tune for an intensified finale. That was the recipe for disco success in the orchestra era.

Going to a disco could mean being subjected to any number of these musical marathons, mixed in with the shorter 12-inchers, scaring the club neophyte and the sadly out-of-shape. The cuts were rarely played in full, though, as many of them became just too repetitive after the first ten minutes. Listening at home was when these classic cuts would sink in indelibly. Since the climactic final sections of the orchestra medleys were always the most effective, deejays usually purchased two copies of the record so that they could skip the boring bits and mould the songs to their personal taste. The episodic Ray Martinez orchestral productions 'If There's Love' and its flip, 'Hazy Shades Of Love' by Amant, were spun in this fashion through most of 1978.

In Europe, the disco orchestra movement did not simply imitate the Big Apple corps. Munich wunderkinds Giorgio Moroder and Peter Bellotte were synonymous with a distinctive violin sound of their own, manufactured by using a single electronically enhanced and magnified instrument. The producers later took on the full symphony orchestra of the Bavaria Studios for their more elaborate Donna Summer showpieces. Their fellow Germans, Charles Orieux and Ingo Cramer of the Hansa Studios, employed the Berlin Opera Strings to sweeten up the Euro hits 'Turn On To Love' and 'City Girls' for their act, Jumbo, persuasive pleasures enough without being any real tours de force of creative innovation.

The first mass rage for British-produced orchestral disco was the work of an ex-lounge lizard from India named Biddu. Weaned on Herb Alpert and MOR Hindi versions of Beatles hits, Biddu had arrived in Swinging London during the late-'60s. Discovered working at a doughnut stand by famed producer Gerry Shury, Biddu's first assignment was recording the score for the Richard (*Shaft*) Roundtree espionage yarn *Embassy* (1972). This soundtrack was followed by a couple of minor Biddu-penned non-hits sung by mod hero Jimmy James, and Carl Douglas, who would find fleeting fame as the 'Kung-Fu Fighting' chart-topper. This huge 1974 hit was released at the tail-end of the martial arts craze but at the beginning of the disco era. It changed a lot for the Jamaican singer – and changed everything for Biddu, who signed a deal with Epic Records on the strength of it.

The resulting 'Blue-Eyed Soul' club hit was the beginning of the British flirtation with New York disco elements and the orchestra vogue. Modelled in 1975 after 'TSOP' by MFSB, the catchy instrumental established Biddu as one of the most prolific purveyors of dance music outside the USA. The Biddu sound incorporated solid playing by a hard rhythm section and fast swirling Northern Soul-style melodies at the precise moment New York disco was being introduced to British dancers by deejay/producers like Ian Levine (future deejay of the premier London gay disco, Heaven) and when the Wigan Casino scene was beginning to divide and diminish as a result of police action. The Biddu Orchestra then tackled the romantic Michel Legrand-composed theme 'Summer Of '42' from the 1971 box-office hit movie of the same name. It reached No. 14 in the British charts in August 1975, and also got Biddu noticed by the hip stateside discos.

The follow-up album, *Rain Forest*, spawned a lesser chart hit with the title track but was nevertheless a formidable and authentic slice of deliberate disco and was, again, accessible to the American market. The notion of relevance and authenticity in dance music, now seen as obvious with continents consistently influencing each other's output, was a major stumbling-block in 1976. Cross-fertilisation and crossover had yet to obtain the all-important American deejay seal of approval which would mean worldwide recognition and a major label supporting the release by actively promoting sales. The title track, 'Rain Forest', was again in the driving MFSB mould with the melodic theme cut into by bounding percussive passages. 'Jump For Joy' and 'Chic-Chica-Chic-Chica-Chic' were substantially successful Latin party flavours and enjoyed an enthusiastic response through US club play.

A high-camp cover version of the old Neil Diamond standard 'Girl You'll Be A Woman Soon' and the brassy 'Boogiethon' were the cream cuts on the next Biddu orchestra album, *Eastern Man*. While this 1977 album did major business in continental Europe, Biddu did have a spring club hit with a fabulous piano-driven version of 'Soul Coaxing' stuffed with soothing strings and piano riffs layered over a lazy shuffling beat building to an uplifting and rousing finale.

The late-'70s saw Biddu tellingly start to incorporate sitars and other Indian instruments into his work, like his last 1978 chart hit, 'Journey To The Moon'. In 1979, after releasing the 12-inch 'Voodoo Man' and composing the title theme for the Joan Collins disco sex flick *The Stud*, he returned to India to continue his career (the 1985 'Dance of Shiva' 12-inch opus) and to work with such local pop acts as Nazia Hassan and Shweta Shetty. This agenda was something he was more than comfortable with after guiding the career of the British disco singer Tina ('I Love To Love') Charles and writing her songs 'You Set My Heart On Fire' and 'Doctor Love'.

The method sound of the orchestra movement was set in stone by Biddu and his contemporaries. A girlie chorus would vaporise in and out of a chugging rhythm track, cooing softly as strings, marimbas, cowbells and a kitchen sink full of percussion instruments targeted the disco mirror ball to be split and reflected into the collective dance consciousness. A British act that tried – and failed – to recreate the Biddu sound was The Armada Orchestra. They offered two albums in the 1975-76 season consisting of fast hustling reworkings of Northern Soul and Philly favourites. Competent enough, and featuring long saxophone solos, The Armada Orchestra just lacked that certain disco savoir-faire.

Italy, Spain and France entered the disco fray with The Botticelli Orchestra, The Sunshine Combo and The Paul Mauriat Orchestra. Canada offered us The Black Light Orchestra in 1977 with their 'Touch Me Take Me' and a beautifully produced Ennio Morricone movie theme medley. There was also the soft-porn effort from the Toronto-based THP Orchestra with 'Two Hot For Love', a sixteen minute Donna Summer-style moan-and-groaner divided into five segments: 'Four Play', two parts 'Excitement', a 'Climax' and a 'Resolution'.

Charlie Calello, who would put an indelible mark on disco by producing the classic 'Native New Yorker' for Odyssey, also had a sizeable hit with 'Sing Sing Sing' by The Charlie Calello Orchestra. Prelude Record label producers Moses Dillard and Jesse Boyce (responsible for the stomping 'Come On Dance, Dance' by The Saturday Night Band) recorded two mesmerising tracks in 1978 as The Constellation Orchestra too. Prelude was noted for its expensively ornate orchestral production, and both 'Perfect Love Affair' and 'Cosmic Melody' were ace examples of this philosophy in epic practice.

Taking their cue from Paul Mauriat and his 'Love Is Still Blue' disco entry, and The New Ventures' 'Superstar Revue' (based on Andrew Lloyd Webber's stage musical *Jesus Christ Superstar*), many other easy-listening war horses climbed aboard the funk-lite train. Respected saxophonist Sonny Rollins presented an ill-conceived 'Disco Monk' project. The endless series of the *James Last Disco Tanz Party* albums from Germany, with their flaccid versions of 'Dancing Queen' and *'El Bimbo'*, were geared to the same MOR market as similar laborious efforts by Frank Pourcel and pianists Ferrante and Teichner. Even Xavier Cugat cranked out a disco disaster in 1975. The Latin bandleader's *Braziliana* was filled with generic banana-boat instrumentals like *'La Nova Cucaracha'* and *'Cielito Lindo'* with a thumping bass drum merely dubbed over each three-minute Cha Cha. No self-respecting deejay ever played these records in a club environment as they were considered kitsch even by OTT '70s standards.

The Disco Godfather

VAN McCOY AND THE HUSTLE

Van (Allen) McCoy was the Chubby Checker of disco. Just as Checker had taken 'The Twist' dance craze from the Peppermint Lounge in New York and popularised it in a '60s song, so McCoy did the same with 'The Hustle' and helped launch '70s disco fever. McCoy was a talented session keyboardist, composer and producer whose life had been devoted to music since the age of four. Born in Washington on 6 January 1944, the engineer's son started piano lessons in infancy and rapidly gained a firm musical foundation for his subsequent career. Van and his violin-playing sibling Norman began touring church socials as The McCoy Brothers, and at the age of twelve Van wrote his first song. As a teenager, he, Norman and three schoolfriends formed a doo-wop group and, later, he sang with Mitch Miller and his Orchestra, of 'The Yellow Rose Of Texas' fame.

Throughout the '60s, McCoy composed songs and produced such acts as The Shirelles (for whom he wrote 'I Don't Think So' and 'Maybe Tonight'), Peaches and Herb and Gladys Knight and the Pips. But it was in January 1975, as he was putting the finishing touches to ten songs he needed for a new album of popular music, that McCoy was told by his deejay friend David Todd about a new dance the Latino kids were doing in the

South Bronx clubs. Todd advised McCoy to hustle over to the Adam's Apple Disco on New York's East Side to witness the phenomenon for himself. McCoy was too busy working on his album arrangements, however, and sent his producing partner Charlie Kipps along instead.

What Kipps saw at the Adam's Apple was kids dancing to choreographed and regimented steps. Communication was back on the dance floor again and such smooth touch-dancing made the wild hippie abandon of the post-Woodstock years seem suddenly, hopelessly, archaic. Clearly lots of thought had gone into working out the moves well before the revellers had arrived at the club to practise further. Kipps was so impressed he arranged for one of the secretaries at their record company, whom he had spotted in the milling club crowd, to demonstrate the dance to McCoy back in the office. As he watched the display, a melody and arrangement surged into his head and an eleventh song was quickly written for the impending album.

As soon as a record company executive heard the bouncy, catchy number, infectiously fusing a Latin beat and rhythm and blues with the seductive invitation to 'Do it, do the hustle', it was rush released as a single, became an instant No. 1 chart hit in America and helped transform disco from a popular Saturday-night pastime into a '70s way of life. Everyone in the world rushed out to take hustle lessons, canny discos mounted early-evening dance classes for the uninitiated, and when the single (credited to Van McCoy and the Soul City Symphony) sold eight million copies, McCoy's album was renamed *Disco Baby* to cash in on its staggering momentum and the subsequent dance madness it engendered.

By the end of 1975, McCoy had been named 'Top Instrumental Artist', *Disco Baby* had gone gold and offers to compose movie soundtracks and TV jingles were pouring in. Sadly, McCoy only had four more years left in which to enjoy the massive success and high profile 'The Hustle' brought him, as he died in the summer of 1979 just after making an appearance in the Mae West cult turkey *Sextette*, playing the minor role of the ambassador from an African republic. McCoy also contributed to the soundtrack of that infamous fiasco in which the former 'Come up and see me sometime' Hollywood goddess gave an incredibly starry cast the octogenarian once-over.

Even if 'The Hustle' were his sole credit, McCoy would go down in disco history as one of the key figures who swept people out of their seats and onto their dancing feet the moment they heard the opening bars of his landmark tune. Happily, McCoy's legacy also includes such other memorable works – admittedly all hustle-influenced – as 'Rhythms Of The World', 'Jet Setting', 'Soul Cha-Cha', 'The Shuffle', 'Night Walk', 'Theme From Star Trek' and 'Change With The Times'.

Van McCoy didn't invent the hustle. All he did was write the tune. He was in the right place at the right time with the right tune to catch his moment of glory in the glint of the mirror ball, for 'The Hustle' was one of the biggest dance discs of the '70s and an epoch-making record in its own right.

52

I've Got the Next Dance

DISCO DANCE CRAZES

As far back as the Dionysian rites of Ancient Greece, dance was about social and sexual release. Dionysus sent women into a state of dancing delirium far removed from the humdrum reality of their daily lives governed by men. In the Middle Ages, people were driven to a 'Dancing Madness' through fear of the Plague, and frenzied gyrating was seen as a liberation from all Black Death worries. When the sexual and worry emancipation are put together, the reason why dance crazes have swept through every culture can be easily discerned.

Whether it was the waltz in the 1800s and the 'ragged time' of 'Alexander's Ragtime Band' in the next century or the 'Tango Teas' that became all the rage in 1912 and the madness of the Charleston which alleviated pre-stockmarket crash fears, the roots of disco emerged from the rhythm that first hit American tourists during the late-'20s in Havana. The Cuban capital had become a dream world of all things lusciously tropical, an island paradise that staggered Western senses with potent rum and vibrant colour.

Then there was the music, the incessant drumming which brought out the sophisticated savage in prohibition thrill-seekers. This hot music was everywhere, an exciting percussive vibration more exotic and sinful than the tango or the

Charleston that had scandalised polite society a decade earlier. The sound had been brought to this melting pot of cultures by West African slaves over four centuries before. The melodic traditions of the Yoruba and Congo races had gradually fused with their Spanish and Arabic equivalents to produce new musical forms like the *habañera*, which later became the tango and was one of the important roots of jazz. As the call-and-response structure common in African music was incorporated further into European measure patterns, the dance steps of the two worlds also began to blend.

The routine that lithe women were now performing on smart nightclub stages was called the rhumba. The top half of the body seemed to be doing a dramatic and controlled flamenco, while the bottom half was indulging in some primitive and exciting mating game. Everyone wanted to learn these moves and soon hips all over the world were swaying more or less in rhythm to such songs as '*El Manicero* – The Peanut Vendor'.

Further south, in Brazil, US millionaires, businessmen and wealthy tourists – cultural imperialists – discovered more rhythm and imported it all back home to Hollywood. Ginger Rogers and Fred Astaire starred in the immensely successful *Flying Down To Rio* (1933) and glided atop a huge drum in a production number built around the samba-based song 'Carioca', while extras undulated around them in Busby Berkeley's kaleidoscopic formations.

The record industry naturally took notice of the new idiom, and Americanised versions of Latin tunes became a permanent feature of the sales chart. American composers such as Cole Porter contributed to the rhumba craze with risqué and romantic numbers, and the Duke Ellingtons of the music world started to incorporate Latin numbers in their sets. Most importantly of all, lured by the promise of the Big City and all the work opportunities to be found there, the cream of the Cuban musicians emigrated to New York. Legendary players like Arsenio Rodriguez mingled jazz and ethnic elements into creative new sounds in the *barrios*, while Xavier Cugat and Desi Arnaz (Lucille Ball's husband both on and off the set of the sitcom *I Love Lucy*) kept High Society entertained in midtown Manhattan's ritzy ballrooms.

The fantasy accelerated during the 1940s when Brazil's most exotic import to date was introduced to America. She was a tiny singer-dancer named Maria de Carmo Miranda de Cunha, a recording star and film actress in her own country. As Carmen Miranda she became a worldwide sensation, wearing gigantic fruited head-dresses and seven-inch cha-cha heels in films such as *The Gang's All Here* (1943), chirping out camp songs by the dozen like 'I Yi Yi Yi Yi Yi Yi Like You Very Much' and 'Chica Chica Boom Chic'.

The major new dance in the late-'40s was the mambo, a fiery mix of jazzy moves and Afro-Cuban rhythms. Developed by the likes of Mario Bauza and Frank 'Machito' Grillo, mambo music was first showcased in New York to a wide public in small clubs like La Conga on Seventh Avenue. During the '50s the action moved to Broadway when an old ballroom was revamped into The Palladium, the Studio 54 of its era. Marlon Brando and Dizzy Gillespie jammed on conga drums while hipsters and society matrons rubbed shoulders on the dance floor with the sharpest mambo dancers from Spanish Harlem and the Bronx.

The Cuban elements were not allowed to be watered down, however, and the Palladium became a temple for all the greats like Tito Puente and Celia Cruz. Then the inevitable happened: the mambo caught the attention of the vast suburban masses of Everytown, America, and the rest of the world soon after that. Like the rhumba and samba before it, this wicked polyrhythmic dance was soon tamed by flat-footed *gringos* and turned into a more easily accessible syncopated set of steps.

This hot Latin impulse was still felt during the late-'50s in popular shows and films like *West Side Story*, but things rapidly cooled down with the bossa nova. Then the Summer of Love and the Woodstock mud baths transformed dancing into an expression of psyched-out ecstasy with no recognisable footwork patterns.

Disco changed all that. In Florida and the New York suburbs, young Hispanics were doing a new step they called 'the hustle', a funky update of all the old moves they had seen their parents dance, filtered through decades of motion refinement. It meant couples stayed in their own area on the crowded dance floor yet moved very fast within it. Basically, the hustle has two people connected hand to hand and sometimes rocking in 'social dance position'- the woman's left hand is placed on the man's arm, his right hand on her waist. The other hands are clasped together. The dance itself involves anticlockwise underarm turns, dramatic dips and lots of posing, as the partners circle each other and try not to cause accidents on the crowded dance floor. Two great examples of the hustle can be seen in the movies *Saturday Night Fever* (1977) and *Carlito's Way* (1993). The former showcases an incredible Puerto Rican couple strutting, swinging and hustling up a storm during the dance contest scenes.

Ask any dance studio-trained teacher about the hustle and you'll get impossibly complicated talk about time signatures, accent patterns and stopping points. Forget all that. This is the way to do the hustle.

THE NEW YORK HUSTLE

Hands clasped, the couple face each other.

The man steps forward with his left foot, very smoothly pulling the woman towards him.

He then steps forward with his right foot.

On count three, he steps back with his left foot, with his hands lightly pushing the woman gently away from him.

On the last count of four, he completes the pattern by stepping back with his right foot.

The woman's steps are the opposite.

Once this basic walking pattern is mastered, start a circular motion, only taking small and accented steps.

The New York Hustle at its best is slithery, subtle and sexy, so remember always to keep your moves cool and collected.

THE LATIN HUSTLE
The man taps his left foot to his left while his weight remains on his right.

On count two, he brings his left foot back and shifts his weight onto it.

During counts three and four, he takes three quick steps. First, he steps backwards with his right foot, takes a quick step back with the ball of his left foot, then takes a step forward with his right foot.

On count five, he takes a step forward with his left foot.

On the last count, six, he closes the pattern by bringing his right foot to his left.

The 'triple step' backwards during counts three and four, when the couple take three steps during two counts of music, may take some extra practice. To make the sequence easier, count the steps as you go along: touch, step, back-back-forward, forward, forward.

The Latin hustle involves the same circling push-pull basic motion as all the other hustle dances. A competent couple of hustlers make fast 360-degree turns with the basic set of six steps. It is also important to vary the speed of the dance and to slow the movement down from time to time as well. Add your own counterclockwise underarm turns, walk-around sequences, dips and pauses, all the while keeping in rhythm.

THE CALIFORNIA HUSTLE/THE BUS STOP
This is a line dance.

Beginning with the right foot, take three steps backwards, right, left, right.

Hit the left foot against the right foot (don't do this too hard!) and clap your hands.

Starting with the left foot, take three steps forward, left, right, left.

Hit the right foot against the left foot and clap again.

Repeat.

Step to the side with the left foot.

Cross the right foot behind the left foot.

Step to the side with the left foot again.

Hit your right foot against the left foot and clap.

Repeat but step to the side with the right foot.

THE TANGO HUSTLE

Keeping your knees bent and body low, take three steps forward starting with your right foot.

Quickly bring the left toe next to the right toe, make it look like you're stopping but don't and . . . step forward on your right foot.

Slightly turn on your right foot and start the whole sequence again.

The continental hustle and the finger-pointing line hustle as seen in *Saturday Night Fever* and *Boogie Nights* require no partner like the California hustle, just a lot of concentration.

The hustle is best done to Latin-influenced disco music, although the hit that made the dance an international favourite in 1975 employed simple drumming, very light choral singing and a lazily skipping flute melody. Van McCoy's 'The Hustle' was followed by a far punchier and longer 'Spanish Hustle' by The Fatback Band and the chugging 'Let's Do The Latin Hustle' by Eddie Drennon & BBS Unlimited. Other more authentic fusions of Latin, salsa and disco can be found in Jobell & the Orchestra de Salsa's 'Never Gonna Let You Go' and the essential all-time classic, Jimmy Sabater's 'To Be With You'.

A Technicolor acid flashback to those Havana dance floors *circa* 1932 is provided by the flamboyant, zoot-suited players of the now legendary Dr Buzzard's Original Savannah Band. The first iconoclastic album of this rhumba-influenced disco revue features sassy Portuguese-Puerto Rican singer Cory Daye on satirical gems, some of them with a social conscience, like 'Cherchez La Femme'. These tracks were all brilliantly arranged in big-band style by the Haitian-born Stony Browder in 1976 and penned by his brother August Darnell (whose alter-ego, Kid Creole and the Coconuts, would keep Latin hustlers spinning into the '80s). The group would often perform with such acts as Gichy Dan's Beachwood #9, and for the avant-garde Ze Records label they appeared on Don Armando's Second Avenue Rhumba Band's No. 1 disco hit, 'Deputy Of Love'.

THE BASIC RHYTHM FOR DISCO DANCING
Close your left foot to your right foot and bend your knees slightly.
Move your right foot to the side and straighten your knees.
Bring your right foot back to the left foot and bend your knees again.
Move your left foot to the side and straighten the knees.
Step to the side with the left foot.
Cross your right foot in front of the left.
Step to the side with your left foot again.
Point your right foot to the side (but don't step down).
Step to the side with the right foot.
Cross your left foot in front of the right.
Step to the side with your right foot again.
Point your left foot to the side.

THE TRAFFIC LIGHT
Step to the side on the right foot and throw both arms upwards into the air with fingers pointing.
Put all the weight on the right leg, bending the right knee and touch the left leg behind on the ball of the foot.
At the same time, throw the right arm to the side, keeping the finger pointed and the left arm behind the body.

Step to the side with the left leg, throwing the right arm up, the
left one out to the side and keep fingers pointed.
Put all the weight on the left leg, touching right foot behind,
and throw both arms down by the side with fingers splayed.

THE POPCORN
Step forward on the right foot, pushing hips forward with a
bounce, and cross arms in front with fingers splayed out.
Touch the left foot out to the side with no weight on it.
Clench the fists with elbows slightly bent backwards and at the
same time push the hips forward with a bounce.
Continue the first move but this time push the left foot forward.
Continue the second move, but with the right foot to the side.
Step forward with a sassy bounce.

THE CORKSCREW
Bend both knees, push the left hip out to the side and swing
the right arm across the chest.

Keeping it loose, and looking over the right arm, swing the left
arm behind the back.
Swing arms loosely out either side and relax the body.
Swing left arm across the chest and right arm behind it.
Always stay relaxed and loose throughout every move.

The freak and the bump are instantly accessible disco dances
for those with lesser terpsichorean aspirations. The bump
involves different parts of the anatomy, mostly the hips, being
thrust against another person's. But you only bump on the offbeat while assuming the Kama Sutra-like positions. Popularised
in 1978 by the *trés élégant* studio band Chic, the freak
resembles a slowed down twist and can be similarly lewd in
form. Raise your arms above your head, bend your hands from
the wrist and wave them sideways from left to right like an
Egyptian, both hands pointing to the same direction. Place
your weight on the balls of your feet. Twist your feet the same

way as the hands, while the body stays in place. If you bend your knees a little and rock sideways like a bell ringing, you are doing the rock freak. You can make a spectacle of yourself alone, as the freak requires no partner; still, doing the dance with someone else doubles the fun. Just position your frame next to the person and do what comes naturally.

Then there was the point. Used as a means of derision or exclamation, the dancer glided around the floor pointing with the fingers of both hands at the worst-dressed person or the best mover in the place. When the pointing came from behind the ears in a swirling motion, the person they pointed to was of exceptional comment in either the good or bad camp.

61

Spaced Out

JET SETTING IN ROME

The year is 1969. Picture yourself lost, wandering aimlessly around the night-time side-streets near the Piazza Navona in the Eternal City. Suddenly there is laughter and a whiff of perfume. You turn around to grab the two girls just about to jump into a dangerous-looking red convertible. Do they speak English? Do they know where the Galleria della Tartaruga is?

'Forget about that Andy Warhol exhibition at the Tartaruga with its endless Che Guevara portraits done in all possible combinations of op-pop colour,' says the girl dressed in the metallic miniskirt. 'Come with us to the Piper Club instead.'

The Piper Club?

'At the Piper you'll find all the cosmopolitan art scene, all the talent from the *biennales* and the metropolitan centres that participate in lively exchanges of artistic activity, the designers, the architects, the musicians, the urban modernists and the up-and-coming international film stars, all assembled for the wild happening. Don't just stand around and stare at dead paintings. Be a work of art yourself!'

And off you go with them in a thundering revving of the red Lamborghini, the girls laughing uproariously.

Outside the club, the parade – a combination of fairground sideshow and haute couture fashion shoot – slowly proceeds through the small, almost undetectable opening. Hippies from the Trastevere area join the swingers in Nehru jackets and obvious jet-setter types arriving in taxis. And, yes, you immediately spot a six-foot fashion model you can't quite name – is it Veruschka, Nicoletta? – walking past you in her bare feet, all in blue against the burnt-umber wall.

As the girls push you inside, you are immediately transported into the kinetic fibreglass future of Roger Vadim's fabulous film *Barbarella*. After a completely dark passage, you enter a psychedelic lobby space, defined into amoeba-like forms by a mesh of elastic cords stretched from floor to ceiling. Electric motors rhythmically deform the structure as it throbs to the music with ultra-violet light. It's as if the whole room is breathing in anticipation of the sensations to follow. You step forward, disorientated now by rapid flashes of colour that are projected onto the wall according to a fixed and ever-changing programme. Images of flowers, comic-strip figures and nudes burn into your retinas. Already this space intensifies your physical and psychic reactions to the point of near panic.

The club is huge. Almost everything is made of shining purple plastic or gleaming stainless steel. All the surfaces that reflect the light and the music have merged into one. Even the ceiling is finished in opaque aluminium panels, reflecting and directing the wash of sound. The neon, the transparent plexi-glass, the abstract forms, the dimensions all accentuate the impression of elastic space and provoke acute perceptual tension. Projections by Ennio Tamburi are slowly metamorphosing into works by Claudio Cintoli on one wall; coloured lights are thrown onto two luminous plastic screens opposite. The tables and the chairs are made of purple transparent PVC. Soap bubbles sparkle in the lights and immense sheets of metachrylate plastic hover over you in the air, treated with chemicals to react to the light and turn violet in time with the music.

This is a new kind of environment for a new kind of

entertainment: a theatre, a dance club and an art gallery all in one. As you make your way below the suspended balcony, you notice there is even a fashion boutique here. Dresses by Paco Rabanne are displayed inside plastic cubes next to silver spacemen overalls. All this constitutes the 'Total Look', the emphasis being on the visual and hyper-modern.

Vibrant new environments like the Piper Club are surfacing as 'The Happening', a form of theatre, and consisting of partly planned, partly spontaneous performances as the participants react as much to each other's actions as to the sound and the light show. Or to the presentations of a band on the stage, or a mime high on the podium. A predetermined musical code or signal programmes the crowd into ritualistic or balletic enactments and different mood changes.

Swinging music as played at the Piper and discos across Europe has played an important role in the emergence of all things revolutionary in the art world. It is a manifestation of a new way of life for the young generation, bringing out bold new forms of fashion and interior design. Now it is possible for an individual to get hold of mass-produced furniture of genuine imaginative quality and to live in a distinctly futuristic setting. You need not go as far as installing a complete Joe Colombo-designed fibreglass living unit; a contemporary space demands just a few well-selected pieces, like a round Eero Aarnio 'Globe' chair or a white Roberto Pasqualetti bed with an attached console.

Besides apartments, two primary examples of new stages for this form research are boutiques and discothèques, providing us with kine-visual objects and more experimental environments. One example comes from the United States. Inspired by the designs of Shiro Kuramata, three students from Pittsburgh created an inflatable club atmosphere with ultra-violet lights, strobe effects, white polythene surfaces, plastic tubing and nine-foot-tall gas-filled silver mylar spheres. As the music played, the participants seemed to float around the throbbing dome lost in the surreal landscape.

64

The Piper Club in Rome, as well as the L'Altro Mondo in Rimini and the Electric Circus in New York, are some of these illustrious spaces that exist only when the rotating lights are switched on. We cannot buy this concept, purchase this new objectless form of art from a gallery or personally possess it in any substantive way. Yet, like an avant-garde film screening or a jazz concert, it succeeds in giving us emotive perceptions in terms of sensations that are as vivid as any that traditional art can give us.

And as the girls push you into the churning mass of bodies towards the heart of the dance floor, the familiar Johnny Halliday yé-yé song abruptly comes to an end. Savage drumming now blasts forth from the speakers and you are plunged into Darkest Africa, assaulted by congas, bongos and a relentless Voodoo-cult chant that pounds right through your skull, taking possession completely, transforming you. 'Jin-go-lo-ba, Jin-go-lo-ba . . .'

DISCO FACT!
The top seven deejays in New York who could make or break a new disco record were Jim Burgess, Kevin Burke, Roy Thode, Rickie Kaczor, Richie Riviera, Howard Merritt and Paul Poulos.

DISCO FACT!
The Ice-Skating Center in California's Conejo Valley became the world's first Icecotèque in the summer of 1977.

Summer Fever

THE SUMMER OF LOVE BEGINS

There are two distinct disco time zones. One is before the first orgasmic gasps of Donna Summer's gigantic club smash 'Love To Love You Baby' began its startling aural assault with a thudding bass augmented by slippery strings. The second is after her series of cadenced climaxes had seduced the satiated sweat-soaked masses into becoming her besotted love slaves.

The Age of Disco Innocence was over! For in the summer of 1975 you couldn't go far without hearing the erotic moans of this mini-masterpiece, which was banned by the BBC and burned by evangelist preachers in the American heartlands. Its impact made Donna Summer the undisputed Queen of Disco, a title she held for well over a decade, and established the Casablanca record label that was to become the premier exponent of dance music.

LaDonna Andrea Gaines was born on 31 December 1949 and grew up in Boston as part of a large family of five sisters and a brother. Her father Andrew was a janitor, butcher and electrician at various different times in his life, her mother a schoolteacher, and her strict church upbringing banned her from even wearing make-up. Inspired by the gospel vocals of Mahalia Jackson, Donna took the first steps towards her singing career at the Grant AME Zion Church where she would often lead the congregation. Lured away from the Lord by white Bostonian rock musicians, and influenced by Janis Joplin and The Velvet Underground, she contemplated a singing career and, as was often the case during this era, also set her starry eyes towards the Broadway stage.

This ambition led her to Manhattan and an audition for the hit musical *Hair* as a replacement understudy for Melba Moore (soon to be a disco diva in her own right with 'Pick Me Up I'll Dance', 'You Stepped Into My Life' and the big hit 'This Is It'). Realising she might never appear on stage unless Moore was taken ill, Donna accepted an offer to play a smaller role (singing the tune 'White Boys') in the German touring version of the show bound for Munich. Because her father had been stationed in Germany during the Second World War and had learnt the language, Donna decided to follow his lead and settle in the country herself. In 1972, while performing in *Godspell*, she met Helmut Sommer. The blond Viennese was a fellow struggling actor who worked part-time as a waiter at the popular Munich disco Why Not?. Soon she was pregnant with her first child, Mimi, and although the couple married in 1973, they would be divorced the very next year.

While starring in *Hair* in Munich, Donna often did the odd studio session for extra cash. During one of these gigs she was introduced to the man who would turn out to be her Svengali and make her an international singing sensation. Producer Giorgio Moroder, owner of Oasis Records with his partner Pete Bellotte, hired her to sing on a demo disc they were preparing at Munich's Musicland Studios for the group Three Dog Night ('Joy To The World'). Once they heard her voice, however, they promptly signed her up, and then searched for suitable songs to show off her talent.

A veteran force on the German music scene since 1966 with his first compositions 'Stop', 'Bla Bla Diddly' and the 1971 hit 'Son Of My Father' on which Donna sang the backing vocals, the Swiss-Italian Moroder made Donna a European smash with her first three releases, 'Hostage', 'Lady Of The Night' and 'Virgin Mary'. 'Hostage' was a No. 1 record in Holland and Belgium, reached No. 2 in France and hit the Top 10 in Spain and Scandinavia. But none of these releases made any impact in America. Moroder knew their first recording geared to vital American and British airplay would have to be really special, and so he decided to write something evocative of the steamy numbers that were much in vogue during the late-'60s, such as the controversial Serge Gainsbourg and Jane Birkin duet *Je T'Aime . . . Moi Non Plus*. (Donna would eventually discofy this song herself in 1978.)

The result was the playfully seductive 'Love To Love You Baby', which Donna found so lyrically embarrassing that she could only sing it in the dark when it was first recorded. On its initial European release, though, the single only found a buying public in Paris. But Moroder refused to give up on the cut and included it in a package of three tracks he submitted to the Los Angeles-based Neil Bogart, who was in the process of setting up a new record label named Casablanca. Bogart loved the 'Love To Love You Baby' track and sensed immediately that it could be a massive hit if it got plenty of what he termed 'bedroom play'. The problem was that the cut lasted only three minutes so Bogart asked Moroder to extend its *coitus interruptus* duration to a more pleasurable length.

Few had ever pushed a pop song beyond the eight-minute mark, but Moroder went back into the studio and, with Donna in the dark again, engineered an unheard-of sixteen-minute-plus version of the song. What was mildly sexy in its original form became a hypnotically erotic tour de force, a *magnum opus* of wanton carnal abandon. Densely orchestrated and deliberately accenting rhythmic thrusts, 'Love To Love You Baby' invited dancers to participate in the sexual ritual of foreplay, fulfilment and post-coital trance. And then held dancers enthralled as it all began again.

Conceptually brilliant, and with an album cover suggesting

masturbation, *Love To Love You Baby* was a formula that would be worth repeating. In the rush to get the Casablanca album into the shops, no one had bothered to check the spelling of Donna's surname, so Sommer ended up as Summer and that became the professional name of the Queen of Disco to every slavering disco queen. 'Love To Love You Baby' not only pushed the limits on the dance floor; it was so often played in its full-length version on the radio that it set a precedent symptomatic of the 'anything goes' spirit of the '70s. The first real rumblings of the coming disco revolution that had been bubbling underground were now being felt beyond its appreciative subculture.

DISCO FACT!
The Sonic Company manufactured a 'Night Fever' pinball machine in 1978 to cash in arcade-wise on *Saturday Night Fever*.

DISCO FACT!
Le Clique was a travelling roadshow of 40 disco fantasy folk hired to create instant atmosphere, theme parties and inject chic excitement into clubs trying to make a trendy name for themselves.

Let Them Dance

THE CASABLANCA RECORDS STORY

Numerous disco record labels exploded onto the scene during the 'thump, thump, thump' '70s. TK, Salsoul, Marlin, Prelude, Butterfly, Solar and Lollipop were just a few of the instantly recognisable logos that dance-floor devotees looked for in the import record shops. But only one label went for disco big time and that was Casablanca Records, the home of Donna Summer, Giorgio Moroder, The Village People, The Ritchie Family, Meco, Love and Kisses, Paul Jabara and practically every other popular dance-orientated artist of the day.

Casablanca Records didn't find its identity until it discovered disco in 1973. But under the visionary eye of owner Neil Bogart the label defined, refined and exploited the genre to its full potential, one that blew its competitors away. Disco music was fun, outrageous and larger-than-life. Under Bogart's innovative guidance, Casablanca spelt Hollywood glitz, glamour and extravagance. The two were made for each other. As each successful month went by, Casablanca rapidly became the MGM of the music industry because Bogart really did have more disco stars than there were in discos like Heaven.

Born Neil Bogartz in 1943, he quickly adopted the name Bogart after his childhood movie idol Humphrey Bogart, star of the classic weepie *Casablanca*. Throughout the '60s he forged a pop promotion career at *Cash Box* magazine, MGM Records and Cameo-Parkway Records and became highly regarded in the industry for his ability to spot a new market and develop music that catered to its tastes. A prime example of this talent came during his tenure as vice-president at Cameo-Parkway; against all the odds he picked out the quirky '96 Tears' by Question Mark and the Mysterians as a major hit.

In the late-'60s, as general manager of Kama Sutra's new independent label Buddah Records, while the rest of the world was into Acid Rock, Bogart realised the gum-chewing teenybopper crowd were being ignored musically. As a result he invented 'bubblegum' music and scored a string of hits with such simplistic songs as 'Green Tambourine', 'Yummy Yummy Yummy', 'Simon Says', 'Chewy Chewy', 'Goody Goody Gumdrops' and '1, 2, 3, Red Light' by groups like The Lemon Pipers, Ohio Express and The 1910 FruitGum Company. When he signed Curtis Mayfield, The Isley Brothers, The Edwin Hawkins Singers ('Oh Happy Day') and Melanie to Buddah, gaining the label a musical credibility in the much-derided 'bubblegum' wake, the rest of the music industry finally woke up to Bogart's perceptiveness.

Just as Bogart scored one of Buddah's biggest successes – 'Midnight Train To Georgia' by Gladys Knight and the Pips – he had a major falling-out with the label's parent company, Viewlex. So he left Buddah in 1974 to set up Casablanca Records and, through sheer reputation alone, quickly found a financial partner in Warner Bros, setting up shop on Sherbourne Drive in Los Angeles. Bogart originally thought of naming his label Emerald City, after *The Wizard Of Oz*, but then he realised Warner's owned the merchandising rights to *Casablanca* . . .

But Bogart really wanted total control over his brainchild and, eight months after signing the Warner's deal, he bought out their share of his company for $1.5 million by over-extending his loans. He took this risk because he was absolutely convinced Casablanca's first album release would be a monster smash. However, *Here's Johnny, Magic Moments From 'The Tonight Show'* sold fewer than half a million copies. To ensure his financial security, Bogart had hoped to shift at least a million of the TV-orientated exploitation item. As bankruptcy loomed on the horizon, he put up everything he owned as collateral to keep his company afloat, and prayed his 'sixth sense' ability to quickly recognise a new trend would not let him down.

Then a package of tracks arrived from the German-based producer Giorgio Moroder and amongst them was the miracle he had hoped for: 'Love To Love You Baby' by Donna Summer. In truth, in any situation other than the dire one in which the company found itself, Moroder, a completely unknown quantity, wouldn't have got past the Casablanca reception desk. (By this time the company had moved to a Moorish-style location on Sunset Boulevard with Bogart's offices being an exact replica of Rick's American Café in *Casablanca*, complete with piano, wicker chairs and birdcages.) But Bogart was desperate and saw Moroder's appearance in terms of divine intervention. In late-1974, as Casablanca looked to be on the verge of early collapse after releasing Gloria Scott's 'Just As Long As We're Together', Bogart had to design the company's Christmas card. Eventually he chose a gold album with snow falling around it and the inscription 'In every desert there is an oasis'. When Moroder revealed his German record label was named Oasis, Bogart was convinced it was some sort of cosmic sign and he bought the rights to 'Love To Love You Baby' on the spot.

Record industry legend has it that Bogart's wife slipped the Donna Summer disc onto his turntable at home during a party. When it electrified his guests into an orgy of dancing, he kept playing the three-minute track over and over again because his party-goers complained it was too short. His subsequent pleas to Moroder to extend the track to album-side length not only assured Bogart disco immortality with Casablanca Records, making his colourful Casbah logo the most recognisable in the dance world, but it also kick-started the international careers of both Summer and Moroder.

At the same time it proved the commercial viability of the genre to the rest of the industry because Bogart sent copies of the song to every deejay in New York's major discos. He knew that if they liked it, he'd have a cross-over hit. After only one week of play in the Manhattan disco area, the album had sold 40,000 local copies and, appropriately, on Valentine's Day 1976, 'Love To Love You Baby' hit No. 1 on *Billboard* magazine's Hot 100, where it would stay for seventeen weeks. Casablanca Records had arrived, saved from extinction by the scintillating spirit of Eurodisco.

It came as no surprise, therefore, that Bogart returned to Eurodisco in its many eccentric forms for further releases. Casablanca launched the continental acts of producer Jacques Morali (Patrick Juvet), Alec R. Costandinos (Love and Kisses) and Adrian Baker (Liquid Gold) on the American market. It would also promote the disco careers of Cher ('Take Me Home'), Lipps, Inc. ('Funkytown'), the Bee Gees protégée Teri DeSario ('Ain't Nothin' Gonna Keep Me From You'), D.C. LaRue ('Let Them Dance'), Dennis Parker ('Like An Eagle'), Pattie Brooks ('After Dark') and many others through the subsidiary labels Millennium and Parachute.

Bogart explained why he had taken so quickly to the disco movement and expounded his overall philosophy at the fourth annual Disco Forum in 1977. 'Disco is a major influence in the world of fashion,' he said. 'It is a dynamic factor in contemporary advertising. It is a message from every consumer that there has been a rediscovery of America's greatest by-product: fun.'

Another label offshoot, Chocolate City, was run by Cecil Holmes, Bogart's close friend and principal partner at Casablanca from its inception in 1973 to its sale to

Polygram/Mercury in 1980. Holmes had been vice-president of R&B promotion at Cameo-Parkway and launched the funk label with 'Find My Way' by a group originally called The New York City Players. Bogart and Holmes changed their name to Cameo as a homage to their '60s roots. Eclectic hits by George Clinton's funkadelic Parliament and Parlet rapidly followed.

As Casablanca's presence in the disco market grew, and money poured in from their major investments Donna Summer and heavy metal rockers Kiss, Bogart decided to extend the company's reach to take in other aspects of the media. Forming a partnership with Hollywood producer Peter Guber (who would later team up with Barbra Streisand's ex-hairdresser Jon Peters to oversee such movie block-busters as *Batman*), the resulting Casablanca Filmworks developed the projects *Thank God It's Friday*, *The Deep* (1977) and *Midnight Express* (1978). Each of the soundtracks became smash hits, helped enormously by the Best Original Song Oscar won for Donna Summer's 'Last Dance' on *Thank God It's Friday* and the Best Original Score Oscar won by Giorgio Moroder for *Midnight Express*.

In 1980, as disco began to dwindle as a mainstream fad, Bogart sold the company to Polygram and set up Boardwalk Records. He hit the American No. 1 chart spot with 'I Love Rock 'N' Roll' by Joan Jett and the Blackhearts in February 1982. Three months later he was dead. Cecil Holmes went straight from Casablanca to Columbia Records where, as a top A&R executive, he oversaw the career of New Kids on the Block.

Bogart and Casablanca were pivotal in the emergence of disco from the gay, black and Latino underground to the commercial mass acceptance of the genre. Bogart pushed disco's innate sensuality, outrageousness, imagination and flamboyance to new levels of symphonic musicality and image-consciousness. And then he went further again with soft-porn album covers. There was no musical experiment or disco act that Casablanca would turn down if the label felt there was a niche for it. A perfect example was the 1978 Christmas sensation 'Hallelujah 2000' by the group of the same name, a pounding fifteen-minute 12-inch version of Handel's Hallelujah Chorus from the brilliant writer/producer team of Joe Long and Robby Adcock.

That each release was so innovative, so well marketed and so timeless in retrospect was the glorious hallmark of a Casablanca record. Play it again, Neil.

Hot Stuff

THE SUMMER OF LOVE CONTINUES

Donna Summer madness continued to capture clubbers' imaginations. The cover of *A Love Trilogy*, her next album after *Love To Love You Baby*, showed her floating in clouds. As a metaphor for her rapid rise to success and newly found goddess status, it couldn't have been a more perfect image. Effortlessly appealing to both straight and gay clubbers, Summer cemented her lofty position with the release of what turned out to be disco dynamite. From the Top 40 hit 'Could It Be Magic' (written by Barry Manilow and revived in the '90s by Take That) to the eighteen-minute marathon 'Try Me I Know We Can Make It', Summer proved she could belt out a song with the best of them, confounding her critics who assumed she could only excel in breathy passion.

Not wanting to rest on their laurels, and anxious to satisfy the growing demands of the discophile, Moroder, Bellotte and Summer would collaborate on an exhausting number of 4/4 beat/song-orientated classics during the golden years. The *Four Seasons Of Love* album quickly followed *A Love Trilogy* and few complained. Even though the slow ballad 'Winter Melody' was the only cut to dent the charts, the album served Yuletide dancers well with 'Spring Affair', 'Summer Fever' and 'Autumn Changes'. The free 1977 calendar which came with the album presented Summer as a Hollywood pin-up for all seasons in various glamorous guises from Marilyn Monroe to Jeanette MacDonald.

For their next theme, the trio came up with a musical journey through the past with *I Remember Yesterday*. Spanning the speakeasy sound of the '20s to Phil Spector's Girl Group era, this pop pastiche continued to extend Summer's range while keeping disco dervishes whirling on the floor. But the tracks 'Love's Unkind' and 'Back In Love Again' paled in comparison with the epoch-making B-Side closer 'I Feel Love'. An industrial Moog mosaic of cosmic vibrations, ethereal vocals and Kraftwerkian electronica, Summer had improvised the song in the studio. Unwittingly, she had created the celebrated pièce de résistance of her career and the single most important composition of the entire disco movement.

'I Feel Love' was crucial in the development of the musical form by introducing a dramatic synthesised soundscape inspired by the 1975 Kraftwerk song 'Autobahn'. Still beloved by contemporary exponents of dance, and consistently reinvented over subsequent years, Summer's anthem remains very much a part of the hip deejay's repertoire. Regarded by many as the perfect disco record, it would steer Moroder into developing and refining his own inimitable brand of sci-fi-influenced metallic grooves, shimmering metronomic sequences, robotic drum beats and mesmeric techno-phunk with 'From Here To Eternity' and other similar seminal trance-like recordings.

Collaborating with legendary Oscar-winning composer John Barry on the blockbuster movie *The Deep* was the next surprising twist to Summers accelerating career. She crooned the sensuous theme song 'Down, Deep Inside'; appropriately the soundtrack was released on transparent blue vinyl.

Once Upon A Time was the next Summer milestone to dominate the disco floors throughout the 1977-78 winter season. It was an ambitious two-record set relating a working woman's Cinderella search for her identity through vividly presented portraits of urban paranoia, drug highs and bitter disappointments on the rocky road to an ambivalent happy ending. The stand-out tracks on this dance-floor fable, co-written by Summer herself, were 'Now I Need You', with its overpowering cathedral choral feel, which segued gloriously into 'Working The Midnight Shift', a sombre lament set against the backdrop of metropolis machinery.

Next, she acted and performed the Oscar-winning song 'Last Dance' in *Thank God It's Friday*, one of the flood of disco movies released in the wake of *Saturday Night Fever*. The album shot to No. 1 in the charts and made Summer a bona-fide superstar with the ability to pack stadiums worldwide on her sell-out tours, as demonstrated by her immensely popular *Live And More* double LP. The 'Live' aspect covered all the hits her fans expected, while the 'More' generated another gigantic crowd-pleasing disco spectacular with 'MacArthur Park Suite' based around the Jimmy Webb easy-listening evergreen classic.

The pinnacle of Summer's career was reached with *Bad Girls* in 1979. A warts-and-all look at the seamy side of Los Angeles, it was *Sweet Charity* goes disco with Donna bumping and grinding her way through the hot and nasty title track, the rock-influenced 'Hot Stuff', the longing 'Our Love' and the rueful disenchantment of 'Sunset People'. She would score heavily with 'No More Tears (Enough Is Enough)', her raunchy duet with Barbra Streisand, the first 12-inch single ever to sell a million copies, but this high point was the beginning of the end for the premier diva.

Greatest hits compilations would continue to sell, as would isolated single releases over the next decade such as 'On The Radio', 'State Of Independence', 'She Works Hard For The Money' and 'This Time I Know It's For Real'. But her alleged comments on Aids in the early stages of the health crisis alienated her enormous gay following and in one fell swoop eliminated her hardcore audience. Despite her fall from grace, Donna Summer's contribution to the entire disco era cannot be underestimated. She semi-started it, she fuelled it, she's written a Broadway musical about it (*Ordinary Girl*) and she'll always be remembered for it, if only for 'I Feel Love'.

Utopia – Me Giorgio

Although Giorgio Moroder was best known for his work with Donna Summer, the producer also had a solo disco career and had a major influence on the work of numerous other artists. Here's a list of Moroder's best non-Donna achievements in the disco field.

- *From Here To Eternity*/Giorgio: a seminal album that had the most impact on the techno-phunk movement and featured the perfect 15-minute 47-second A-side medley of the title track, 'Faster Than The Speed Of Light', 'Lost Angeles' and 'Utopia – Me Giorgio'
- 'Get On The Funk Train'/Munich Machine
- 'I Wanna Funk With You Tonite'/Giorgio
- 'Evolution'/Giorgio Moroder: a moody side-long slice of pre-electronica from the *Battlestar Galactica* album
- E = MC3/Giorgio: 'Baby Blue', 'What A Night', 'If You Weren't Afraid' and the title track
- 'Zodiacs'/Roberta Kelly
- *A Whiter Shade Of Pale*/Munich Machine introducing Chris Bennett: the title track, 'It's For You' and 'It's All Wrong (But It's Alright)'
- *Love's In You, Love's In Me*/Giorgio & Chris: the title track, 'Keep It Together' and 'I Can't Wait'
- 'Call Me'/Blondie (theme from *American Gigolo*)
- 'Chase'/Giorgio Moroder (from *Midnight Express*)
- 'Harmony'/Suzi Lane

- 'Beat The Clock'/Sparks
- 'The Runner', 'Set Me Free', 'Jump The Gun'/The Three Degrees
- 'Fire In My Heart', 'Playing For Time', 'You Can'/Madleen Kane
- 'Let The Music Play'/Giorgio: rare analogue synthscape released as a seven-inch single only in 1977

After composing the soundtrack for Paul Schrader's film *Cat People* (1982), Moroder teamed up with Human League lead singer Phil Oakey for 'Together in Electric Dreams' from the *Electric Dreams* (1984) soundtrack. 'Goodbye Bad Times' was their follow-up. He also composed a whole new score for the 1926 Fritz Lang science-fiction movie classic *Metropolis* when it was reissued in 1984. Songs by Bonnie Tyler, Pat Benatar, Adam Ant and Freddie Mercury were integrated into the score. In 1990 Moroder wrote the official World Cup song for Italy, 'To Be Number One'. The original Italian version, *'Un' Estate Italiana'*, was sung by Edoardo Bennato and Gianna Nannini.

In 1992 Moroder had a sizeable European hit with the album *Forever Dancing*, which featured updates of the classic disco tunes 'Boogie Oogie Oogie', 'That's The Way (1 Like It)', 'Don't Leave Me This Way', 'Born To Be Alive' and his own 'I Feel Love', intermingled with the new compositions 'I Can See You Dancing, 'My Secret Wish', 'In The Name Of Love' and 'The Party Goes On'. The lead song on the album was 'Carry On' by Donna Summer which has had an extended club life by being remixed on countless occasions ever since. Donna, Giorgio and disco have happily gone full circle.

DISCO FACT!
Actor Jeff Bridges wrote the disco tune 'Do the Kong' while shooting the remake of *King Kong* in 1976.

DISCO FACT!
Slim Hyatt is the man credited as being the first ever disco deejay. He began his career in 1962 at Oleg Cassini's Le Club in New York. When he moved on to Shepheard's, he was the first deejay to take on the Musicians Union and their argument about whether spinning records in clubs was putting those who played live out of work.

*Parlez-Vous Français?

EURODISCO

Ursula and Ulla are are models. To help them keep the rhythm on the catwalk, you play them something with a metronomically thumping beat. The record has to have a pretty melody they can hum while they pout and pose. The lyrics need to be in very simple English, nothing too complex or confusing. To get the girls in the mood for the party later on, choose a tune that is sexy in a dreamy way, think of '*69, Année Érotique*' by Jane Birkin and Serge Gainsbourg, or the intoxically sensual theme tune from the film *The Story of O*, only with a stronger beat. Something with the pulse of 'The Theme From Shaft' by Isaac Hayes but simpler, more like the poppy chart hits the girls like to hear on your car radio. Something like 'Turn On To Love' by Jumbo '76, an album recorded in Munich, sent to New York and then sold back to Europe as an import. What you need is Eurodisco.

America may have first defined disco, but it was the European connection that expanded its repertoire with a coolly refreshing sound, derived from various ethnic sources and filtered through years of the Eurovision Song Contest, European Union debate and Eurotrash culture. The Eurodisco style evolved from a confused desire by the 'big fish in a small pond' to be as fabulously fêted internationally as they were on their home turf. But their desperate attempts at 'Americanisation' would usually be so wide of the mark that they remained essentially even more European than ever. This gave Eurodisco its clearly identifiable sound – one where the producer's role was the most important and where the singer was relegated into second place. Often the results of this mind-bending common market melding of foreign accents, bad diction, bizarre arrangements and lightweight production, usually top-heavy with strings, were headache-inducing (Germany's Dschinghis Khan with 'Moscow' and its gob-smacking chorus 'Ha, ha, ha, ha, ha', for example) or hilariously funny (like Holland's Luv and their pedantically enunciated 'You're The Greatest Lover').

But sometimes the united colours of *bene* tone efforts would resonate with signature melody, production zing and mesmerising power, and hit the irresistible D spot of electric ecstasy. A prime example is the Spanish duo Baccara with their enormous pan-European hit of 1977 'Yes Sir, I Can Boogie'. It was the '70s disco era which gave rise to what is still termed the 'summer hit' in music business-speak. More people were travelling to more exotic places and dancing to a wider selection of music than ever before during those defining years. When they returned home they wanted to relive their holiday memories as a sonic postcard and the pop charts would reflect their imported tastes. Other instances of this phenomenon were 'Magic Fly' by Space, '*Y Viva España*' by Sylvia, '*Dolce Vita*' by Ryan Paris and 'Bimbo jet' by El Bimbo.

Some Eurodisco mavens would have a far-reaching impact on all aspects of global dance culture: Giorgio Moroder, Alec R. Costandinos, Cerrone, Amanda Lear and Jacques Morali were just the tip of the iceberg. But we mustn't overlook all those quirky, tacky, camp, half-forgotten and blissfully wonderful Euro arias which continue to sparkle, or which had a brief magical moment before landing squarely in the guilty-pleasure disco void.

Baccara was the brainchild of Dutch producer Rolf Soja. He put singers Maria Mendiola and Mayte Mateus together (is the latter's surname the reason why the duo's logo was a single red rose?) and, with co-writer Frank Dostal, crafted some of the most memorably Kontinental Kitsch Klassics of the decade. 'Yes Sir, I Can Boogie', with its instantly engaging harp opening, breathy lyrics, anti-feminist subservience, peripatetic violin cadences and daft lyrics, meant the Baccara formula was set in stone. It was one Soja would relentlessly mine for all it was worth over three fun albums and a Eurovision Song Contest entry for Luxembourg in 1978 with '*Parlez-Vous Français*?' (it came seventh).

Because Baccara were the first ever Spanish duo to top the charts in Britain, the Soja factory churned out one soundalike cut after another until 1980 and created as many delights as disasters in the process. Examples of the former were the Soja/Dostal compositions 'Koochie-Koo', 'Sorry, I'm A Lady', 'Don't Play Me A Symphonie' [*sic*], 'Ay Ay Sailor', 'My Kisses Need A Cavalier' and 'By 1999'. Soja came unstuck when he tried to broaden the duo's appeal with disco versions of such diverse evergreens as 'Light My Fire', 'La Bamba', 'Granada' and 'Yummy, Yummy, Yummy'. Each fell horribly flat and was hampered further by the autocue cuties murdering the lyrics with their Costa Brava inflections.

This touches on one of the more diverting aspects of Eurodisco. It was one thing garbling 'Boogie Woogie' as 'Boogie Voogie' in 'Yes Sir, I Can Boogie'. But when the girls pronounced words totally wrongly because of bad English translation and/or tuition, it was another giggle-inducing thing altogether. For example, in their western-themed 'The Devil Sent You To Laredo', complete with scintillating honky-tonk piano and gunshot sound effects, the word 'desperado' is mispronounced 'desper- *ay* -do' to rhyme with 'Laredo'.

And so it was with the German threesome Arabesque who, on their 'Midnight Dancer' hit single, had the brain-freezing rhyme of 'tequila', with 'Venezuela'. The South American country was pronounced 'Venezwheeler' to rhyme with the alcoholic beverage. Arabesque were typical Baccara clones of the day and their record arrangements would slavishly ape those of their Spanish counterparts. While their songs were in the main gimmick-ridden glamour galas with about as much substance as the glitterdust painted on their faces, the jet-set fantasy 'High Life' and the ethereal 'Bye Bye My Love' stand out from the disco dross of 'Parties In A Penthouse', 'Make Love Whenever You Can' and 'Hello, Mr Monkey'. 'High Life' sports another mispronounced howler in the vague rhyming of 'Barbados' with 'alligators'. And does lead vocalist Sandra Lauer sing about 'hounding' or 'hounting' or 'hunting' alligators?

Arabesque's legacy to dance culture had nothing to do with their erratic releases, but everything to do with Sandra Lauer. Using just her Christian name, Sandra would have enormous club hits in the '80s and '90s with such songs as '(I'll Never Be) Maria Magdalena', 'In The Heat Of The Night', 'Innocent Love' and 'Everlasting Love'. Her producer, Michael Cretu, would then recast her as the voice of Enigma for his multi-million-selling global Gregorian Chant project of the same name.

Other German disco acts include Eruption ('I Can't Stand The Rain'), Gilla ('Bend Me, Shape Me'), Champagne ('Rock 'N' Roll Star), Amii Stewart ('Knock On Wood'), John Paul Young ('Love Is In The Air'), Roberta Kelly ('Zodiacs'), drag queen Louise Leshter ('*Deshabillez-Moi*'), The Munich Machine ('Get On The Funk-Train') and Lipstique ('At The Discotheque'). Silver Convention were one of the first groups to break out of the German ghetto and take their lightly choppy disco message to America, garnering seventeen gold discs in the process. Produced by Michael Kunze and studio muso and arranger Sylvester Levay, Silver Convention came about when the duo teamed up in 1974 to write and record some disco instrumental backing tracks together. Overdubbing female session singers on one track they considered particularly commercial, they coined the name Silver Convention (taken from Levay's own nickname, Silver) and had a massive and immediate hit in Europe with 'Save Me'.

Demand for an album quickly followed and, using the same anonymous session musicians and singers, Kunze and Levay cobbled together the *Save Me* LP which sold a million copies worldwide. One Levay-penned track had been recorded as 'Run, Rabbit, Run', but when it was pointed out the title also referred to an old English music-hall standard, it was changed to 'Fly, Robin, Fly' and the result was their biggest-selling record ever. A huge chart hit in 1975 that crossed over into the clubs and got the early mirror ball rolling, it sold a million copies in Germany alone.

Soon an actual group was needed rather than just session talent, and the Silver Convention line-up was put together from German singers Penny McLean and Ramona Wolf, and former Les Humphries Singers member Linda G. Thompson (who had a minor solo disco hit with 'Ooh What A Night'). Not a lot of variety or content was heard in Silver Convention's output, but the mood evoked was consistently spacy, ecstatic and heavily orchestrated with sweetly ephemeral vocals bouncing off the tight production. 'Get Up And Boogie', 'Save Me', 'I Like It', 'Tiger Baby' and 'No, No, Joe' kept the group on most disco turntables throughout 1976 while Penny McLean (real name Gertrude Munzer) also had her own solo disco hit with 'Lady Bump' in 1975, a shrieking, raucous barnstormer that would be immortalised as part of The Ritchie Family's classic medley, 'The Best Disco In Town'.

By 1977 Thompson had quit the group to resume her solo career and was replaced by New York *chanteuse* Rhonda Heath. But Silver Convention were on the decline by then despite some great tracks like the underrated gems 'Dancing In The Aisles', 'Always Another Girl', 'Everybody's Talking 'Bout Love' and the Eurovision Song Contest entry 'Telegram' (it came eighth for Germany) being taken as singles from their third and fourth albums *Madhouse* and *Golden Girls*. Their swan song was the superb 'Spend The Night With Me' which kept the glittering threesome in the disco public's eye during the summer of 1978. Its failure to chart, however, caused the trio to break up soon after its release. Producer Michael Kunze went on to translate several hit musicals such as *Cats* and *Sunset Boulevard* for German audiences. Together with Sylvester Levay he arranged and composed a new take on the opera *The Magic Flute* called *Mozart!* for Vienna's prestigious Theater an der Wien in 1999.

The most famous German disco group of all would be put together by producer/composer Frank Farian, the man behind Gilla, Eruption and, in the modem era, ace mimers Milli Vanilli. From the very beginning, in the looks department, Boney M were always a source of cringe-inducing embarrassment. Not since Abba had a group edged so close to self-parody. Three girls and a guy outlandishly abusing gold lamé, steel chains and winged silver spacesuits in an attempt to acquire an air of international sophistication, Boney M always got it wrong. They always got it wrong in exactly the right way, however, and no one could ever hope to match the jolly-holiday mentality and brain-curdling catchiness of their songs, which won them grudging respect from even the harshest of the rock press critics.

The whole Boney M success story came about because Farian had thrown the song 'Baby Do You Wanna Bump' together in 1975 and performed the lead vocals himself. When it became a surprise hit in Holland, he quickly needed to form an actual group for those vital television appearances. After careful consideration he selected four attractive West Indians in search of a German career. Liz Mitchell came from the Hamburg production of *Hair*, Marcia Barrett and Maizie Williams hailed from London, and the gruff-sounding male vocalist Bobby Farrell was recruited from a local soul group.

It wasn't until late in 1976 that Farian and Co came up with 'Daddy Cool', their first international smash. Radios around the world repeated its maddeningly nagging refrain for months on end and, when New York's prestigious Paradise Garage club included it on its playlist, Boney M's disco career was assured. The album *Take The Heat Off Me* offered a rendition of the Bobby Hebb 1966 hit 'Sunny', while the British pressing of the disc had to replace 'Baby Do You Wanna Bump' with 'Help Help', a remix of a Gilla track, for copyright reasons.

Love For Sale was released in 1977 and contained the hook-filled hits 'Ma Baker' (another example of the continentals getting it wrong, as the real-life '30s criminal the song referred to was actually called Ma Barker) and 'Belfast', an unlikely choice of subject matter for a singalong crowd-pleaser. The disco-crazed summer of 1978 saw the release of the group's biggest success. Their music-box version of The Melodians' reggae spiritual 'Rivers Of Babylon' shot straight to No. 1 in most charts around the world. In Britain, once the song had peaked at the top of the charts, the single was flipped over so the former B-side 'Brown Girl In The Ring' could be offered as the next big hit. Amazingly, this devious device worked and Farian scored again. Not surprisingly, the tie-in album *Nightflight To Venus* turned out to be a massive seller as well.

The shimmer of Boney M never dimmed as amiable Euro hits like 'Gotta Go Home', 'El Lute', 'Painter Man' and 'Kalimba De Luna' consolidated the band's cult fan base. While a 'Rasputin' or a 'Mary's Boy Child – Oh My Lord' might not be anybody's idea of a perfect four minutes on a serious dance floor, the free-for-all party atmosphere of the whole Boney M repertoire has survived remarkably well.

Like Frank Farian in Germany, producer Jacques Morali, together with Henri Belolo (his partner in Can't Stop Productions), were adding a distinctive touch to French Eurodisco. After devising The Village People and outing gay disco from the club closet, Morali and Belolo launched the disco career of firm French favourite Patrick Juvet. The handsome blond had recorded a breakneck speed ten-minute French-language disco stormer with Jean-Michel Jarre called 'Paris By Night' and had been a constant feature in the Gallic Top 10 with 'Magic' (a cover version of the 1974 Pilot hit), 'Sonia' and *'Rappelle-Toi Minette'*, and Morali and Belolo quite correctly divined his international appeal given the right contemporary material.

All that came from brainstorming sessions between Morali, Juvet and ex-Village People lead singer Victor Willis. Together they wrote the first Juvet jingle to chart internationally, the blatantly commercial 'I Love America'. 'Got A Feeling' from the *I Love America* album made inroads too. But it was the follow-up album *Lady Night* which delivered the delicious Eurodisco goods. The title track with its impossibly swirling violins, 'Swiss Kiss' and the medley 'The Gay Paris/French Pillow Talk' floated dancers off the floors towards nighttime Nirvana in 1978.

Morali would have less success with the career of Phylicia Allen. The wife of Victor Willis, she released her *Josephine Superstar* album in 1978, a disco homage to the showbiz life and eyebrow-raising loves of Josephine Baker, the famous black American dancer who emigrated to France and found stardom on the Pigalle cabaret circuit. The title track and 'Two Loves Have I' had their diehard fans but it wouldn't be until her appearance as Bill Cosby's wife in the hit American sitcom *The Cosby Show* that Allen, under the name Phylicia Rashad, would find the fame eluding her under the disco spotlight.

Away from the Morali music machine, three other French groups made a deep impact on the international scene. Space were conceived thanks to a French television programme on astrology after the series producer approached singer/songwriter Didier Marouani to compose the theme tune. The idea of composing a melody with space connotations greatly appealed to Marouani because he had been experimenting with synthesiser and keyboard techniques in an attempt to create a 'new' sound. The result was a demo tape which so excited everyone who heard it that Marouani eventually took it to French record producer Jean-Paul Illiesco for his opinion on just exactly how commercial it was.

The slice of classical futurism which Marouani had composed immediately impressed Illiesco, who quickly hired three other musicians – John Flying, bass keyboards, Pierre Alain Dahan, drums (later replaced by American drummer Joe Hammer), and Roland Romanelli, clavinette and Korg synthesisers – and the end result was the magnetically echoing 'Magic Fly'. Even though Illiesco claimed the intensely rhythmic track wasn't specifically aimed at the disco market, it became an instant dance-floor hit before achieving massive crossover success in the pop market. Ironically, the astrology show never did use the theme. Kebekelektrik also scored a hit with a 1977 cover version of the tune.

The ensuing album contained the follow-up singles 'Tango in Space' and 'Carry On Turn Me On' with vocals supplied by superstar session singer Madeline Bell. She also featured on the second album *Deliverance*, an even stronger disco seller, and the title track, with its synthesiser melodies augmented by heavy drums and a full choral chant, was an all-enveloping stunner. Other Space odysseys were 'Save Your Love For Me' and 'Air Force'.

The reason drummer Pierre Alain Dahan left Space was so that he could join the group Voyage, the second major force in *le monde du disco français*. With their very first release, the sweet harmonious sounds of producer Roger Tokarz's combo filled the world's airwaves and dance floors in the latter part of the '70s. To front the group he picked Sylvia Mason, fresh from singing lead vocals with Cerrone, and surrounded her with keyboard player Marc Chantereau, bass player Slim Pezin, and Dahan. Collectively they wrote and produced their material which, as their name suggested, zipped around the world of music and nabbed every available rhythmic inspiration from the Orient ('Orient Express'), Scotland ('Scotch Machine'), the Pacific Islands ('Tahiti, Tahiti') and South America ('Latin Odyssey'). These 'Souvenirs' of their *bon voyage* into the 'From East to West' hemispheres of disco were a delight and guaranteed the group a first-class passage into dance history.

As did 'Don't Let Me Be Misunderstood', the first major release from Leroy Gomez and Santa Esmeralda. Gomez, a Cape Cod native of Portuguese descent, had moved to Paris in the mid-'70s and found himself working consistently as a session musician thanks to his talent with the guitar, flute and saxophone. His idea to update The Animals' classic 1965 hit with Latin licks, flamenco frissons and a driving disco beat broke record sales all over Europe when it was released in 1977, achieving pole chart position in Germany, Spain, France and Holland. It proved to be disco dynamite when Casablanca Records picked up the stateside rights and it has since become a dance staple.

Gomez was also voted the Best Live Act of 1977 in France thanks to his energetic concerts but soon left Santa Esmeralda to pursue a solo career with the album *Gypsy Woman*. The best track on that 1978 release was 'Spanish Harlem'. Jimmy Goings filled his place in the Santa Esmeralda line-up and, naturally, after hitting disco pay-dirt with one Animals song, they decided to try it again with 'The House Of The Rising Sun', but to lesser success, and 'Sevilla Nights' which ended up on the *Thank God It's Friday* movie soundtrack. But in 1979 the group bounced back with the irrepressibly infectious 'Another Cha Cha + Cha Cha Suite', undoubtedly the best Santa Esmeralda disco attraction of all.

Other French acts worth mentioning include La Belle Epoque ('Black Is Black' and 'Miss Broadway'), Kongas ('Africanism/Gimme Some Lovin' '), Don Ray ('Got To Have Loving'), Sabine Sauvant ('Casbah In Cairo'), Michel Polnareff (the entire soundtrack to the violent 1976 thriller *Lipstick* starring Margaux and Mariel Hemingway), Afric Simone ('Ramaya'), 'Ça Plane Pour Moi' *homme* Plastic Bertrand ('*Tout Petite La Planètte*'), Monserate featuring Lyda Zamora ('When The Sun Goes Down'), Crystal Grass ('Hot Love In Spain'), France Gall (the *Dancing Disco* album), Ottawan ('Hands Up (Give Me Your Heart)' and 'D.I.S.C.O.'), the Liberace-styled Claude François ('Alexandrie, Alexandra' and 'Magnolias Forever'), The Gibson Brothers ('Come To America', 'Non-Stop Dance' and 'Cuba') and Alain Chamfort ('Manureva' co-written and produced by Serge Gainsbourg).

The brief disco career of Sheila B. Devotion is worth noting in the French arena. Her unremarkable version of the classic Gene Kelly Hollywood anthem 'Singin' in the Rain' had hustlers unfolding imaginary umbrellas in 1978 and paddling across the neon floors. But the '60s survivor (she had the French cover hit of Cher's 'Bang Bang') would actually have her biggest dance-floor success the next year with the Chic-penned hypno-trancer 'Spacer'.

But the all-out French diva was another Parisian survivor from an even more distant era: Egyptian-born Yolanda Gigliotti changed her name to Dalida and had her first hits in the '50s (such as 'Bambino' in 1956 and '*Histoire D'Un Amour*' in 1957). But the Grande Dame of Notre-Dame, who was dubbed Mademoiselle Bambino for years after her splashy début, would transform herself into France's premier disco queen through being a permanent fixture on the top-rated Sacha Distel TV variety show and then via a mythical clutch of Maxi Club versions of her chart-toppers.

Her least interesting cut 'The Lambeth Walk' aside (purloined from the ancient British stage musical *Me And My Girl* and shockingly discofied to within an inch of its sorry life), Dalida's major releases were musical manna from disco heaven. '*Laissez-Moi Danser*/Let Me Dance', '*Rio Do Brasil*', '*Confidences Sur La Fréquence*', 'Gigi In Paradisco', '*Soleil Soleil*', 'Generation '78' and 'Ça Me Fait Rêver' were all exceptionally produced by her brother Orlando. Each kept dancers stuck to club floors like magnets to a fridge and were brilliantly executed by the silken-voiced *chanteuse*.

Even though she committed suicide in tragic circumstances in 1987, Dalida's work lives on in modern France thanks to her brother's tireless efforts to keep her past glories alive. Every jewel-like track is continually being remixed by producers inspired by her unique disco *joie de vivre*. Her legacy also continues in the songs she made famous being translated into other languages – such as the soft disco epic *'Mourir Sur Scene'*, about a diva wanting to die on stage, being turned into the MOR ego-trip 'I Was Born To Sing Forever' for Shirley Bassey.

Dalida also contributed to the disco medley craze that swept Europe following the success of Ritchie Family's international 1976 hit 'The Best Disco In Town'. On her lushly produced *Generation '78* album she emoted through such diverse standards as 'Where Have All The Flowers Gone', 'Look What They Have Done To My Song Ma' and 'Dream Lover'. Hundreds of other artists and studio troupes had already followed suit with their own *mélanges,* excerpting everything from Gallic drinking songs to the chart hits of The Rolling Stones. Sabine Sauvant's 'To The Music Hit-Makers' listed a bewildering amount of '60s million-sellers as did Veronica Unlimited's 'What Kind Of Dance is This?' and Theo Vaness's 'Back To Music'. Cafe Creme's 'Disco Unlimited Citations' focused on Beatles songs, Melophonia's 'Limelight Disco Symphony' strung Charlie Chaplin tunes together and 'Nostalgia Medley' by The Chocolat's did the same with Cole Porter's back catalogue.

The Chocolat's were fabricated in Brussels, and Belgium was also churning out Eurodisco product to meet the insatiable demand. 'Kings Of Clubs' by The Chocolat's, 'Euro-Vision' by Telex (it came seventeenth for the country in the 1980 Eurovision Song Contest) and 'Born To Be Alive' by Guadeloupe-born Patrick Hernandez were highly

93

representative of what was happening disco-wise in the land of Hercule Poirot.

Two Man Sound were to score Belgium's major worldwide hit with 'Disco Samba', a medley of Latin-American carnival favourites including 'Ay Ay Caramba', 'Brazil', 'Charlie Brown' and their own self-penned chart success 'Copacabana'. The latter became a hit at the Rio de Janeiro Festival in 1971 where songwriters Sylveer (Sylvain) Vanholme and Francis Pop (Lou) Deprijck won third prize for their sterling effort. Vanholme had left the popular Belgian group The Wallace Collection to join up with Deprijck and form Two Man Sound after the high point of Charles Aznavour covering three of his compositions in a home-grown movie. The enigmatic Pipou was the third member of the group who also hit big with '*Que Tal America*' in 1979 but couldn't match that success with their follow-up releases 'Samba Samba' or 'Brazil O Brazil'.

Mondo Disco in Italy provided few worldwide hits because the industry was geared very much towards its home shores. Every now and again a pizza platter would become a global chart sensation, but most spaghetti sounds would remain underground favourites for the discognoscenti only. Breakout cuts include La Bionda's 'One For You, One For Me' – even though the duo's 'Sandstorm' was better crafted for disco play – and Raffaella Carra's impossibly catchy '*A Far L'Amore Comincia Tu*', The latter track was re-recorded in English as 'Do It, Do It Again' by Carra, best described as Italy's Cilla Black for having a long career in film (*Von Ryan's Express*), music and as a television presenter of popular programmes, and became a huge European smash reaching No. 9 in the British charts in 1978. Carra continued to release further disco-orientated records of which '*Rumore*', 'Black Cat', 'Male' and '*Felicita, Ta, Ta*' are notable.

Other Italian celebrities weren't so lucky with their disco releases in the international arena. The 1960s icon Bobby Solo (he covered 'If You're Going To San Francisco' for the Italian market) also adapted one of his greatest hits, '*Una Lacrima Sul*

Viso', to the beats-per-minute format. Lucio Battisti, a '70s icon, had *'El Velero'*, and his chart companion Umberto Tozzi provided *'Tu'* and 'Gloria' for his fans, but it would be Laura Brannigan who would have the international hit with the latter song in 1982, three years after its Italian sell-by date. Celebutante supremo Heather Parisi scored two major hits with the expertly crass 'Disco Bambina' and infinitely superior *'Ti Rockero,'* with its shivering violin break, too.

But while amazingly operatic and Giorgio Moroder-influenced releases would appear from time to time (such as Baciotti's thundering slice of electronica 'Black Jack' and The Rings 'Savage Lover), Mondo Disco seemed to be reserved for three writer/producer/arranger twosomes only. The most important of these were Celso Valli and Quelli Del Castello who were responsible for the *Disco Fizz* album by Azoto, *'Amado Mio Amore'* by El Pasador, 'Hot Leather' and 'He's Speedy Like Gonzalez' by The Passengers and their directional masterpiece, 'Hills Of Katmandu' by Tantra. The Tantra cut, one of the major club hits in 1979, was an entrancing seventeen-minute opus of melodious mysticism, choral chanting and hypnotic momentum. Once heard, 'Hills Of Katmandu' is never forgotten and would be remixed by gay disco guru Patrick Cowley for further club success.

Jacques Fred Petrus and Mauro Malavasi were the second powerhouses of Italian disco pop. They produced 'Music Man' in 1979, 'It's Dancing Time' by Revanche and 'I'm A Man' by Macho, but found more success with The Peter Jacques Band releases 'Fire Night Dance', 'Counting On Love – One Two Three', 'Welcome Back' and 'Exotically'. This four-man band comprising lead vocalist Jacob Wheeler, Sandi Bass, Dianne Washington and Von Gretchen Shephard were cynically modelled on Boney M and even beat that outfit in the outlandish lurex, satin and glitter stakes. 'Welcome Back' was co-written by Luther Vandross, and the future multi-million-selling recording artist would join Petrus and Malavasi to notch up their biggest success as part of the group Change. 'A Lover's Holiday', 'Glow of Love' and 'Searching' were as big on the dance floor as they were in the charts.

The third team, Giancarlo Meo and Claudio Simonetti, produced their fair share of dynamo disco ditties, like 'Fear' by Easy Going and 'Give Me A Break' by Vivien Vee. But Simonetti would achieve more lasting fame and celebrity as a film composer. His disco-orientated scores would grace the soundtracks of Italian horror maestro Dario Argento's *Tenebrae*, *Demons* and *Opera*.

Still, it was always Ennio Morricone who has really waved the flag for Italy on the international film soundtrack scene. When the composer's first scores arrived during the mid-'60s, people were immediately struck with his offbeat, almost expressionistic use of the orchestra and the groundbreaking introduction of abstract female voices, eerie whistling sounds, harmonicas and twanging electric guitars to classically handled themes. Besides the music for the Sergio Leone Westerns, for which he is most famous, Morricone painted sonic collages of '60s pop art to cult films like *Danger: Diabolik,* composed huge sweeping symphonies for baroque melodramas directed by the likes of Bernardo Bertolucci and managed to express a perfect early-'70s lifestyle in audio form in countless slickly filmed *giallo* thrillers. There were also the Morricone disco records. Several of his mid-'70s scores contained short discofied takes on the main themes of the films, but in 1977 he released a separate 12-incher aimed directly at the clubs, a remoulded earlier work called 'Come Maddalena'. This especially haunting mid-tempo tune, featuring the wordless cathedral wailings of Edda Dell'Orso, was a welcome change to express in full the delicate, sensuous detailings of the maestro's music in body language. Impeccably designed for maximum cinematic effect, the new version had the power to turn the dingiest disco into a perfectly spotlit private club in the heart of Milan.

Another Italian composer whose film scores surveyed the

decadent '70s scene was Nico Fidenco. His best work was for the *Black Emanuelle* films, a series of soft-core sex traveloques manufactured to cash in on the worldwide success of Just Jaeckin's 1973 film *Emmanuelle*. While the films themselves hit mainly low notes, the Fidenco soundtracks came across as ambitious productions gathered together from global beat collections as well as from the composer's own bongo-driven fusions of easy listening and Santana-styled Latin rock. 'Emanuelle In America Theme' from 1976 is especially memorable. Evoking visions of Cinzano sunsets or undercover reporters performing stripteases for expensively clad human traffickers, this suggestively grinding yet beautifully melodic dance track blurs the distinctions between elegantly poised sound imagery and glossy sleaze.

Aside from Baccara (who continued to have club hits until the early-'90s with the Modem Talking-influenced 'Fantasy Boy' and 'Touch Me'), Spain offered a few one-hit disco wonders: 'Bandolero' by Juan Carlos Calderon, 'Big Bamboo' by Georgie Dann (who co-wrote the French hit 'Soul Dracula' for Hot Blood) and the cover version of Bimbo Jet's '*El Bimbo*' by La Balanga. Bebu Silvetti recorded 'Spring Rain' in Spain which Tom Moulton remixed for Salsoul Records into a disco smash thanks to its instantly recognisable piano riff. Silvetti's other two disco cuts created less fuss but 'Primitive Man' and 'I Love You' are highly interesting nevertheless.

Barrabas, too, managed to rack up a sizeable number of disco hits. With their biblically inspired name, the six-man Spanish group were a prime example of the Eurodisco eclectic style at its most accessible. Their tried-and-tested formula was rough vocals overlaying a heady mix of Latin jazz, Philly soul and LA rock. Barrabas supplied breezy dance-floor fodder via 'Wild Safari', 'Woman', 'Hijack' (which Herbie Mann covered for America and garnered the most successful single of his career) and from their album *Heart Of The City*, 'Family Size, 'Checkmate', 'Along The Shore' and 'Mellow Blow'.

97

Just as they left their indelible mark on the pop charts of every country in the world, the Swedish supergroup Abba would invade dance floors with their particular brand of pure Eurodisco. Although not a disco hit per se, Abba's 'Dancing Queen' would often be used by deejays as the wind-down song at the end of a frantic evening. The Scandinavians' only American chart-topper had actually been inspired by George MacRae's 'Rock Your Baby' as songwriters Benny Anderson and Bjorn Ulvaeus lifted the disco founder's drum part for their much loved anthem. Their serious forays into danceland include 'Summer Night City', 'The Visitors', 'Voulez-Vous' and 'Gimme! Gimme! Gimme!' However, Abba's undoubted disco masterpiece is the 12-inch version of 'Lay All Your Love On Me' taken from their *Super Trouper* album, a galloping ode to tuneful romance, juiced up with reverberating frills and stop-start gimmicks. It's also the purest slice of Eurodisco it would be possible to find anywhere in the Common Market of clubland.

98

Pleasure Island

In the anthem/rave '90s it was Ibiza. Back in the heady disco years it was the Mediterranean island of Capri in the Bay of Naples in Italy. That's where the neo-*dolce vita* set went to top up their tans, sit around in nightclubs sipping champagne with other people's husbands or lovers, and dance to the best imported sounds from New York, London, Paris and Munich. Everybody would be talking about pop music.

July 1977: The night begins with a three-hour dinner at the Ristorante Capannina surrounded by monochrome photographs of Jackie O and Ari dining alfresco, Brigitte Bardot walking down the town's narrow lanes and Alain Delon hiding behind dark glasses and a cigarette. Then it's on to have a midnight espresso in one of the tiny central piazza cafés where lingering glances are exchanged from table to table as you wonder exactly which route Bardot took under the luxuriant vegetation in order to check out her reflection in the windows of the exorbitantly priced boutiques.

First stop is Club Number Two, directly opposite the Quisisana Hotel, for a quick peck to see what's happening. Nothing! This small, mirror-walled *discoteca* never really gets started until after four in the morning, so it's back up the stairs and a further few minutes along the picturesque cobblestoned lane. Your heart quickens as the heavy thump from the Piranha Club becomes increasingly audible in the velvet night air. Is that *prima* diva Amanda Lear being escorted through the door to this minuscule version of Studio 54? You hurry straight in to find out as there are no rude doormen here to block your way. There's no need. Everyone on the island is beautiful and ready to play.

The decor of the tiny Piranha Club is a glitzy mix of black, white and gold, with low satin banquettes and soft lighting through cream lampshades that makes everyone's skin gleam against their crisp, cool and clean summer white ensembles. More like an expensively furnished living-room than an actual club, the ambience here is that of a private party Amanda is laughing at the next table and refusing to get up and dance as the deejay cues her new Eurodisco hit 'Tomorrow'. Naturally, she finally gives in and the lights catch her famous silver sequins as she shimmers to the lyrics of the song. Everyone else surveys the sexy in-crowd and mouths the same words to the object of their desire in between sips of Martini.

Wait a minute! Aren't those American tourists doing a new hustle step? I've never seen that one before. This could be their only night on the island – maybe I should ask for some private lessons right now? But hold on. There's that gorgeous German model from the Caffè Vuotto I saw earlier with some guy who looked like a Greek god. Is she really making eyes at me and smiling? Her partner can't dance so perhaps I should cut in and . . .

Everybody screams. The big summer disco hit suddenly

blasts forth – 'Zodiacs' by Roberta Kelly, one of Donna Summer's former backing singers. Everyone puts their hands in the air as they dance and sing along.

The ensuing catalogue of impossibly good music at the Piranha Club is played to perfection. With his endless can't-stop-dancing-no-matter-what medley of the latest disco dynamite, it's as if the deejay has somehow connected with everyone personally. You love each and every record played and every single person in the place is your best friend. And two breathless, exhausting and sweaty hours later after dancing up a storm on the tiny floor, you really do earnestly begin to search for the sign that goes with your own sign of the zodiac.

DISCO FACT!
In 1974 there
were 1,500
discos in
America. By
1975 the number
had jumped to
10,000.

The More I Get, The More I Want

DISCO IN OVERDRIVE

The year 1977 was a momentous one for the music industry. While the Queen celebrated her Diamond jubilee, The Sex Pistols released their punk anthem 'God Save The Queen' in cynical commemoration. The Clash opened The Roxy club in London's Covent Garden on the site of the former gay bar Chaguaramas. Elvis Presley died. T Rex glamster Marc Bolan died. Opera diva Maria Callas died. And *Saturday Night Fever* was released, igniting a disco boom beyond anyone's wildest dreams.

Saturday Night Fever was so commercial, so pop and so everywhere that it couldn't help but turn the genre into a mainstream fad. Disco élitism quickly mutated into popular music's chosen form in the next phase of the genre's life. Once the major record labels, who had originally seen disco as a minor glitch on their planned horizons, collectively said, 'Okay, we can make money now,' the genre became a huge commercial money-making roller-coaster.

It was revealed at *Billboard* magazine's Third Disco Convention at the Americana Hotel in New York that dance music had generated over $4 billion since appearing on the scene. This figure may have included club revenues, bar tallies, purchases of lighting and sound equipment as well as record sales, but it placed disco a startling second only to Hollywood movies within the communications sphere of big money-earners in 1977.

Disco was also changing the face of the music industry in unconventional ways, too. Unknown artists were having hits virtually overnight with sensationally commercial product, alongside small record labels and production companies in tune with the new musical trends.

What caused the major labels concern as disco touched the mass audience was that track exposure in a hip and happening club didn't necessarily translate into record sales. The majority of deejays (who saw themselves as artists in their own right, anyway) never announced the title of a song they were playing. Nor did they display a list of favoured tracks. If the deejay booth was at floor level, the ardent discophile could often crane their neck and make out the record title spinning away on the turntable before it was whisked off and replaced in its generic sleeve. Unlike the Northern Soul deejays in Britain, who jealously hid the identity of their records by erasing the titles on the labels to prevent punters buying them and therefore making them too popular, the disco deejay didn't purposely keep his 12-inch singles a secret. Yet, more often than not, the casual disco-goer had a hard time identifying what was being played.

When a song like 'I Love the Nightlife (Disco Round)' by Alicia Bridges reached a high chart position based on both massive radio and club play, the rewards could be staggering. And that's why the major disco labels in 1977 (Casablanca, Salsoul and TK) committed themselves to serious campaigns involving T-Shirts (Salsoul's 'Dance Your Ass Off'), display posters (Donna Summer's 'I Feel Love') and visual aids of all kinds to attract disco patrons to their product. Slide shows of artists and promo ads became part of the lighting design in some low-rent clubs around this time too when it became clear that deejays were never going to announce the titles of the records they were playing because they felt they were running the risk of turning into radio announcers. The best the deejays did was print out playlists and distribute them amongst discerning disco lovers.

Disco also invaded the home, and not just through radio. In the USA, *Soul Train* had gone on television in 1971, and artists from Kool And The Gang to David Bowie had lip-synched their danceable hits for the 'Soul Train Gang' members, rubber-legged boys and girls who strutted their new moves on the floor. A couple of these, Jody Watley and Jeffrey Daniels, were discovered by the show's host and producer, Don Cornelius, and along with two more newcomers, Gerald Brown and Howard Hewett, became the group Shalamar. The American Bandstand/Soul Train concept worked for the disco-age Dance Fever too, while in Italy spectators were bewitched by the outrageous Stryx. In six episodes that got aired before the show was cancelled, flamboyant artistes Grace Jones and Amanda Lear emerged from clouds of purple smoke dressed in next to nothing, posing and undulating in strangely lit medieval settings, while topless girls gyrated in the background.

Symptomatic of the times that were incessantly thumping along at 125bpm was the fact that, when interviewed by the press, practically all the main disco artists of the day professed to be widening their repertoire into musical areas other than their trademark disco one. Everyone from Gloria Gaynor to Andrea True stated that they didn't want to be artistically stifled by restricting themselves to one musical formula. Only Grace Jones gleefully admitted to loving the 'stomp and grind' and refused to be a rat deserting the disco love boat. The old school were eyeing the new disco upstarts very warily and making contingency plans for the approaching day when the music would die. Bye bye, Miss American Pie!

But the next three years saw some of the most classic disco music ever released thanks to producers becoming more adept at their trade and the featured artist/session singer learning to be comfortable with their secondary position in the grand scheme of things. Aside from the major names launched on the scene, Giorgio Moroder and Pete Bellotte produced the magnificent Munich Machine track 'Get On The Funk Train' (backing vocals by The Midnite Ladies which included Madeline Bell, Sue Glover and Sunny Leslie). 'I Gotta Keep Dancin' by Carrie Lucas came along with that fabulous intro, as did the incandescent stomper 'Lovin' Is Really My Game' by Brainstorm and Claudja Barry's 'Sweet Dynamite'.

'Instant Replay' by Dan Hartman came out in 1978, as did 'I Love New York' by Metropolis, a brilliantly tuneful cash-in on the Big Apple's tourist slogan of the day, 'Boogie Oogie Oogie' by A Taste of Honey, 'Love Is In The Air' by John Paul Young, 'Standing In The Shadows Of Love/Love Shadows' by Deborah Washington and 'Copacabana (At the Copa)' by Barry Manilow. The stand-outs from 1979 were 'Touch Me In the Morning' by Marlena Shaw (taken from her absolutely stunning album *Suite Seventeen*), the classy 'This Time Baby' by Jackie Moore, 'Come To Me' by France Joli, 'Sugar Pie Honey Bunch' by Bonnie Pointer, 'Love Attack' by Ferrara and 'Like An Eagle' by Dennis Parker.

At one point in early-1979, it seemed that an outrageous outfit and glitter eye-make-up or an old Hollywood diva dusting off her famous movie songs and adding a disco beat would guarantee a chart hit. Soon everything was becoming tacky and disco was tarred with the same brush, rapidly beginning to equal mass-produced overkill in the mind of the general public. Punk music was gaining a hold for being controversial and dangerous – the antithesis of the disco mindset. With such a confluence of gathering popular distaste, fuelled by the mistaken belief that all disco records sounded the same, despite revellers still dancing themselves dizzy, the 'Disco Sucks' movement began to gather alarming momentum.

Hot Shots

THE PRODUCERS BEHIND THE GROOVE

Meco Monardo

The big story of 1977 was *Star Wars*. Over one memorable weekend, director George Lucas invented the summer blockbuster movie, created a whole new special-effects industry, brought back epic action adventure to the cinema and revolutionised the science-fiction genre with his 'May the force be with you' space opera. His outstanding achievement took a fortune at the box-office and made overnight stars of Harrison Ford, Carrie Fisher and Mark Hamill.

And Meco Monardo.

The trombonist, record producer and sci-fi fan saw *Star Wars* on its opening day in May and went back to see it four more times the following day too. Then he queued up and saw it again as many times as he could. The orchestral soundtrack by John Williams (composer of *Valley Of The Dolls* and *Jaws*) had Meco hooked. Only after repeated viewing did he realise that Williams had composed the music in a classical thematic form with separate leitmotifs for Darth Vader, Princess Leia and the other main characters. It was then that he had the idea to turn the ultra-melodic themes into the popular dance idiom of the day – disco! But who would back such a crazy idea?

Meco Monardo was born in the Pennsylvanian coal and

papermill town of Johnsonburg in November 1939. His father was a trombone player in a small Italian band and Meco himself eventually took up the instrument at the age of nine after scotching the idea of being a drummer. Throughout high school he won numerous musical competitions and, although his father wanted him to train as a tailor, Meco won a scholarship in 1957 to the Eastman School of Music in Rochester, New York, to set the seal on his musical fate. It was there he met his fellow students Chuck Mangione and Ron Carter, the future jazz greats.

He joined the West Point Army Band as a way to work out his military service and gain musical experience in the process. After that, he ended up playing in bandleader Kai Winding's four-trombone ensemble thanks to an introduction from Mangione. At the same time, Meco began studio session work and, between 1965 and 1974, learned all about arranging. One of his high-profile arrangements was the featured horn section on the Tommy James and the Shondells No. 2 hit 'Crystal Blue Persuasion' in 1969. Meco's major career breakthrough came when he co-produced the seminal disco classic 'Never Can Say Goodbye' for Gloria Gaynor with his regular partner Tony Bongiovi and Gaynor's manager Jay Ellis. This was followed by another surefire stormer, 'Doctor's Orders' by Carol Douglas, and a cover version of The Casualeers' Northern Soul classic 'Dance Dance Dance' by Liquid Smoke.

Meco had been caught in a legal wrangle barring him from producing for a year when he had the idea of turning the *Star Wars* music into a disco dance marathon. The first person he pitched the project to was Neil Bogart, head honcho at Casablanca Records. Bogart said no at first, but when the film shattered every known box-office record over its first weekend, he changed his mind and approved the idea, putting Meco in touch with the company's Manhattan-based offshoot label, Millennium.

In the following hectic three weeks Meco talked Tony

Bongiovi and Broadway arranger *extraordinaire* Harold Wheeler into joining him on the project. Then, using seventy-five musicians (with Meco himself on keyboards and trombone), the entire 15-minute 47-second cut of 'Star Wars' on the *Star Wars And Other Galactic Funk* album was recorded at MZH Studio in New York. The B-side of the album – the 12-minute 30-second 'Other Galactic Funk' – was basically a jam session by five high-school kids spotted by Meco in Central Park playing jazzy drum beats with a separate music track put underneath.

Thanks to Meco's stellar arrangements, Wheeler's feel for the theatricality of the endeavour and Bongiovi's studio tape effects, ranging from animal growls to electronic blips, 'Star Wars' is a masterpiece of disco dynamism. Perfectly capturing the excitement, drama and thrills of the film experience for a totally different aural assault, the complete 'Star Wars' suite – comprising the 'Title Theme', 'Imperial Attack', 'The Desert And The Robot Auction', 'The Princess Appears', 'The Land Of The Sand People', 'Princess Leia's Theme' (misspelled *Leis's* on the original album cover!), 'Cantina Band', 'The Last Battle', 'The Throne Room' and 'End Title' – is a brilliantly conceived and utterly captivating slice of sonic space fantasy. From the opening blare of the impressive main theme to the majestic finale, 'Star Wars' is a disco delicacy of rare quality.

Even John Williams was impressed. 'I hadn't heard of either disco or Meco,' recalled the Oscar-winning composer when Meco also decided to discofy his *Superman* soundtrack in 1979. 'When I was asked to listen to Meco's now-famous recording, I was a little apprehensive, wondering how a pop record could be made from "The March From Star Wars" and what it would be like. I immediately liked what I heard and sensed that a genuine communication was taking place. Meco took things forward another step by bringing *Star Wars* to a vast audience who otherwise would not have heard it in its original symphonic setting. I am most grateful to Meco for all of this and I am delighted that "disco" and "Meco" are now household words.'

A three-and-a-half-minute-long single was carved out of the album-length suite and entered the charts on 6 August 1977. Two months later 'Star Wars Theme/Cantina Band' was at the top of the American charts. It reached No. 7 in the British charts eight weeks after that – a full two months before the film itself was released, thanks to extensive play in the clubs. 'Star Wars' made Meco a very rich man indeed, so it isn't surprising that he looked at every major science-fiction release thereafter as potential disco gold. 'Theme from Close Encounters Of The Third Kind', 'Music From The Black Hole', 'Star Trek Medley', 'Superman And Other Galactic Heroes', 'The Empire Strikes Back Medley' (unusually released as a ten-inch EP), 'Ewok Celebration' (from *Return Of The Jedi*) and 'Impressions Of An American Werewolf In London' all tried to mime the same seam, with varying degrees of success.

But when the producer decided to apply his 'Star Wars' disco formula to an old favourite film classic from Hollywood's golden era, the endearing result was a superior slice of club culture whimsy. The *Wizard Of Oz* album kept gay dancers in Judy Garland fairyland during late-1978 with its marvellous medley of the popular songs 'Over The Rainbow', 'We're Off To See The Wizard (The Wonderful Wizard Of Oz)' and 'Ding Dong, The Witch is Dead'. Meco called this disco panto his 'crowning glory' and even today many would argue that it was superior to 'Star Wars'.

Another commendable off-shoot of the Meco/Bongiovi/ Wheeler triumvirate resulted in the *A Disco Symphony* album by Camouflage, featuring Mysti, in 1977. Together with producer Jay Ellis, they orchestrated a magnificent pastiche of well-known classical themes, riffs from George Gershwin's 'Rhapsody in Blue' and original material to put over an easy-going flow of aural candy. Interwoven through its slow middle section was the very first use of the Jimmy Webb standard

'MacArthur Park' in a disco record, a full year before Donna Summer got around to using it for the same purpose. It was probably *A Disco Symphony* which gave her producer Giorgio Moroder the idea.

Meco would write some original material himself ('Moondancer') use Harold Wheeler's compositions ('Meco's Theme') and discofy musical classics from other genres (Cozy Cole's 'Topsy') to flesh out his later albums. When he moved from Millennium to Arista Records and released the *Pop Goes The Movies* album in 1982, however, it was very much business as usual. Endless medleys incorporating everything from 'Tara's Theme' and 'Zorba The Greek' to 'The Godfather' and 'The Pink Panther' were stretched out over the two MOR album sides. The same year brought *Swingtime's Greatest Hits* – two sides of medleys incorporating 'Patricia', 'Cherry Pink And Apple Blossom White' and other Harry James favourites.

Meco left the music business in 1985 to become a commodities broker in Florida. It was a fitting end, since what else did Meco see the science-fiction film soundtrack as other than a commodity to be tailored to his own pop-culture requirements? That his ambitions and good taste dovetailed with the disco vogue was serendipity for the *Star Wars* fan, the cutting-edge clubber, the record retailer and the Garland brigade. Art Meco lives!

Boris Midney

On the Mount Olympus of disco there are numerous gods but there is only one Zeus and his name is Boris Midney He's the Stephen Sondheim, David Hockney and Stanley Kubrick of the disco genre all rolled into one. The enigmatic producer's output quickly became the yardstick by which all other disco deliveries would be measured, as each loving opus released to his acolytes was a superbly crafted, earbending and unique original, unafraid to scale the slinky and surreal heights of the dance format.

As directional and fresh-sounding today as they were the first time they were heard, every Midney album is a masterpiece which oozes clean-cut style and daring technique from every silky groove. The Emphatic producer minted new disco sounds based on variations of symphonic themes for an ever-eager, open-armed dance culture and was entirely responsible for updating the genre by giving it a more sophisticated and avant-garde patina.

Boris Midney's was the thinking dancer's disco. The sparse, ethereal space effect he created was instantly recognisable and completely his own. It was technically advanced disco to drool over while you were being transported to uncharted havens of fantasy resonance on the twinkling platforms of cavorting self-expression in clubland. You took your place in Midney's hyper-realistic disco theatre and became Pinocchio, Evita, Luke Skywalker and more, ready to take your place centre stage as each of his poperettas enfolded you in aural sensations and cosmic vibrations.

Midney first burst onto the scene in 1978 with co-producer Peter Pellulo. The *Come Into My Heart* album by USA-European Connection was, as the session group's name suggested, a blend of driving rhythm *à la* American mode with a Eurodisco slant towards lilting melody. Side One belonged to the fourteen-and-a-half-minute 'Come Into My Heart/Good Loving' while Side Two's thirteen-minute 'Love's Coming/ Baby Love' compounded the unique in-house Midney style with sensuous vocals provided by Leza Holmes, Renne Johnson and Sharon Williams. Their sparsely produced vocals in amongst absolutely gorgeous choral lines, wild percussion, peripatetic strings, shrieking *Psycho*-style violins, pounding reverberations, ingenious use -of harps, xylophones and wind instruments, and discordance made to sound sweetly harmonious, all combined with an echo valley ambience to present a totally new disco sound.

The next album with the magic Midney touch was *Make*

That Feeling Come Again! by Beautiful Bend with vocals by Xo-Xo. All the songs were composed, arranged and produced by the disco maestro on his own, and he outdid himself on 'That's The Meaning' mixed with 'Boogie Motion' and the title track segueing into 'Ah-Do It'. Midney also played on keyboards and saxophone (no one could blow an instrument better than Midney!) and the hypnotic result was another exemplary delve into luscious melody and dazzling harmony driven by a hypnotic beat that did exactly what the group's name hinted at. Each track was beautifully bent out of shape and then back into dazzling form by Midney's miraculous production skills on fortyeight-track stereo recorded at his favourite studio, Eras at 226 East 54th Street in New York.

The patent 'Mi Sound', as he began to label his prolific output, was next applied to *Caress,* which was written, produced and arranged by Midney under his own name. 'Catch The Rhythm/Charmed By You' and 'You Got It Too Uptight/Love Spell' had every dancer shaking, shivering and shimmering to each cadence in the first medley and totally agreeing with one of the lyrics in the latter alluding to what Midney did, he did so well. Next up was the second USA-European Connection album, featuring the cuts 'I'd Like To Get Closer/Do Me Good' and 'Join The Dance/There's A Way Into My Heart'. With vocals provided this time by Chequita Jackson and Kevin Owens, a duo who would continually be employed to convey the crisp trademark Midney sound, USA-European Connection hit the disco spot once more especially with the haunting plea to take a chance on love in 'There's A Way Into My Heart'.

The third 1979 release from Midney found the tireless producer changing direction thematically as opposed to musically. Obviously noting the success his contemporaries were having with such concept albums as *Romeo And Juliet* by Alec R. Costandinos, *Wuthering Heights* by Ferrara and *The Wizard Of Oz* by Meco, Midney dusted off the old Carlo

Collodi Italian fairytale *Pinocchio* and went to disco town on the subject matter. This is how he described it on the album sleeve:

THE BEGINNING

Scene I: A small, shabby room with a fire and a steaming kettle painted on the wall. Old Gepetto makes a funky puppet and nobody believes him ('Wooden-Wooden Puppet')

Scene II: The wooden puppet shows his first steps.

>Girls: Take a step now,
>
>Shake a leg out,
>
>Twist that body,
>
>Wow, leap into the crowd!

Scene III: Pinocchio doesn't know much about love yet, but sings a love song ('I'm Attached To You')

Scene IV: Trouble, trouble, trouble . . . This part of the tale is very hairy cats and foxes ('Cat-Tails')

Scene V: L.O.V.E. and *Répondez S'il Vous Plaît* ('L.O.V.E./R.S.V.P')

Scene VI: Two bad guys leave the puppet hanging on a tree. The girls sing 'Don't Leave Me Hanging', but it's no fun for Pinocchio. He wants to get down!

Scene VII: THE LAND OF MIRACLES. Pinocchio finds out (the hard way) that money doesn't grow on trees and falling stars aren't diamonds ('The Land Of Miracles')

Scene VIII: After all this the wooden head decides not to go by the book. Instead he turns back home. The same, small room with its painted fire and steaming kettle. Gepetto and Pinocchio finally got together; still poor but happy. Thinking to find food, the puppet pokes his nose into the painted kettle and sees a light. Gepetto tears the painting off the wall. A SECRET DOOR! At the end of the tunnel, they find all their friends in A GREAT MASQUERADE! ('Open The Secret Door')

Credited to Masquerade, another of Midney's alter egos, *Pinocchio* was a daring experiment in filtering his eclectic musical influences through a narrative fable. The results were spectacular. Once heard, 'The Land Of Miracles' and 'Open The Secret Door' are never forgotten for their lyrical inventiveness, wailing vocals and mini arias of astral disco beauty. Chequita Jackson and Kevin Owens come into their own as the Masquerade singers giving loads of oomph to the project by actually acting it out in a highly believable fashion. *Pinocchio* is one of the best disco fairytale concepts because Midney has as much fun with the mythic Collodi symbolism as he does with all his unusual orchestral-manoeuvres-in-the-dark story to paint a funky Europop pantomime.

The fourth release bearing the maestro's name was the Theo Vaness album containing such soundalike gems as 'Thank God There's Music' and 'I Can't Dance Without You', on which Midney was credited as associate producer. But his magnum opus was his fifth release. The musical *Evita* had already been a popular concept album and then a smash hit on the West End stage before it arrived on Broadway in September 1979. In order to cover as many markets as possible, impresario Robert Stigwood (who had clearly learnt his PR lessons after producing *Saturday Night Fever*) and his RSO record label got Midney to tailor an *Evita* album for the disco market to get the cross-promotional message across. The show's anthem 'Don't Cry For Me Argentina' by Julie Covington had not been a chart hit in America and it needed as much exposure as possible.

Midney was definitely the right man for the job. He succeeded in moulding Andrew Lloyd Webber's and Tim Rice's songbook biography of Eva Perón so expertly to the disco medium that it became a separate work of mellifluous musical art in itself. A primer in how to adapt such baggage-laden material to an alternative musical macrocosm, *Evita* by Festival is a solid thirty-six minutes of innovative variations on the Webber/Rice theme with pertinent tweaks, audacious arrangements and rewritten lyrical content to reflect the disco delineation.

Beginning with a long piano intro, the journey starts with an atmospheric 'Buenos Aries', full of Latin inflection and crowds yelling out in Spanish, moves into a jaunty 'I'd Be Surprisingly Good For You' and ends Side One with 'Don't Cry For Me Argentina' complete with an electrifying tango break. Side Two starts with an adventurous take on 'High Flying, Adored' and soars with the stupendously orchestral 'Rainbow High'. After Kevin Owens sings 'She Is A Diamond' in the way the show's Juan Perón always should have done, the impossibly fabulous album ends with the Midney original, 'Eva's Theme: Lady Woman'. Midney was no fool for including this flaming flamenco fantasy. He knew the album was going to sell well, so why should Webber and Rice get all the royalties from his hard work?

Evita was a stunning achievement and its reputation amongst the discognoscenti was enough for a CD reissue in 1997 as part of the promotional package for the belated film version starring Madonna. Most Midney fans would have preferred to have seen the Material Girl appear in a film of his disco drama than the musical they actually did get. A spectacular work of sound and visionary artifice, *Evita* is the definitive Midney album.

Midney's next project had an air of commercial desperation about it. One can only guess that he was forced into producing *Music From The Empire Strikes Back* in an attempt to match the commercial success of Meco's 'Star Wars' triumph. The 1980 summer release was everything one had come to expect from a Midney album, yet 'Yoda's Theme/The Imperial March (Darth Vader's Theme)' and 'Han Solo And The Princess (Love Theme)/Star Wars (Main Theme)' feels too restricted by its pedigree and John Williams's bombastic original movie score. It's Midney-Lite aimed at the *Star Wars* fan for easy listening at home rather than for bopping to at the disco.

Significantly, too, the album cover was not designed by Midney himself. Throughout his entire producing career, his insistence on designing the cover art for his albums was another example of how involved Midney was in the total concept of each project. He photographed every cover from the first USA-European Connection album, featuring hands almost touching in that popular Michelangelo/Sistine Chapel imagery, to their second LP showing an aeroplane wing over an ocean of water. *Caress* carried the most startling image; a naked woman with a boa constrictor crawling down her back. Midney trainspotters also quickly noticed that he recycled the first USA-European Connection back cover photo of twinkling lights for both *Pinocchio* and *Evita*. The *Empire Strikes Back* album sported a tacky *faux* '40s movie poster illustration by Gribbitt (the design group favoured by Casablanca Records) even though the back cover did feature a rare photo of Midney himself perched on the studio console at Eras.

Midney's best cover photo also graced his most unusual offering: 1981's *Companion* featured a gatefold sleeve depicting a naked female body stretched out against a starry space vista with an asteroid floating to the left of her breast. The musical content was equally bizarre. A surreal roller-coaster of ethereal instrumental snatches set against divine disco clusters of airy melody (vocals by Charmaine and Kevin Owens), 'This Is A Test', 'Living Up To Love (Companion)', 'Step On Out', 'There's A Way' (a stripped-to-disco-essentials version of 'There's A Way Into My Heart' from the second USA-European Connection collection) and 'I Feel Delight' are five authoritative cuts of unequalled disco peculiarity and free musical association from the Midney *oeuvre*.

Only three 12-inch singles followed this extraordinary example of the all-encompassing Midney cosmos in disco action: 1982's poptastic 'Can He Find Another One?' by Double Discovery carried one of Midney's loveliest tunes; 1983's 'D-D-D-Dance' by Midney (supposedly taken from a disco musical show, *Pushkin – The Black Russian*, which never materialised); and the same year's 'Living Up To Love' and 'Step On Out' compositions re-orchestrated, remixed and credited to USA-European Connection.

Apart from a snatch of 'Beautiful Bend' played on the soundtrack of the arty science-fiction underground punk movie *Liquid Sky* (1983), Midney vanished from the disco landscape only to surface later in the techno arena. But it was a terrain that belonged to him alone as the most gifted producer to grace the disco era. Jimmy James and the Vagabonds sang it first in 1976, but 'I'll Go Where Your Music Takes Me' could have been written with Boris Midney in mind. 'Make That Feeling Come Again!' indeed.

Michael Zager

Bodytalk was on every clubber's lips during the 1977–78 season as the anthem 'Let's All Chant' by The Michael Zager Band ricocheted off the disco walls of sound. Supremely catchy and melodic, with a quite miraculous classical chamber-music-style break in the middle, 'Lets All Chant' became an international hit and remains a key recording which instantly defines the disco era.

It was the high point in the extraordinarily versatile career of producer, arranger, pianist and songwriter Michael Zager. Born in Passaic, New Jersey, in 1943, Zager grew up listening to jazz greats Miles Davis, Oscar Peterson and Maynard Ferguson. Graduating from the University of Miami with a degree in communications, he followed this up with a major in composition from Mannes College of Music after studying under the tutelage of legendary Broadway composer Stephen Sondheim for two years.

With Aram Schefrin, his best friend from college, Zager then formed the heavily jazz-influenced pop band Ten Wheel Drive in 1968. The ten-piece ensemble performed an oratorio with lyrics by Schefrin at Carnegie Hall with the American

Symphony Orchestra and pre-dated Blood, Sweat and Tears and Chicago with their blend of jazz and rock music. Ten Wheel Drive released four albums in all (three on Polydor, one on Capitol), featuring Zager on keyboards, Schefrin on guitars and Genya Ravan on vocals. They toured for five solid years, eventually losing Ravan to a solo career with Columbia Records (Ann E. Sutton replaced her for their last album), which the duo co-produced. By this time, Schefrin had had enough of being on the road and retired from the music business to become a lawyer.

Zager needed a new partner. He teamed up with Jerry Love, the former head of A&R for A&M Records, setting up the New York-based Love/Zager Productions company. Signed to Bang Records, the first fruit of their labours was the *Out Among 'Em* album by Love Child's Afro Cuban Blues Band which included the cuts 'Honeybee', 'Bang Bang', 'Life And Death In G&A', 'Black Skin Blue Eyed Boys' and 'Jerry's Theme'.

Love Child's Afro Cuban Blues Band went on to release two other albums: *SpanDisco* featuring 'Oye Como Va', 'The Speak Up Mambo' and the 'Spanish Harlem/Dancin' To SpanDisco' medley; and *Rhythm Of Life* with the tracks 'Black Widow Woman', 'Baila' and 'The Moon Is The Daughter Of The Devil'. The production duo then formed Michael Zager's Moon Band and their debut release was 'Do It With Feeling' in 1976 featuring singer Robert 'Peabo' Bryson. Zager also arranged Bryson's first solo album.

By 1978 the studio group's name had been shortened to The Michael Zager Band and they had signed a deal with the Private Stock label (home of Walter Murphy and the Big Apple Band's 'A Fifth Of Beethoven') on the understanding that a disco album would be forthcoming. And that's where 'Let's All Chant' began life, featuring Zager and the song's co-writer, Alvin Fields, sharing lead vocals with session singers Dollette McDonald and Billy Baker.

The story goes that Studio 54 *habitué* Jerry Love noticed

how the revellers gyrating on the crowded dance floor would continuously chant a rhythmic 'Ooh, Ooh!' to whatever track was thumping through the speakers in order to increase their participation and enjoyment. When Love described the scene the next day to his partner, and suggested he write a song to cash in on the fad, Zager thought he was crazy. But he wrote 'Let's All Chant' with Fields anyway, along with a B-side, the effervescent and zingy 'Love Express', and recorded the tracks at the Secret Sound Studios in Manhattan.

Nobody expected the amazing impact that 'Lets All Chant' would have on dance floors or charts around the globe. If Zager was flabbergasted, Private Stock were delighted as now they had a hit focal point for the band's first disco album. To accompany the two tracks already recorded, Zager went back into the studio and, with mostly the same musicians and vocalists, created a disco homage to one of his favourite jazz heroes, Dave Brubeck. The 'Take Five' guy had once recorded an album of jazz variations on classic themes from Walt Disney cartoon feature films. Zager did the same thing, only in disco. The resultant Mouse House salute was entitled *Dancin' Disney Medley* and included the evergreens 'Heigh Ho', 'Whistle While You Work' (from *Snow White And The Seven Dwarfs*), 'Give A Little Whistle' and 'When You Wish Upon A Star' (from *Pinocchio*).

As the *Let's All Chant* album climbed the charts, Zager branched out and took on production duties for a variety of disco acts. For porno actress-turned-singer Andrea True, he produced the *White Witch* album from which 'What's Your Name, What's Your Number' became a sizeable dance-floor hit under her Andrea True Connection banner.

Then he supervised Emily 'Cissy' Houston's comeback to popular music. Zager had met Houston while producing Genya Ravan's solo project and really respected her backing-vocal work with such artists as Wilson Pickett, The Drifters, Esther Phillips and Aretha Franklin. Houston, the mother of Whitney, the sister of Thelma ('Don't Leave Me This Way', 'Love

Masterpiece') and Lee Warrick (herself the mother of Dionne and Dee Dee Warwick) had also been a prominent member of '60s girl group The Sweet Inspirations. Along with part-time members Doris Troy and Judy Clay, the group recorded such soulful ballads as the Isaac Hayes-penned 'When Something Is Wrong With My Baby' and the Gamble and Huff composition 'Gotta Find Me A Brand New Lover, Parts 1 & 2'. Together they collaborated on the *Warning Danger Cissy Houston* album of 1978 featuring the classic cut 'Think It Over'. (A year before Grace Jones grabbed it, Houston had had the first hit with 'Tomorrow' from the Broadway musical *Annie*.)

Cissy's fourteen-year-old daughter Whitney was to play a pivotal role later the same year on The Michael Zager Band's follow-up album to *Let's All Chant*. She sang a lead solo alongside her mother on 'Life's A Party', the title track of what was another sensational artistic success for Zager. The exceptionally tuneful Zager/Fields composition 'You Don't Know A Good Thing' followed the title track on the album's A-side. But it was the absolutely haunting four-part B-side which made disco devotees dance to attention. 'Love Love Love', 'Still Not Over', 'On And On' and 'Using You' were all part of an emotionally wrenching torn marriage manual set to a disco beat and sung to soap-opera perfection by Kay Garner, Stephanie De Sykes, Chas Mills and Stevie Lange. Adult, ear-bending and eye-opening, this bittersweet suite is one of the all-time disco masterpieces.

The Michael Zager Band's third album, 1980's *Zager*, featured vocals by Deniece Williams on 'Time Heals Every Wound' and by Luther Vandross, who shared the lead with band member Alvin Fields, on 'Don't Sneak On Me'. Other acts that Zager produced around this time included The Spinners, Johnny 'Guitar' Watson, The Elusions, Fontella ('Rescue Me') Bass and the M-Zee Band. He also supplied music for the film soundtracks of 1978's *The Eyes Of Laura Mars* (the reason why 'Let's All Chant' is used as background for a model shoot), *Inside Moves*

(1980) and *Friday The 13th Part 3 3D* (1982). Zager was also a much sought-after composer of music for TV commercials and some of his more memorable jingles include Schlitz Malt Liquor (sung by Kool & The Gang) and Bounce (Whitney again).

Let's All Chant was just the tip of the Michael Zager iceberg. He was a disco mentor and his stated ambition was to make music to make you feel good. In that endeavour he succeeded beyond his wildest dreams and indeed made sure life was a party that everyone came to in 1978.

Patrick Adams

It did not matter that Side One of the Patrick Adams-produced album *Keep On Jumpin'*, an effervescent delight released by the group Musique in 1978, only lasted thirteen minutes. Or that one of the tracks on the four-cut album existed in two versions. With smooth, hook-filled vocal melodies and funky tribal percussive dubs, the album would demonstrate to the full what the producer and songwriter is famed for – beautiful songs and brilliant arrangements. What you had in your hands was a Patrick Adams record and you knew it would deliver screams of ecstasy on the dance floor.

While almost all traditional disco music used eight beats to a rhythmic sequence, Adams introduced weird time changes, adding or dropping bars to great effect. The album's title track, a No. 1 worldwide club smash, begins as a classy-sounding melodic galloper. As it reaches the expected rattling middle break, a whirling string section suddenly dovetails into the mix. Arranged in a speeded-up 8/10 time, the music now seems to get under your feet and lift you off the floor. The pounding 'Push, Push, in The Bush' uses similar time changes – the brass figures at the end of the sections being in a 5/4 count. Adams himself described this as 'a stop-break effect, something like taking a sip of wine during a good meal. When you go back to the food it tastes even better.'

Drawn to music from an early age while growing up in

Harlem, New York City, Adams cited the Stax output of the '60s as well as The Beatles as major influences. After travelling as a young musician and opening for Jerry Butler, and later The Commodores, he set up his own production company. Entering the disco era, Adams immediately perfected the elemental mix of the mid-'70s dance equation and possessed an uncanny knack of producing future cult items like 'Love Bug' by Bumblebee Unlimited. This was a stripped-down and simple rhythm track with synthesised strings and an irritatingly infectious female voice on top buzzing the stinging lyrics. The song is as light as a feather yet it bops along in a curiously funky manner. In complete contrast, his 1976 Philly-styled 'My Baby's Got ESP' by Four Below Zero already showcased harmonious vocals and the intricate string figures that were to become his trademark. They would be heard in further Musique releases and in the elegant 'Night Rider' by Venus Dodson, another cult favourite.

Adams gained a solid reputation as a producer as disco became a trend to watch. Sine's 'Just Let Me Do My Thing' was a Top 40 hit for Prelude, a label which prided itself on expensive orchestrations and cross-over disco hits. Despite a hideous cover image of the slightly built flautist Herbie Mann ripping his suit off to reveal a *Superman* costume underneath, the 1978 'Super Mann' project was a big commercial success for him and Adams too. Thanks to producer Meco Monardo beating the team in the rush to get a discofication of the then hot John Williams-scored movie out in the marketplace, listeners were unexpectedly treated to an urgently hustling version of the similarly named, but quite different, Celi Bee and the Buzzy Bunch hit of the previous summer instead. The album turned out to be an exquisite blending of Mann's fusion jazz and Adams's sleek and slinky instrumental disco. it was perfect for home listening.

One of the featured vocalists in the 'Super Mann' chorus, and one of Adams's long-time muses, was session singer Jocelyn

Brown, a formidable talent still active in the music business today. Whether intoning the most gentle of chants, trembling in anticipation of yet another heartbreak to come, or screaming out in unrestrained joy, Brown always makes her presence felt with her unmistakable gospel-trained voice. She had worked with Adams on Musique and other memorable projects like Inner Life's 'I'm Caught Up (In A One-Night Love Affair)' where she vocalised a mid-tempo tale of turmoil and starved emotions which sent shivers down the spines of disco lovers everywhere during late-1979. This track and another hit from the album, an epic reworking of The Supremes' 'Ain't No Mountain High Enough', also contained one of Adams's most complex orchestral arrangements.

In 1997 Jocelyn Brown appeared on a Todd Terry re-recording of 'Keep On Jumpin'' alongside Martha Wash of The Two Tons Of Fun and The Weather Girls fame, bringing the tune once again into mass consciousness. Patrick Adams has successfully continued his career producing, arranging, writing and engineering music for various acts, from old-school legends Loleatta Holloway and Gladys Knight to rap superstars Salt 'N' Pepper, Eric B & Rakim and Coolio.

Cerrone

Already high on champagne and no doubt dubious cigarettes, a group of five women lounge in a Paris discotheque, perhaps Le Main Jeune. As they buzz with excitement and size up the talent in the bar, one of the women comes up with an idea – what would it be like if they all shared a man; could they imagine all five of them teaming up on one guy? A distinctive candidate immediately catches their eye. Though apparently rich and gorgeous to look at, there's still more to the man, as one of the women points out – just look at the front of him, that's no banana! The ladies explode in lascivious laughter, bringing them to the attention of the gent in question, Cerrone himself. As the first heavy beat of the snare drum shakes the room, the five predators start to descend on their more than willing prey.

Thus begins 'Love In C Minor' (1976), a cinematic tour de force of a record and one of the most recognisable dance classics of all time. Taking their cue from Donna Summer's 'Love To Love You Baby' and expanding on the premise with their own ornate brand of baroque orchestration, masters at work Jean-Marc Cerrone and his co-writer, Alec R. Costandinos, first offer the famous one minute, twenty-one second prologue described above, which deejays would lay on the track playing before it to tantalise the dancers with a taster of the pleasures to follow. After the beat commences, layer upon layer of guitar riffs and cadenced violins are introduced to the mix to illustrate the intensifying sexual activity of the narrative. The excitement seems to peak after the women's orgiastic screaming gives way to a long sigh and traditional romantic melody, but as the refrain ends and all the brass instruments and strings drop away, the phallic thrust of the drum and the probing bass-lines remain. There is no release from the heat as the record continues to build up the momentum again. With Monsieur Cerrone, once is never enough.

Jean-Marc Cerrone was the youngest of three children born to a small Parisian shoe manufacturer. His musical bent was noted at school where he would snap his ruler in time to an imaginary beat on his desk. At home he did the same thing with cutlery at the dinner table until his father bought him a drum kit, and set him on his musical career. By the time he was fourteen years old Cerrone was working with neighbourhood groups; at eighteen, after getting a hairdressing diploma for security, he decided to try and make it as a professional musician, becoming an orchestra leader at the Club Mediterrane. By the age of twenty, Cerrone had landed a lucrative producing contract with the French label Barclay.

In September 1976 he went to London's Trident Studios to produce 'Love In C Minor' and when every French label turned down the chance to release the epic composition, he returned to England and pressed the record himself. He sold the albums individually to the clubs and tirelessly promoted it twenty-four hours a day until Atlantic Records issued 'Love In C Minor' on their subsidiary label Cotillion in February 1977. Unfortunately, during this delay a halfway decent, more Philly-inspired cover version by The Heart and Soul Orchestra had appeared. But it was the original Cerrone which became a permanent fixture on the dance floors and in the Top 3 slot of the *Billboard* Disco charts for two solid months. Simultaneously it also made the Top 30 ranks of the R&B best-seller charts.

Cerrone further consolidated his premier disco position with the *Cerrone's Paradise* album, a hypnotic desert island fantasy containing pointed references to the Garden of Eden, which floated dancers effortlessly around the flashing floors in the latter half of 1977 with sensual feelings of ecstasy. 'Disco is easy,' said the French press, 'but disco Cerrone-style – only one person can do it.' They did have a point as Alec R. Costandinos conceded when he left Cerrone's One Man Paradise to pursue his own musical identity in the same glittering genre.

Cerrone's third album was the incredible *Supernature* which took him fourteen months to perfect and broke from the rigid disco formats of the time to craft a more Giorgio Moroder-influenced electronic base from which all the other vibrating melodies flowed. A fable about good and evil infused with H.G. Wells's *The Island Of Doctor Moreau*, *Supernature* took a once-upon-a-time look at scientific cross-breeding and playing God and the dire results for mankind if such things weren't kept in check. Dark, sinister lyrics dove-tailed the cautionary disco fairytale with issues the avid discophile recognised as part of his or her world as life imitated art imitated life in the narcissistic mirror ball of creativity.

Cerrone would also produce records for other artists, among them Don Ray's 'Got To Have Loving, Kongas' 'Africanism', Pado and Co's 'You Keep Me Hangin' On' and Revelacion's 'House Of The Rising Sun' (segments of which were recycled by the producer for the Philippe Monnier-directed crime movie soundtrack *Brigade Mondaine – Vaudou Aux Caraïbes* in 1978. Cerrone also scored two other films in the series, *Brigade Mondaine* (1978) and *Brigade Mondaine: La Secte De Marrakech* (1979) with electronic rhythms far ahead of their era). But it was the trademark sound of his own compositions that the disco crowd loved the most, such as 'Music Of Life', '*Je Suis Music*', 'Give Me Love' and 'Call Me Tonight'. By the time of the release of *Supernature,* Cerrone's albums had sold over ten million copies and in 1978 *Billboard* magazine's Disco Forum IV named him Disco Artist of the Year, Male Disco Artist of the Year, Disco Composer of the Year, Best Producer of a Disco Record, Disco Music Arranger of the Year, and Disco instrumentalist of the Year. It was an incredible achievement.

Numerous other albums of various quality would follow: *Golden Touch* and *Cerrone V: Angelina* (1979), *Cerrone VI* (1980), *Cerrone VII: You Are The One* (1981 and featuring future diva Jocelyn Brown on 'Hooked On You'), *Cerrone VIII* (1982) and *Cerrone IX: Back Track* (1982), along with the obligatory live recordings, a proper film soundtrack (*Dancing Machine* in 1990) and a New Age opera entitled *The Collector* with vocals by Lene Lovich. None would hit the heights of his original trio of consummate classics pounding out sex and lies on audiotape. Still working in the industry, Cerrone is arranging sell-out concerts in grand scale with his son, as well as putting out excellent nu-disco CDs like *Hysteria,* the cover art of which managed to outrage shoppers even in France. Trust Jean-Marc to keep the sexy spirit of 'Love In C Minor' alive!

Alec R. Costandinos

'Love In C Minor' burst onto the world's dance floors in early-1977 and raced up the singles charts in March on both sides of the Atlantic in abridged form. Written by Jean-Marc Cerrone and Alec R. Costandinos, the full-length 16-minute 16-second definitive French disco classic set both men on the path to fame

– but separately It was never intended to be that way for the dynamic duo. Cerrone was the sole featured artist on 'Love In C Minor' and because he never seemed to give Costandinos any credit whatsoever for the part he played in its production, the miffed Cairo-born Armenian (who had written Euro hits for Henry Mancini and Paul Anka and also produced two disco tracks by Demis Roussos on the Greek star's *Souvenirs* album) parlayed his contribution into a solo contract with the Casablanca label to release his future works.

The most influential of these were his three albums for the group Love and Kisses (which was made up of the cream of Britain's session singers) and all recorded at London's Trident Studios. A foreigner recording in London was typical of disco's cross-cultural momentum at the time and pre-dated the world music trend of the '80s. Over the next few years Costandinos (and other big producers in the field) would regularly provide work for Sue Glover, Sunny Leslie, Vickie Brown, Katie Kissoon, Tony Burrows, Stephanie De Sykes and Madeline Bell, and their harmonious contribution to his overall symphonic sound cannot be over-emphasised.

A brief summary: Sue and Sunny started life as The Myrtelles in 1963 and their first record release was a cover version of Lesley Gore's 'Just Let Me Cry'. But although they would play a key role in propelling Joe Cocker's 'With A Little Help From My Friends' to No. 1 in 1968 and became part of the line-up of the original Brotherhood of Man (for 'United We Stand'), only Sunny would find lasting fame, with her 1974 Top 10 hit 'Doctor's Orders', which American diva Carol Douglas would further discofy the next year.

Vickie Brown (née Haseman) was an original member of the Vernons Girls ('Only You Can Do It') and she regularly appeared on the British TV pop show *Oh Boy*. She married singer Joe Brown, formed a girl group named The Breakaways in 1962 and their continually shaky singles career began with a decidedly odd cover of The Crystals' Phil Spector classic 'He's A Rebel'.

When work dried up in the early-'70s, Vickie became one of the most sought-after session singers – as did her partner on the 1973 flop 'It Happened On A Sunday Morning', Stephanie De Sykes. Stephanie was one half of Tree People with Vickie for this rare Polydor single but she only had to wait a year before having her own No. 2 British hit, 'Born With A Smile On My Face'.

Trinidad-born Kathleen Kissoon started off in the group The Marionettes in 1964 singing the Marty Wilde-produced song 'Whirlpool Of Love' with her brother Jerry. She soon sported the name Peanut for 'Home Of The Brave' (a cover version of the 1965 Phil Spector classic recorded by Ronnie Spector of The Ronettes under the alias Bonnie and the Treasures) and then Mac and Katie Kissoon with Jerry for the two Eurosoul pop hits 'Sugar Candy Kisses' and 'Don't Do It Baby' in 1975.

Madeline Bell arrived in Britain from New Jersey in 1962 with the touring gospel spectacular *Black Nativity* and quickly acquired a record contract. The best of her early recordings was 'You Don't Love Me No More' from 1964 before she cut the original version of 'I'm Gonna Make You Love Me', which was quickly swiped by Diana Ross and the Supremes and The Temptations. Joining the group Blue Mink in 1969, Madeline and company had hits with 'Melting Pot', 'Good Morning Freedom' and 'Banner Man'.

Tony Burrows was in so many bands during the '60s and '70s that it's impossible to list them all, but he did contribute to The Flowerpot Men ('Let's Go To San Francisco'), Pipkins ('Gimme Dat Ding') and Edison Lighthouse ('Love Grows Where My Rosemary Goes'), and he was famous for appearing in three different group line-ups on one single edition of *Top Of The Pops*.

Each of these individually talented session singers was brilliantly used by Costandinos and the entire disco industry as a separate vocal instrument in his or her own right to fabulous choral effect.

The first Love and Kisses album in 1977 featured side-long suites arranged and conducted by Don Ray (singer on the smash

Cerrone production 'Got To Have Loving'). But Side One's 'Accidental Lover' was overshadowed by the flip's 'I've Found Love (Now That I've Found You)'. Beginning with an instantly foot-tapping piano crescendo, Costandinos himself sang lead vocals on this swooping declaration of true devotion. Using the weird device of fading out the chorus to nothing, before bringing the chanting to the fore again, 'I've Found Love' earned disco respect from the cognoscenti who realised Costandinos was deliberately entering exciting and uncharted musical waters.

However, it was Side One of the second album *How Much, How Much I Love You* the next year that set the seal on the typical Costandinos production. Even more blatantly romantic in lyrical content than their first outing, with rhapsodic talk of the wonderful moments and beautiful seasons contained in the cycle of every love affair, and repetitive to an ethereally delicious extreme, the 16-minute, 21-second magnificent miniature was jam-packed with soaring strings (Courtesy of The Pat Halling String Ensemble) and vibrant brass sections and deviously scattered with duelling banjos. If Mozart had been alive in 1977 he would have composed 'How Much, How Much I Love You'. It is one of the most perfectly crafted disco idylls of the entire era.

'You Must Be Love' from the third Love and Kisses album in 1979 tried to copy the same formula and almost pulled it off despite having an inferior melody. It wasn't a big dance-floor hit as a result of this musical mimicry and Love and Kisses faded into obscurity after supplying the so-so title track for the film *Thank God It's Friday* as well as another amiable sing-along ditty 'You're The Most Precious Thing In My Life'.

There was something else that set the three Love and Kisses albums apart too. The cover designs were eye-opening soft-porn images that would not have been out of place in top-shelf girlie magazines, and did wonders in establishing the disco=sex formula. The first album had three sets of male hands tearing off a girl's T-shirt with a subtle hint of nipple showing through one rip; the second (and most outrageous) had a blonde model astride a white horse and wearing nothing but riding boots and carrying a whip (supposedly to illustrate Side Two's major cut 'Beauty And The Beast'), and the third featured a semi-naked girl riding a motorbike down an American highway. In a politically incorrect era of sexist images (and Casablanca would always be the main offender with their controversial album covers), the Love and Kisses trilogy were explicit to a groundbreaking degree.

If Love and Kisses represented the viciously commercial side of the Costandinos *oeuvre*, the composer clearly wanted to apply his romantic ethos to something with a little more personal weight. At the same time as he was working on the first Love and Kisses album he'd crafted the religious disco epics 'Judas Iscariot' and 'Simon Peter` for the session group Sphinx and was looking around for further inspiration. Major advances were being made in the music industry itself and at Trident Studios the possibility of forty-eight-track recording finally became a reality. During a crucial ten days of mixing and recording in early-1978, Costandinos and the Trident engineers put a new coding system to the test, synching two twenty-four-track tape-recorders to within 1/2000 of a second.

The result was first heard in all its glory in the most popular of all Costandinos releases, *Romeo And Juliet*. Together with the Syncophonic Orchestra, Costandinos put all five acts of Shakespeare's classic love story to a disco beat and the result was a shimmering cascade of melody, harmony and poignancy that incredibly set much of the Bard's own text to music. 'Two households both alike in dignity, In fair Verona where we lay our scene, From ancient grudge break to new mutiny, Where civil blood makes civil hands unclean' were odd yet evocative words to be echoing around the disco speakers in 1978, but Costandinos pulled off the eyebrow-raising coup. *Romeo And Juliet* is always being redefined for a new generation. Film director Franco Zeffirelli did it in 1968, as did Baz Luhrmann in

1997 (using Candi Staton's 1976 dance anthem 'Young Hearts Run Free' in the process), so why not a disco version?

Four other albums followed in quick succession. The French movie soundtrack *Trocadéro Bleu Citron*, the space soap opera *Golden Tears* by Sumeria (clearly inspired by *The Man Who Fell To Earth*), *Hunchback Of Notre Dame* by Alec R. and the Syncophonic Orchestra, and *Paris Connection* by Paris Connection featuring maxi-length disco updates of Barry Ryan's 1968 hit 'Eloise' and The Righteous Brothers' classic 'You've Lost That Loving Feeling'.

In 1979 Alec R. Costandinos and the Syncophonic Orchestra released an album featuring guest musicians Alirol and Jacquet performing cod classical pieces with the titles 'Benedite', 'Mangareva' and 'The Rite Of King Gymenaud'.

The producer/composer's life then took an unusual turn with an experiment that would have ensured his mainstream breakthrough had it worked. The United Artists label was desperate to reinvent the image of Tina Turner at the time. Ike's former partner had been given a heavy image in 1978 with the album *Rough* but it had failed to work. So UA brought Tina to London and teamed her up with the disco eminence and let him try his hand at producing the larger-than-life future megastar in his idiom. The resulting 'Love Explosion' track from the album of the same name had a good tune but Tina's voice was clearly not right for the genre. Despite the album containing an acceptable salsa version of The O'Jays' hit 'Backstabbers', it flopped and Tina returned to America.

The same year Costandinos was commissioned to write a score for an animated movie from Japan, *Winds Of Change*. The resulting album's side-long totally instrumental title track proved to be an unexpectedly complex symphonic work, with deep-toned and ominous passages darkly coloured by the lower instruments, lighter horizons characterised by typically beautiful string arrangements and even leaps to jazz with a zonked-out-sounding piano. Multifaceted, provocative and satisfying even to those who thought they had danced to everything, *Winds Of Change* is now considered by many to be the artist's most momentous masterpiece.

Americana came in 1980, along with *Burnin' Alive* by Tony Rallo and the Midnite Band, which spawned the popular British dance hit 'Holdin' On', a typical Costandinos production in the style that had made him a household name in the disco world. By blending compelling rock beats, fabulously mellifluous orchestrations and flowing poetic metres, Costandinos created a sound that was perfectly in tune with the times. In 1978 he said, 'I'm a musician, an expressionist . . . perhaps a little of everything, which makes me a good producer.' Those all-round talents shine through his three masterworks 'How Much, How Much I Love You', *Romeo And Juliet* and *Winds Of Change* and provide him a place in the hallowed halls of disco divinity

Rinder And Lewis

Young W. Michael Lewis and middle-aged Laurin Rinder were nothing if not versatile and they provided the disco era with an eclectic series of sounds under the names El Coco, Le Pamplemousse, Tuxedo junction and Saint Tropez as well as their own solo ventures. The two session musicians met in the late-'60s after paying their dues on many recordings in a number of studios, especially Detroit's Tamla Motown, and joined the American Variety International label as house producers. The Ray Harris-owned label scored heavily with the likes of camp MOR pianist Liberace and soulster Rufus Thomas, but Rinder and Lewis were restless any wanted to broaden their horizons by trying their hand at prime disco.

Their first effort was in 1975 with El Coco and the cut 'Mondo Disco'. The sound was pure disco with Lewis providing the heavy bass-line on a synthesiser and hi-hat drumming, strings and a girlie chorus layered over the top. The second so-so El Coco album was *Brazil*, but 'Let's Get It Together', from the third album, sold over 800,000 copies on

12-inch single alone, mainly through word of mouth having received very little radio air-play. The same album provided another disco chart hit with '*Fait Le Chat*'. 'Cocomotion' was a huge British disco hit in 1977, as were 'Dancing In Paradise' and 'Under Construction' in 1978. In 1977, Rinder and Lewis took the more R&B route with '*Le Spank*' by Le Pamplemousse (it means 'grapefruit' in French!) and scored a hefty disco hit as well as reaching No. 6 in the R&B charts.

The producers' most commercial venture was with Tuxedo junction and their Glenn Miller disco concept. The group's lead singer, Jamie Edlin, had grown up with the big-band sounds of Miller, Tommy Dorsey and Artie Shaw, and he figured the music they made would adapt perfectly to the disco vernacular and vibe. Under the direction of Rinder and Lewis, wartime standards, '20s froth and Broadway torch songs came alive for a new dance generation. 'Chattanooga Choo Choo', 'Toot Toot Tootsie Goodbye', 'Rainy Night In Rio', 'That Old Black Magic', 'Take The A Train', 'Begin the Beguine' and, most startling of all, 'Volga Boatman' floated clubbers along on a wave of meaty, beaty, big and bouncy ballroom nostalgia. The producers actually used some of the original musicians from many of the Miller recordings for their venture and were grateful when the seasoned professionals fixed the complicated string charts in a few seconds after they themselves had spent eight days trying to crack the orchestrations.

For the Butterfly record label (home of the superb disco version of Curtis Mayfield's 'Move On Up (Suite)' by Destination), Rinder and Lewis produced the Saint Tropez girl group and scored three massive disco hits with a densely orchestrated, string-heavy and orgasmically sung '*Je T'Aime*' (the first dance version of Serge Gainsbourg's '60s erotic classic), and the bubblegum crowd-pleasers 'One More Minute', '*On A Rien A Perdre*' and 'Fill My Life With Love'. All four tracks were recorded at London's Trident Studios and were big on the gay disco circuit because they were defiantly romantic and melodically fullblooded. They

132

were also risqué in quite a unique way. Saint Tropez released three albums in all, *Violation, Belle De Jour* and *Femmes Fatales*, and on each was one cut that played out a soap opera serial about a *ménage à trois* between passionately emoting characters Jean, Nicole and a lesbian assassin.

After putting out the *In Search Of . . . Orchestra* album in 1977 containing disco versions of popular television themes, Rinder and Lewis's own *Seven Deadly Sins* album was a more jazzy and spacy affair than anything they had attempted before, and spawned a decent-sized hit with a cover of the Cliff Richard (and others) standard 'Willie And The Hand Jive'. The 1979 *RinLew All-Stars* album continued that funkier trend. At the height of their success, Rinder and Lewis were producing two albums a month for their array of artists, with the addition of solo ventures by Dave Williams and Dave Benoit, both from the Le Pamplemousse line-up. An excellent example of journeymen producers, Rinder and Lewis gave each of their acts a highly distinctive sound that kept rivalry at bay but revelry at full blast.

DISCO FACT!
'60s singer Paul ('Diana') Anka was the first person to install an airport-style metal detector at his $3 million Las Vegas disco, Jubilation, to make sure no knives or guns were brought into the place.

DISCO FACT!
The best discos in 1978, according to America's *Discothekin* magazine: Best Nationwide: Studio 54. Best Regional: Studio One (LA), Limelight (Florida) and Limelight (Montreal). Best for Style: New York New York. Best Gay: The Loft (NYC). Best Women's: Sahara (NYC). Best Latin, Black and Rock: Les Nuages, Pippin and Ashley's (all NYC).

I Need A Man

GAY DISCO

What was the first gay discothèque? Some say it was The Sanctuary on West 43rd Street in New York which opened its doors in 1970 to platters spun by the revolving deejay trio of Francis Grosso (from The Haven), Steve D'Aquisto and Michael Cappello (from the crucial uptown venue Tamberlaine). Others argue it was the Ice Palace in mid-town Manhattan. Or was it any venue on Fire Island, the popular gay weekend resort beach in New York? After all, Paul Jabara wrote his 1978 hit 'Pleasure Island' as a homage to that dune-and-disco retreat. After cruising in secluded sandy secret, wearing the latest Hom swimwear, it was an easy segue into swishing around darkened disco confines hoping for another glimpse of the unattainable object of your lust-ridden affections spotted earlier on the beach.

Others are convinced it was the Manhattan restaurant/discothèque Aux Puces, a chic watering-hole fitting the late-'60s brief of what a dance club often aspired to be – somewhere plush to eat fine French food, relax over Irish coffee and possibly jive around a postage-stamp-sized floor between courses or whenever the mood took you.

In London, the gay district of Earl's Court offered the mirrored chi-chi club The Masquerade. Part of its charm, due to Britain's weird licensing laws at the time, was that the price of admission had to include some sort of meal, otherwise alcohol couldn't be sold. The ridiculous situation arose of having to redeem your entrance ticket stub at some stage during the evening for a tiny plate bearing a moth-eaten lettuce leaf, half a tomato, a blob of coleslaw and a slice of processed ham served up by very harassed and embarrassed waiters.

A minute around the corner from The Masquerade, on the same block as the notorious gay pub The Colherne, were The Catacombs. This glorious basement dive was unlicensed (no Spartan salad!), served Italian coffee and toasted sandwiches, and could only stay open until midnight. It should only have held a hundred people really, but three times that number regularly crammed into the place between 11 p.m. and closing time. Yet it was where many big-city homosexuals lost their disco virginity to deejay Chris, and the one regulars used to call Pamela Motown, while wandering through the dimly lit cave-like tunnelled pick-up area just beyond the dance floor. Afterwards they'd continue to wander around the nearby Wharfedale Street if they hadn't cruised successfully indoors, which was why the council finally closed the place down.

Further up the road, on Kensington High Street, behind a very discreet doorway distinguished by its famous Mexican hat sign, was The Sombrero, or Yours and Mine as it was often called because it set the London trend for a gay/mixed ambience. There was no grand reception area – you just paid your money and descended the long staircase to the shadowy depths below. But whereas The Catacombs catered to the sleazy Joe Orton/leather brigade, The Sombrero was strictly piss-elegant queens, Chelsea rent boys and bisexual glam rock wannabes (all captured perfectly in Todd Haynes's 1998 glitter gala *Velvet Goldmine*).

The smell may have been more Habit Rouge than the sweaty amyl nitrate of The Catacombs, but The Sombrero did have something extra that none of the other few exclusively gay venues had. It sported one of the first flashing under-lit disco floors, resembling a large Trivial Pursuit game counter with neon-coloured segments. Lighting wasn't that important in the fledgling days of gay disco, though. Knowing that the person dancing next to you to Marvin Gaye's 'I Heard It Through the Grapevine' and Desmond Dekker and the Aces' 'The Israelites' shared the same sexuality and had the same nomadic bedsit lifestyle was more than enough. The gay mantras 'San Francisco (You've Got Me)' and 'I Wanna Funk With You Tonight' (Giorgio Moroder's classic cruise cut where 'funk' was always mispronounced in a cacophony of giggles) would come later.

The Sanctuary actually epitomised New York in the post-Stonewall/ camp bitch *Boys In The Band* era. Stonewall was the legendary queer hangout in Greenwich Village where the first rumblings of the modern gay rights movement began in 1969. At this tacky bar, drag queens, pseudo-militant fags and other homo habitués took a stand (significantly, on the night Judy Garland died) against a corrupt police force who regularly busted the place due to ludicrous discriminatory laws regarding single-sex fraternisation. The ensuing riots and media coverage changed attitudes towards homosexuals virtually overnight and laid the foundation for the disco demolition of accepted family values, the 'more more more' 1970s orgy mentality, and the eventual Caligula-esque extreme spectacle floor shows of The Anvil and The Mineshaft clubs, where 'How Many Beer Cans Can You Shove Up Your Ass?' nights became de rigueur. (The record stood at six for many weeks!)

When gay men won the right to dance intimately together without worrying about police interference, the disco boom really couldn't be too far behind. The two cultures were waiting for each other to propel both lifestyles into the spotlight. Gays were always responsible for setting fashion trends in motion, anyway. The non-stop party ethos that disco magnified was also down to the fact gays never ever intended to grow up, and the subculture would redefine ageism. as the era progressed. Soon the burgeoning number of private pleasure palaces became not only sites of liberation away from the judgmental straight world but also desert islands of like-minded desire where the very act of dancing became a democratic decree of tribal transcendence and catwalk consciousness.

That's why The Sanctuary was the perfect starting point for the roots of gay disco to take hold. It was a former Baptist church in New York's Hell's Kitchen area where deejays Francis Grosso et al. pumped out homo hymns from the altar turntables to those gathered for communion on a Saturday night. Here the holy wafer was a quaalude and the sacred wine a can of Budweiser. Confessions clearly took place in the club's dark recesses – why else were the choir boys on their knees? – and adoring parishioners wouldn't leave the wild frenzied scenes of druggy abandon until they heard those heartfelt sermons of the day 'Spirit in the Sky' and 'Band of Gold'. Heaven and marriage Hell in one pro-gay disco package.

During the early-'70s, being gay was a major part of the disco experience. Any new venue worth its salt paid a fortune for gay mailing lists to put on their invitation Rolodex. Straights therefore adopted a gay persona (glam rock providing the perfect alibi) to enter the hallowed halls of homo, heaving. Soon clubs had to come up with a door policy that meant exclusion and exclusivity without going broke in the process. Fag hags were fine. (As a contemporary joke went at the time, why did God invent gay discos? So fat, ugly, straight women would have somewhere to dance!) Models and low-rent starlets were okay, too. They wanted to pose and take a central place in the self-obsessed musical fantasy world as much as any metropolitan fairy did.

Clearly heterosexual men (spotted instantly via their uniform of South Sea Bubble flared jeans, grubby tank tops and cheap aftershave) were the problem. Convinced they were the answer to every gay guy's dream and therefore had to protect themselves at any cost, they would often become abusive and belligerent when surrounded by platoons of poofters. While that attitude would always remain a problem in suburban areas, straight men who were confident in their sexuality soon realised that instant hipness was granted once they gained access to the gay disco environment. They loved the free-for-all orgy mentality exuded under the spinning lights and, even though instant sexual gratification will always be easier in the less-inhibited gay world, they wanted to entertain the possibility of perpetual pleasure. They mainly loved the music, though. No straight club ever mixed the records as well as deejays did for the gay crowd.

It was the gradual incursion of the blinkered straight world into gay disco which caused the 'Disco Sucks' movement to gain ground in America in the late-'70s. Socially constructed differences are often associated between high and low culture. The former is seen as masculine, active and being able to provide intellectual stimuli. The latter is generally considered to possess feminine qualities such as heightened and 'needless' emotionality. Low mass culture, especially popular music, is something the élite intellectual would never admit to allowing himself to enjoy outside camp slumming. The mundane pleasure of relentless self-induced trance states, like dancing in clubs, to 'manufactured' dance music, is seen as a sure sign of regressive listening habits and declining tastes. Therefore the representations of consumers of 'low' disco music are marginalised by social and sexual categories – culturally deprived working-class men, emotionally fickle women and homosexuals.

So attempts were made to de-gay disco because the straight world found it impossible to reconcile the alluring *joie de vivre* sensibility within mainstream culture. How could the straight disco establishment cope with the early-morning Sunday ritual of hosing down the cum and Crisco in the balcony area of The Saint (the legendary East Village gay disco)? Disco as a corporate money-maker was wanted but not the vitally orgasmic lifestyle that defined it in sexual ecstasy terms. That's why The Village People in the movie *Can't Stop The Music* became straight pop stars, why the live-and-let-live gay atmosphere of Paradise Garage was replaced with angst-ridden sexually tormented straight youths cruising the 2001 club in *Saturday Night Fever*, and why disco diva Candi Staton sang about 'Young Hearts Run Free' in 1976 but being a 'Victim' in 1978.

As the straight world turned more homophobic through jealousy and petulant annoyance, discophobia waited in the wings. Only by killing disco could rock music reaffirm its threatened masculinity and could straight men – strong-armed by their girlfriends into dancing next to mustachioed clones, and continually 'castrated' by nightly choruses of 'I'm Every Woman' and 'Knights in White Satin' – get their balls back with some pride intact. The 'Disco Sucks' division (and the fact that the very sexual word 'Sucks' was chosen is revealing) culminating in the 'Disco Demolition' rally in Chicago's Cominskey Park, home of the White Sox, in July 1979, wasn't so much an assembly against mindless plastic music but more about putting gay liberation back in its nocturnal niche.

It was a deliberate heterosexual exorcism of an increasingly *mucho* macho twilight society that could play the 'masculine' game better than any straight man ever could. This was also the reason why the Aids epidemic was leapt on with such gruesome glee by straight society too. Gays had been having their cock and eating it for far too long as the only dangers lurking in the safe '70s were treatable ones like crabs, herpes and doses of the clap. It was about time they suffered for all the fun, filth and fist-fucking they got up to in the deliciously sleazy '70s, the last entirely sexually free decade of the twentieth century.

While disco would continually raise such profound sexual and social issues from its innocent inception to its move back underground in the early-'80s, the contours of the movement remained predominantly gay throughout the era. Straights adopted a temporary gay persona to fit into the quintessentially queer milieu everywhere from The 10th Floor and The Loft in Manhattan to Glades and Rod's in London and Le Sept in Paris. If voyeurism was mainly what it was all about from the heterosexual perspective, it was the music that carried the melodic ebb and flow of simple desire for the gay contingent. The song titles really said it all: 'Don't Leave Me This Way', 'I Love To Love', 'To Each His Own' and 'Lovin' Is Really My Game'.

Disco is concerned with collage, pastiche and quotation, with a selective pasting together of different musical styles. It showcases a flawless approach to production values while rejecting divisions between serious and fun popular music. Much of disco is unabashedly camp and while the camp phenomenon was subjected to a pop homogenisation during the '60s by Susan Sontag and her contemporaries, it is still largely seen as a specifically gay agenda. That's why disco is often said to be an extended 4/4 soulful beat conversation between black female divas and gay men who fully understand the lingo, the swooping sexual innuendo and the tragic emotions evoked, as the classic gay disco cuts 'Love To Love You Baby' by Donna Summer, 'I Need A Man' by Grace Jones and 'I Will Survive' and 'I Am What I Am' by Gloria Gaynor prove beyond any doubt. That's the way they liked it, uh-huh, uh-huh!

These songs mirrored the frenzied, posturing, arrogant, primadonna-ish, ego-deifying, self-protective, super-compensating principles that psychologists have identified as vital components of the homosexual lifestyle and psyche. More politically skewed cuts came from producer August Darnell and his group Machine. Their profoundly moving song 'There But For

The Grace Of God Go I' dealt directly with homophobia and racism. Carl Bean proudly stated 'I Was Born This Way' too. But for the most part the gay disco approach was straightforwardly more camp and frothy fun. 'Abdullah's Wedding' by Orient Express neatly summed it all up. Sung by an all-male cast over eastern-tinged instrumentation, this six-minute aural drag show episode tells the story of a hesitant veiled bride who gradually succumbs to the charms of the groom's old father.

But as all these songs crossed over into the mainstream very quickly, should they really be classed as bona fide gay disco records? Definitely. What became clear as the '70s marched towards the homogenised output of obviously gay-orientated groups looking for cultural cross-over, The Village People being a prime example, was that hardcore clubbers, needing a cogent alternative to mainstream chart dance music, went further into niche disco subterrania than ever before. Anything with a dangerous, exotic, underground sensibility – gay or otherwise – was fine according to the club cognoscenti. Hence the popularity of Amanda Lear, Pattie Brooks, Sylvester, Claudja Barry and The Village People on the straight circuit while they remained very much a part of gay disco furniture.

Gay disco had cheeky humour in song titles ('Push Push, In the Bush' by Musique being a glorious example), thinly veiled eroticism in dance movements (the bump), outrageous flaunting of sexuality (the fan as an accessory with which to keep cool in those dim and distant pre-air-conditioned times) and a savvy sense of underground élitism. But above all it was the universal dedication to partying with which every cultural group could empathise that gave gay disco in all its varied forms such an edge.

I Can't Dance Without You

FOUR FACES OF GAY DISCO

The Village People

The Village People are easily the most famous gay disco group. Not only did they come along at precisely the right time to capitalise on the new air of gay liberation blowing around the world, but they also adopted a macho image and stance that many gay men responded to after years of being labelled effeminate nellie queens. Gay French record producer Jacques Morali and his partner Henri Belolo put the act together after touring some of the more notorious Christopher Street dives in Greenwich Village and, realising macho drag was trendy in a big way, assembled a group of male stereotypes including a biker, policeman, construction worker, cowboy, soldier and Red Indian. Singer-songwriter Victor Willis (star of the Broadway musical *The Wiz*) was Morali's first recruit as the cop lead singer – the Officer of Love – and his back-up support vocalists and dancers were Randy Jones (in Stetson), David 'Scar' Hodo (in hard hat), Glenn Hughes (in shades and Muir cap), Alexander Briley (in fatigues) and Felipe Rose (in full feather).

Launched in October 1977 (after ironically making their try-out live stage debut on 28 February that year at 2001 Odyssey in Brooklyn, soon to be made world famous by *Saturday Night*

Fever), The Village People were an instant hit with their 'San Francisco (You've Got Me)/Hollywood' medley. The sex six-pack then began their spectacular run of hits, peaking with the super-catchy British No. 1 (American No. 2) chart hit 'YMCA'. Composed on a whim as Morali passed by the New York YMCA, with the lyrics just coming into his head, the song is still a strong club/party anthem today complete with ritual arm movements spelling out the title letters. The group collectively put their success down to their over-the-top image being like 'the cast from a Broadway show or a Hollywood movie'. They also called themselves a 'People's Liberation Group' as opposed to anything political for selling a 'don't dream it, be it' philosophy more than a sexual lifestyle.

Other hits followed: 'Macho Man', 'In The Navy' (which the US armed forces seriously considered using as a recruitment jingle until they realised exactly where the boys were coming from), 'Go West'(based on the same chord progression as classical composer Pachelbel's 'Canon in D'), 'Can't Stop The Music' (the title track of their much-maligned movie and their last Top 20 hit), 'Just A Gigolo/I Ain't Got Nobody' and 'Ready For The '80s'. All were strong gay disco cuts which kept the dance floors smelling like new car upholstery thanks to the sudden surge in sales of leather chaps, jackets and arm-band accessories.

Victor Willis eventually got tired of the group's gay associations (he was married to Casablanca diva Phylicia Allen) and was replaced by Ray Simpson, brother of composer/singer Valerie Simpson of Ashford & Simpson fame. Willis's career would take a further severe downturn after being charged with abduction and drug offences. After a dreadful New Romantic/Visage style makeover in the early-'80s on the album *Renaissance*, The Village People bounced back with 'Sex Over The Phone' and, their last recording to date, 'Far Away In America'.

Still going strong today and better live than ever, the group flaunted their outrageously camp sensibilities as an anti-establishment act even as the same establishment wholeheartedly embraced them. They were gay disco personified and the perfect example of the dichotomy inherent in that label. They sold a very positive male, if not macho, image to those willing to fantasise about pan-sexual possibilities. The Village People were dangerous and revolutionary despite ending their chart days appealing to the predominantly female teeny-bop audience of the time.

Amanda Lear

Playing the gender game in an altogether different way was Amanda Lear, cover girl, fashion model, muse of artist Salvador Dalí and enigmatic disco queen. Was she or wasn't she? That was the question on everyone's lips when *I Am A Photograph*, her first album on the German Ariola label, was released in 1977. Was she or wasn't she what? A transsexual, that's what! The rumour mill ran riot over that particular question. Tongues wagged about secret sex-change operations. Friends of friends of boyfriends knew someone who knew for a fact that Amanda was born a man in 1947. And topless photos were scrutinised with magnifying glasses for any possible telltale scars or hints of five o'clock shadow.

The haughty and remote Amanda herself barely acknowledged the question and, like 'The Sphinx' of her 1978 soft disco classic, never answered it, cannily playing on the word-of-mouth publicity for all it was worth. It only added to her mystique, as gay disco did so love a scandal, a heartbreak or a skeleton in the closet served up with their fame whore glamour. What tended to get lost amongst all the whispering and straight sniggering was that Amanda's musical output was of an extraordinarily rare vintage. Each of her major disco cuts was a high-class production in every respect.

Amanda has a deep, smoky, masculine voice, not unlike that of Hollywood star Marlene Dietrich. She would often conjure up the Marlene comparison herself in her *Blue Angel*-inspired album photos and the two disco cover versions of the wartime Dietrich standard 'Lili Marlene' (1979 and 1993). And like Marlene, Amanda was canonised by the besotted coterie of Eurodisco fans who worshipped the ground her stiletto heels touched. And they still do. Looking as glamorous as ever, Amanda is today active in all areas of the European entertainment industry, releasing excellent records geared towards the dance market, appearing in films and, as an expert on Salvador Dalí, attending openings of art exhibitions around the globe.

She started her modelling career in 1965 in the pages of *Marie-France* magazine wearing an Yves St Laurent outfit, and throughout the '60s would also work with such noted designers as Paco Rabanne, Mary Quant and Ossie Clark. In 1967 she appeared as a Martian in her first French movie, directed by Henri Lanoe, and then found herself representing Hippie Youth in 1968 thanks to a front-page *Daily Telegraph* photo accompanying a Malcolm Muggeridge essay entitled 'The Summer of Love'. Amanda wore a purple minidress in the spread because Dalí had told her purple was the colour of the church.

The first time she entered the international collective public consciousness in any major way was when she posed for the cover photo of Roxy Music's album *For Your Pleasure* in 1973 wearing an outfit designed by King's Road fashion guru Anthony Price. In 1975 she tested the music business waters with the single '*La Bagarre*', but it wasn't until the release of 'Blood and Honey' from *I Am A Photograph* that her singing career took off like a rocket and flung her headlong into disco divadom. 'Blood and Honey' was an instantly beguiling bisexual vampire disco lament produced by Anthony Monn, the man often called Amanda's alter ego, and arranged by Harold Faltermeier (who would soon spell his surname Faltermeyer and become a Hollywood film composer of renown, scoring a major hit with 'Axel F' from *Beverly Hills Cop*).

Other supremely confident disco tracks from *I Am A Photograph* include the dreamy date jape 'Tomorrow', the pounding opium/white slave fantasy 'Queen of China-Town', the extraordinarily autobiographical litany 'Alphabet' and the camp *Come Dancing* come-on 'Blue Tango'. *I Am A Photograph* was an amusingly pleasing disco &but from Amanda and Monn. Amanda had co-written most of the album with Monn, too, a rare feat at the time, and she continued in the same capacity throughout her career. If 'The Lady In Black' and the strange reworking of 'These Boots Are Made For Walking' didn't quite cut the disco mustard, the album had an overall quality which ensured it a place on every Euro gay turntable throughout the season.

What came next from the Amanda/Monn camp blew everyone away. *Sweet Revenge* was not only one of the key albums of 1978, but it has become an ageless classic and is the

one recording Amanda will always be remembered for. The reason for this is the sensational A-side, a Faustian fable enlivened by one of the most fabulous orchestral disco productions the entire era had to offer. Recorded between December 1977 and February 1978 at the Arco, Trixi and Ariola studios in Munich, and Sound Studio N in Cologne, the twenty-minute marathon began with a shimmering gong that galvanised the attention of every dancer and then swept them along on a melodic suite of soaring violins, punchy percussion, hard rock and relentless choral magnificence.

Amanda described the unbearably beautiful disco odyssey this way: 'This album is the story of a girl who sold her soul to the Devil and won. A lonely child, disenchanted by the society she lives in, she has no friends until the day she listens to the tempting offer of the Devil who promises her anything she wants ['Follow Me']. Her first wish is for riches ['Gold'] and then for fame. After turning to her mother for help ['Mother, Look What They've Done To Me'], she runs away ['Run, Baby, Run'] and retires into solitude and memories. Renouncing her selfish need, she offers her love to a man who really needs her ['Follow Me' reprise], her sweet revenge over the Devil's offer . . .'

The B-side of the album (sporting a cover photo of Amanda in leather trousers and torn vest brandishing a whip), featured the popular 'Enigma (Give A Bit Of Mmh To Me)' and 'Hollywood Flashback', but these flippant fillers took a back seat to the triumph of the eternal 'Follow Me' side and its mysteriously haunting web of love, seduction and disco. 'Follow Me' was everything a great gay disco record should be, and its continuing popularity – you can't find a jukebox anywhere in Germany that doesn't have a copy – is a testament to its timelessness and distinguished disco craftsmanship.

The languid sensuality of La Lear's performance in 'Follow Me' made an impression among record labels in America too, where for some inexplicable reason the artist's releases had been all but ignored. The track was given to Wally McDonald to reconstruct, in the hope of securing an entry to the Billboard charts with the resulting 12-incher. What the re-mixer delivered turned out to fulfil all expectations – except getting the singer noted in America. More a luminous, trancey exercise in breathless euphoria than a dance track meant to induce heavy perspiration, the ten-minute symphony now pulsated with additional analogue synthesizers and swelled up with extended string passages. On top of the violins, Amanda seemed to hover above the subtle chord changes, a bio-morphic figure drawing us into her world of limitless luxuries. In America, only the more adventuresome clubs programmed this new deluxe edition, while in Europe the few pressings available quickly became alluring objects of desire.

The next year Amanda built on her growing diva reputation with the album *Never Trust A Pretty Face* which, along with the title track, offered the dance evergreen 'Fashion Pack' (in the French version 'Disco Jet Set'), a fun list of contemporary celebrities and haute couture haunts (Marisa Berenson, Zoli, Regine's, Studio 54, Andy Warhol, Paloma Picasso, Le Sept). 'Black Holes' and 'The Sphinx' put science-fiction morality and Egyptian exotica on the dance floor, the latter disco drone one of Amanda and Monn's more unforgettably eerie high points.

The following year, 1980, brought a change of direction with the spikier and more electronic Monn production *Diamonds For Breakfast*. Amanda remarked on the liner notes, 'To me, every tear, every frustration, every heartache is a precious diamond which lingers in my mind. Good and bad experiences, pleasure and pain, are the richness of which I am proud. I pity people without feelings, they don't have diamonds for breakfast.' And those diamonds on this album (with early cover artwork by Pierre & Gilles) included the feisty 'I Need A Man', 'Oh Boy', 'Diamonds', 'Insomnia' and 'Fabulous (Lover, Love Me)'.

Incognito was the next album and, quoting Robert Sheckley with 'Hell Is Who (Where) You Really Are', Amanda took the dancer on a spray-can tour through the Seven Deadly Sins. Laziness was represented by 'Hollywood Is just A Dream When You're Seventeen', fear by 'New York', pride by 'Egal', greed by 'Nymphomania' and envy by 'lf I Was A Boy'. Even at this late stage in her career Amanda was still keeping the gender guessing-game going.

Anthony Monn went on to supervise the HI-NRG career of Fancy and his prolific output included 'Chinese Eyes', 'Slice Me Nice', 'Flames Of Love' and the superb 'Bolero'. He then retired from the industry. Amanda Lear, however, has continued in the public eye and in the European music charts through her Italian television career (she presented the top-rated variety shows *Viva La Donna* and *Ars Amanda*), concert tours and a steady stream of well-received records.

The *Tam Tam* album in 1983 revealed yet more tuneful sides

to the diva's pen with such ace numbers as 'Bewitched', 'Magic', 'No Regrets', 'Gipsy Man' and 'Music Is'. The 12-inch single 'Love Your Body' in 1983 cashed in on the aerobics craze, 'Assassino' followed in 1984, 'No Credit Card' the next year, and the album *Secret Passion* appeared in 1987 featuring the 1986 HI-NRG hit 'She Wolf' as well as 'Mannequin' and 'I Want My Name On A Billboard'. More recently Amanda has reached a whole new Euro gay handbag/MOR audience with 'Fantasy' in 1993 and 'Alter Ego' in 1995. The former cut is from the album *Cadavrexquis* on which she updated 'Fashion Pack' to include Madonna, Elton John and Naomi Campbell. The next release arrived in 2001. In addition to the popular no-frills club cut 'I Just Wanna Dance Again' and the expectedly camp update of the Muzak theme from the TV show *Love Boat*, the CD *Heart* also contained several deliciously dramatic half-whispered, half-sung *chansons* such as '*L'Invitation au Voyage*' and '*L'Importante e Finire*'. After two decades of totally electronic dance material, these moody cabaret-style performances were further proof that the diva would never lose the power to make us fall into her tender trap over and over again. Three years later, 2004 saw the publication of an extended edition of her autobiographical book, *Mon Dali*, a beguiling journey through scandalous gallery openings, fashion shoots and phantasmagorical parties staged by the famed surrealist.

Amanda Lear is one of the dominant success stories of disco. She changed along with the disco trend long before people like Madonna cottoned on to redefining their image with each successive album release. Retaining one's hardcore fans in the image-engineering process is often what makes or breaks an artist. But Amanda Lear said 'Follow Me' in 1978 and, because it was such a powerfully breathtaking plea, everybody has done precisely that. We didn't dare not to!

Sylvester

Sylvester didn't need to tell anyone he was gay. He assumed everyone knew. The perfectionist camp singer with the lisp and falsetto voice exploded onto the gay disco scene in the summer of 1978 with 'You Make Me Feel (Mighty Real)'. The early rock video that accompanied the track was shot in London's trendy Embassy disco and featured the glaring singer daring you not to take him seriously as he walked down the club's theatrical staircase wearing a gob-smacking array of '70s fashion-queen finery: first a black dress over leather trousers, then a white suit and fans, and then a sequinned gown and turban ensemble. Sylvester knew he was superstar material from an early age and his knack for feverish and sophisticated disco, with an all-important underlying tinge of gospel rhythm and blues, instantly endeared him to the adoring gay masses.

Born into a bourgeois family (the actual date was kept a closely guarded secret), Sylvester James was raised in Los Angeles where he learned to sing gospel in church. He shared much of his early life with his grandmother, Julia Morgan, a celebrated '30s jazz singer, and it was through her that he became interested in blues, singing professionally and the theatre. At the age of eight, he travelled America's gospel circuit, and by twelve had fallen hopelessly in love with the music of Bessie Smith and Billie Holiday.

He impersonated Smith and Holiday as well as Lena Horne in a stage show called *Women Of The Blues* which he put together at The Rickshaw Lounge when he moved to San Francisco in the late-'60s. Here, Sylvester lived as a woman in the soon-to-be gay capital of the world, calling himself Ruby Blue. In 1970 he rose to major gay fame as the star of The Cockettes, an outrageous musical revue, which rapidly became the toast of the town amongst the acid-dropping hippie contingent. He left the troupe in 1973 to become lead singer with The Hot Band for Blue Thumb Records. The group recorded three albums – *Lights Out In San Francisco*, *Scratch*

My Flower (the cover had a scratch-and-sniff patch which smelled of gardenias) and *Bazaar* – and throughout The Hot Band years Sylvester indulged his passion for wearing women's clothes and gaudy jewellery.

It was producer Harvey Fuqua who recognised Sylvester's raw talent, insolent manner and stage presence. Fuqua signed him to Honey Records, a label he owned with Nancy Pitts, and which was licensed to Fantasy Records. The trio worked on the 1978 *Sylvester* album which included the Ashford & Simpson track 'Over And Over' as well as 'Down, Down, Down' written by the singer himself. Then came the massive success of 'You Make Me Feel (Mighty Real)', which was originally conceived as a gospel track until finally given the dance treatment to send it happily soaring into gay disco history. The phenomenal success of the hit, which was co-written by Sylvester, got the singer a unique gig performing at The War Memorial Opera House in San Francisco. Halfway through the two-hour set, backed by a twenty-eight-piece orchestra and his two backing singers, Martha Wash and Izora Rhodes collectively known as The Two Tons of Fun (who would later transform into The Weather Girls and have a major gay disco hit with 'It's Raining Men'), Sylvester was given the keys to the city; 11 March 1979 was also proclaimed 'Sylvester Day' as San Francisco rewarded one of its own international star emissaries for taking the communal happiness ethic on the global gay circuit.

While also packing the dance floors with 'Dance (Disco Heat)' in 1978, a rattling version of 'I (Who Have Nothing)', the Jerry Leiber and Mike Stoller standard, and 'Stars (Everybody Is One)' in 1979, Sylvester managed to find time to make his movie debut in *The Rose* alongside another gay icon, Bette Midler. He played Pearl in the tragi-musical and sang the Bob Seger song 'Fire Down Below' with his co-star. That year he also won a succession of awards including three at the *Billboard* Disco Forum and for Best Disco Male from *Disco International* magazine.

Gays loved Sylvester because he would always speak his mind and didn't care whom he shocked in the process. He once told a journalist he wanted to marry Prince Charles so that he could become Queen of England. He would also reveal he was having major surgery. Not the anticipated sex change, though – a nose job!

Further success would come Sylvester's way with a cover version of the Brainstorm classic 'Lovin' Is Really My Game', 'I Need You' and 'Do You Wanna Funk' which he performed with '80s HI-NRG icon Patrick Cowley in 1982. An updated version of Freda Payne's 'Band of Gold' would be his last British Top 100 chart showing before he died of Aids in 1988.

Sylvester was an artist who refused to conform. That's why gays loved him. He had a flamboyant image and carefree attitude they desperately wanted to copy. But it was his passion and respect for disco music that earned him a place in the gay disco Hall of Fame. 'I realise that gay people have put me on a pedestal,' he said in 1979, 'and I love it. Of all the oppressed minorities, they have to be the most oppressed.' With speeches like that, Sylvester couldn't fail to make a gay disco impact.

Boys Town Gang

Despite The Village People's huge accomplishments, very few managers tried to copy the formula, which is surprising considering the sheep mentality of the music industry. When Take That became stars, for example, twelve other boy bands were instantly groomed, choreographed and marketed to appeal to the same audience. In Britain, a leather-clad duo tried to copy The Village People's gay-orientated success, but The Poppers and 'Take It To The Top' never made it past the demo stage.

But eventually cloned from the same mould as The Village People were Boys Town Gang who crossed into mainstream pop with considerable aplomb and success. The brainchild of producer Bill Motley, Boys Town Gang reflected his

152

preoccupation with instrumental and vocal harmony highlighting lyrics of love, companionship and good times. Another artistic success to come from the San Francisco talent pool of Sylvester, Two Tons of Fun, Paul Parker and Patrick Cowley, Boys Town Gang started off as a studio session band put together by Motley to record 'Remember Me/Ain't No Mountain High Enough' in 1981 as a homage to Tamla Motown and Diana Ross.

Although a sizeable dance-floor and chart hit, it was the flipside of that fifteen-minute medley which really raised eyebrows. 'Cruisin' The Streets' was the *Deep Throat* of disco, a thirteen-minute mass market gay porno fantasy which had the most sexually aggressive and four-letter-word peppered lyrics of the era. On this cutting-edge record, it's Motley's voice you can hear as the lonely cruiser who seems embarrassed when a rather rude suggestion is whispered in his ear by a fellow Castro clone. 'I didn't think anyone was into that!' he says in hilarious hushed tones.

This leads to an open-air orgy complete with orgasmic sound effects, watched by a masturbating female hooker, which the police bust up and then decide to join in. Singer Cynthia Manley took the lead vocals on the track which, naturally, quickly became a gay disco mantra. Lyrics containing the words 'asshole', 'cunt' and 'dick of death' were very unusual ones to be heard coming from the speakers even in those sexually liberated times and 'Cruisin' The Streets' sold an amazing quarter of a million copies in the UK alone, thanks to its inclusion on a Ronco compilation album, mainly because of this high-density shock factor.

Jackson Moore was drafted in as the lead vocalist on the next Boys Town Gang release, a superb disco take on Frankie Valli's 1967 standard 'Can't Take My Eyes Off You'. Considered the last great disco record because very few after it used an orchestral backing (from 1982 onwards computer keyboards would steadily take over), 'Can't Take My Eyes Off You' is upbeat and classily constructed to hit every gay disco nuance. The Top 10 track appeared on the *Disc Charge* album (the cover photo featured stripped-down sweaty hunks fixing a car in a greasy garage setting) along with the scintillating sing-along 'Disco Kicks' and the 'Signed, Sealed, Delivered (I'm Yours)' chart hit.

The resulting success of the album meant Motley had to put together an actual touring group to support the numerous single releases. So Jackson Moore, Tom Morely and Bruce Carleton were sent on the road under strict instructions to present a wholesome, clean-living image, laced with polite but subdued virility. It was important for Motley to show the world a gay disco group of mixed sexuality and race who fully supported each other and their lifestyle choices. Both Motley and Tom Morely were lost to Aids but the message in Bill's music endures, as 'Can't Take My Eyes Off You' remains one of the most popular disco songs of all time and regularly appears on compilations celebrating the era.

154

Sorry I'm A Lady

SATURDAY NIGHT DIVAS

Grace Jones

Fetishised by influential photographers and artists like Jean-Paul Goude and Guy Bourdin, the statuesque Grace Jones was the ultimate disco diva. Her panther-like face leered from the covers of magazines from *Elle* and *GQ* to *After Dark* and Andy Warhol's *Interview*. She luxuriated in the limelight at swank soirées and fashion-pack openings, and struck arrogant Bitch Goddess poses at her favoured watering holes, Le Jardin and Studio 54.

And her records weren't half bad either.

Her craving for glamour had already manifested itself at the tender age of twelve as she moved with her parents from Jamaica to Syracuse, New York. She instantly recognised the new possibilities for all things different and theatrical and started to experiment with clothes and styles. After high school – where she held the record for the long jump – Grace was drawn to the stage, and after a period of musical comedy her tutor suggested she try her luck at modelling. Proud of her imposing frame and completely at ease with her body, she went for it and also started auditioning for movie roles too.

Although she gave the impression of being about six foot tall (she was in fact five foot nine), her ferocious looks – something she blamed on a genetic mix-up between herself and her twin brother – were deemed too wild for American model agencies, although she did land a bit part in the blaxploitation film *Gordon's War* (1973). So she packed her bags and left for Paris where her head-turning style soon got her noticed by the top European fashion magazines and led to her first *Elle* cover.

Now in hot demand, Grace was invited to club openings and posh parties around town. It was during one glittering bash that she got carried away by 'Dirty Ol' Man' by The Three Degrees and jumped up on a table to sing along. Well aware of her vocal restrictions, she was surprised that, instead of being escorted off the premises for causing a riot, she found herself with a record deal.

The first track she released was the superb mantra 'I Need A Man', which became a huge gay disco success in France and Holland thanks to the merciless repetition of the title backed by a rock hard rhythm. After appearing in the Italian crime movie *Colt 38 Special Squad* (1976) and singing 'I'll Find My Way To You', Grace co-wrote and recorded two more cuts, 'Sorry' and 'That's The Trouble', for Island Records in London which were remixed by maestro Tom Moulton. Thanks to his reputation, they managed to get vital radio airplay in America. 'That's The Trouble' became Grace's first stateside hit as a result and Moulton then produced her first album, *Portfolio*, with the cream of Philadelphia's studio musicians in 1977.

Arranged by Vincent Montana Jr, the record included the three hits plus a medley of soft discofied Broadway show tunes: 'Send In The Clowns' from *A Little Night Music*, 'What I Did For Love' from *A Chorus Line* and 'Tomorrow' from *Annie*. It was also Moulton who came up with the idea of Grace doing a disco version of the beloved Edith Piaf classic torch song *'La Vie En Rose'*. It turned out to be the perfect after-hours disco wind-down, the French vocals delivered in what would become Jones's trademark flamboyantly off-key manner.

An instant club hit, the album and her outrageous live-performances made Grace the darling of the more theatrical avant-garde disco cliques worldwide. Usually dressed in skimpy animal skins or a slash of fabric exposing her breasts, Grace would roar up a ramp onto disco stages on a motorbike, or be carried on by half-naked, jock-strapped slave boys. Then she'd grab the microphone like it was a velvet vibrator and fling her campy lyrics sung by her 'not too anything voice' into the adoring faces of her audience. The reaction would always be the same – howling, stomping, screaming pandemonium. Notably, *Portfolio* had a sleeve painted by *Interview* magazine cover artist Richard Bernstein who was instrumental in creating her quintessential 'Queen of Mean' look.

Fame, the spectacular 1978 follow-up album, found Grace selling Eskimos snow in the opening hit 'Do Or Die'. Arranged and grandly orchestrated by John Davis (of Monster orchestra fame), Side One's big production medley portrayed the diva as a desperate superstar longing for lost love as it continued through 'Pride' and 'Fame'- highcamp tales of loneliness at the top and the price of celebrity. The elaborate folding album sleeve, again by Bernstein, this time featured Grace in Marlene Dietrich mode.

The next year's *Muse* was a curiously less-inspired affair despite containing such infectious tracks as 'On Your Knees' and 'Suffer', complete with sobbing and nasty whiplash sound effects. Her next album, however, 1980's *Nightclubbing*, was an artistic and musical triumph spawning the bawdy chart hit 'Pull Up To The Bumper'. The acclaimed video work *One Man Show* by her Parisian paramour Jean-Paul Goude further developed Grace's neo-cubist image with a collage of colourfully stylised performance clips which, with her own inimitable sense of the theatrical, ensured her smooth shift from dominatrix diva to formidable '80s club icon.

Madleen Kane

Like Grace Jones, Madleen Kane was another model-turned-singer who found fame in the hallowed Halls of Disco Delirium.

Madleen was born in Sweden (her father was a piano-maker, her mother a native of Sari Francisco) and her early years were marked by overseas travel, music and dance lessons, luxury living and hanging out with Monaco's royal family After becoming one of the hottest European models and gracing over a hundred magazine covers, Madleen lived for a while at the home of Eileen Ford, head of the very successful Ford modelling agency.

It was while on one Ford assignment that she met record producer Jean Claude Friedrich and established successful dual careers, all before the age of eighteen. She burst onto the international music scene in 1978 with her first album *Rough Diamond*, which spawned a No. 1 club hit and was followed by a string of dance classics including eleven chart-toppers.

Madleen never really liked modelling. She always wanted to sing and would use her modelling earnings to pay for singing lessons. Nor did she fancy a Hollywood career, even though Jack Nicholson offered her a chance to be in one of his movies. In truth, Madleen had a limited vocal range and her thin, breathy voice would often sound slightly tinny. But her gorgeous looks, fabulous choice of material, superior production from Eurodisco's best engineers (like Thor Baldurson and Juergen Koppers) and excellent back-up from the usual Sue/Sunny/Tony Burrows contingent all added up to a potent formula which appealed across the board to all disco lovers, regardless of sexuality or gender.

The title track 'Rough Diamond' certainly laid bare Madleen's vocal deficiencies but made up for them with ornate orchestrations and ear-catching flourishes. That was the secret of her celebutante success and she would repeat it throughout her amazingly long career. The first album also contained a disco version of another evergreen that would clearly position Madleen as a lower-echelon Siren of Song – Peggy Lee's 'Fever'.

It was her second album, 1979's *Cheri*, that made both the casual and die-hard disco admirer really sit up and take notice of the imagined candy Kane. Side One contained the meltingly mellifluous and magical 'Forbidden Love (Suite)', nearly eighteen minutes of romantic highs and lows, ebbing and flowing violins, unbelievably catchy melodies and pulsating emotions all wrapped up in gorgeously clichéd piano rolls and cascades. 'Forbidden Love' was so generic, it shouldn't have worked. But its clever balance of Mills & Boon sentiment, disco schmaltz and epic *Imitation Of Life* production was every tear-jerker from *Casablanca* to *Gone With The Wind* pummelled into a mirror-balled Valentine card and posted through the club speaker-system. All sealed with a loving kiss from heartbroken citizen Kane.

Had *Cheri* been Madleen's only musical effort it would have been enough to ensure her disco immortality, but in fact she would continue to release one memorable track after another, including 'Cherchez Pas' and 'Move Me With Your Love' from 1980, and the Giorgio Moroder-produced 'Fire In My Heart' from 1981, before becoming a major force in the HI-NRG arena with such smashes as 'I'm No Angel' and 'Ecstasy'. There were better singers around who never got the chance Madleen Kane did thanks to her privileged modelling position and moneyed background. Sure, it was her looks that got her noticed rather than her voice, sold her records to a disco ignorant Joe Public and made her good tabloid copy. But it's what finally happens on the disco floor that counts, and Madleen Kane's brand of bubblegum bravura was a 'Secret Love Affair' everyone could indulge in and enjoy. In 1978, life was 'suite'.

Pattie Brooks

Casablanca Records seemed to have the copyright on divas throughout the second half of the '70s, and like Roberta Kelly (of 'Zodiacs' fame) Pattie Brooks was also plucked out of Donna Summer's backing vocals line-up and given a stab at solo stardom. Born in Fort Riley, Kansas, to a military family always on the move, Pattie began singing professionally in 1968 after a brief stint working at a telephone company. Winning a spotlight segment on *The Smothers Brothers Comedy Hour* she went on to sing with Henry Mancini's Young Generation and also guested on Bobby Darin's TV series and *The Pearl Bailey Show*.

A sought-after session singer throughout the '70s, she was hired by Donna Summer to sing and help find all the backing vocalists for the *I Remember Yesterday* album recording session at Munich's MusicLand Studios. Pattie was only too happy to oblige. She had followed Donna's career with keen wannabe interest – many thought their vocal ranges were similar – and lined up the services of Petsy Powell, Dani McCormick and Marti McCall as well as herself.

It was when Pattie met Northern Soul maven and UK deejay Simon Soussan, who had gone to the States to record Shalamar's disco Motown medley 'Uptown Festival', that everything clicked into place and her connections paid off with an album contract at Casablanca. Soussan expertly produced Pattie's debut album *Love Shook* and beautifully tailored all the tracks to the dreamily commercial end of the disco pop market. The first big club hit from the album was a gleaming disco reworking of an old Northern Soul favourite originally recorded by Timebox in 1968, written by the soon-to-be-famous Philly producers Kenny Gamble and Leon Huff.

In Soussan's hands 'Girl Don't Make Me Wait' eschewed its tinny '60s flavour to become a bouncy flamenco sizzler complete with gypsy violins, reverberating xylophones and a relentless build towards a wailing, scorching climax. The album's title cut, the 'Pop Collage Medley' – linking the 1972 'Popcorn' instrumental sensation by Hot Butter to other '60s hits 'Black Is Black' and 'Na, Na, Hey, Hey, Kiss Him Goodbye' – were also much-played club favourites.

The *Our Miss Brooks* album was released the next year. Produced again by Soussan, it shared its most popular cut with the *Thank God It's Friday* soundtrack. That song, 'After Dark',

160

also shared its title with the name of a trendy, gay-orientated entertainment magazine. Not slow to realise the obvious cross-over potential, the magazine used the album as part of a promotional give-away to new subscribers. The song itself was another brilliantly crafted sultry slice of Soussan syncopation (written by Simon and Sabrina Soussan) – a whipped-cream confection with knives of stabbing sound poking through *glissando* peaks – and it enjoyed as much disco attention as Brooks's earlier releases.

The same could not be said about 'Got Tu Go Disco', her last major release, in 1979. Brooks had been passed the poisoned chalice of promoting the title song from the ill-fated Broadway musical because of a show-track deal with Casablanca. But even she couldn't help save it and punter disinterest soon showed on the dance floor. Pattie also made a brief appearance in the 1980 horror movie *The Fifth Floor* as a disco floor-show artiste.

Simon Soussan, founder of the Harem record label, went on to score many disco hits with Jessica Williams ('Queen of Fools') and the groups Arpeggio ('Love and Desire', of which Williams was the lead singer), French Kiss ('Panic'), Romance ('Dance My Way To Your Heart'), Charisma ('You're My Fantasy') and The Simon Orchestra ('I Close My Eyes And Count To Ten'). Meanwhile, Pattie continued to do session work for other Casablanca artists, like Paul Jabara, broadening her musical scope to back Olivia Newton-John, Weird AI Yankovic and Paula Abdul (on 'Opposites Attract').

Pattie Brooks made disco seem an effortless doddle, rather than the difficult and demanding job it actually was. Her music has stood the test of time precisely because it communicates a sense of casual wellbeing and saucy fun – the hallmark of her hot and distinctly humid delivery.

Andrea True

Probe the back catalogue of producer/arranger Gregg Diamond and you'll find an eclectic list of names from highly regarded session singers like Jocelyn Brown and Luther Vandross (both of whom would later define the cutting edge of dance music with their solo careers), to personalities not readily associated with the kind of classy music Diamond provided throughout the disco era. His two Bionic Boogie albums (*Bionic Boogie* and *Hot Butterfly*) and his brilliant *Starcruiser* offering of 1978 are exceptional in the field.

One of the more outré acts he produced was Andrea True. The icy blonde porno queen, with her studio backing band, Connection, oozed a mature and predatory sexuality the like of which had never been seen in disco before and proved Diamond was a girl's best friend. Like her *Behind The Green Door* rival Marilyn Chambers, Andrea True gravitated towards disco music, had worldwide recognition for a short period of time and then faded into supper-club obscurity.

Born in Nashville, Tennessee, Andrea True moved to New York in 1968 to study acting. After landing the odd job as an extra in legit motion pictures (such as the Barbra Streisand/Robert Redford soaper *The Way We Were*), she was recruited into the adult-movie circle and first displayed her naked talents to a wide public in the 1972 production *Illusions Of A Lady*. This film was made at the height of the short-lived porno-chic period when it was erroneously predicted that every major legit movie star would have to follow suit, strip to the buff and display their wares in action.

During her screen career, Andrea True was presented with a 'Most Versatile Actress' award by the Adult Motion Picture Association of America in 1975. However, by now well into her mid-thirties and only commanding $500 a flick for standard hardcore fare like *The Seduction Of Lynn Carter* (hailed as her best performance), she tried her hand at writing commercials and producing her own adult features. *Once Over Lightly* was one result of the latter, which she juggled with appearing in the sado-masochistic roughie-and-kinky *Devil's Due*. She also took to making appearances at pricey restaurants as a cabaret singer, luring in the curious by the lascivious promise of her scandalous past.

In 1975 she travelled to Jamaica to work in a local television commercial project. As the political climate suddenly deteriorated into a state of emergency, she found herself stranded on the island, forbidden to leave with her salary. So she called producer Gregg Diamond and asked him to immediately fly over to the island with a multi-track master tape recorder. That way she would be able to give him the money, realise her ambition to sing a pop song and then ship it out of the country as her first legit recording. In spite of never having actually heard the woman sing, Diamond duly arrived and wrote the tune 'More More More' for her within an hour of landing. Once Andrea had recorded the vocals and an additional horn section dub, the tape was sent to New York for legendary disco producer Tom Moulton to remix.

The catchy piano-driven track was a tongue-in-cheek autobiographical statement about her own brand of expertise – making love in front of the camera. It scored a No. 5 chart position in Great Britain despite the fact that none of the actress's shocking screen antics had ever been seen there. *A More More More* album naturally followed with a hilarious picture sleeve depicting the enraptured singer gracefully floating above the clouds like a vision of the Virgin Mary. While 'Party Line' and the house-esque 'Call Me' got most of the club spins, the ethereal 'Fill Me Up' was later covered by producers Rinder and Lewis for their Saint Tropez project.

The next year Andrea True returned with the *White Witch* album produced by Michael Zager. 'What's Your Name, What's Your Number', a single carved from both rock and disco aesthetics depicting a sleazy singles bar seduction scene, impressed the fans to a lesser degree despite capturing the mood of the moment perfectly. The album also contained another moderate crowd-pleaser, the Gregg Diamond-produced '(New York) You Got Me Dancing' cataloguing the city's disco action hot-spots such as Regine's, 12 West and The Silver Dollar.

At the 1977 Disco Convention held in Manhattan's Americana Hotel, Andrea True announced her departure from dance music and the disco scene with immediate plans to conquer the world of rock 'n' roll. And apart from a sparsely attended gig at the Richard Branson-owned Venue club in London, that was the last anyone saw of her. As for Gregg Diamond, his 1979 release *Danger* on the TK label saw the musician also moving more towards the rock 'n' roll vein with the cut 'Tiger Tiger' in an effort to break from the disco mould.

The Ritchie Family

'Soul rhythm, somewhere between the Philly sound and Barry White', is how independent producer and arranger Ritchie Rome described his luscious, ridiculous and enduringly enjoyable namesake 1975 project *Brazil*. The overblown disco reworking of the old Ary Barroso standard '*Aquarela Do Brasil*' was Rome's first collaboration with Parisians Henry Belolo and Jacques Morali (the men behind The Village People). Together these three would outrage and annoy mainstream critics, while keeping smiles on the faces of hardcore dancers, with four glamorous Ritchie Family albums without which any disco library is incomplete.

In its original, and beloved, line-up, the Family consisted of Philadelphia session musicians assembled by Rome and three singers, Cassandra Ann Wooten, Gwendolyn Oliver and Cheryl Mason-Jacks. A soul affair this was definitely not! The first album, *Brazil,* is orchestrated with gorgeous lush excess, with seemingly enormous numbers of string and percussion instruments all playing at once, creating a huge Les Baxter-lounge-core-style wall of sound.

Side One kicks off with a mid-tempo rendition of 'Peanut Vendor' complete with risqué suggestions from the softly chanting ladies. A rattling bongo break leads dancers into an eight-minute 'Frenesi', another Latin standard, followed by the famous satisfaction-guaranteed title track itself. Side Two contains a selection of original compositions – five forays into swinging disco lounge full of catchy cha-cha rhythms.

The Ritchie Family's second disco extravaganza arrived during the summer of 1976 and *Arabian Nights* is magnificent from start to finish. The travelogue begins at 'Istanbul (Not Constantinople)', moves on through the theme from *Lawrence Of Arabia* and closes 'In A Persian Market'. The feel was Hollywood soundtrack meets disco glamour spiced up with percussion and uncharacteristic male voices joining in the chant. This album also contained the massive chart hit 'The Best Disco In Town', a medley of club favourites (such as 'I Love Music', 'Lady Bump' and 'Turn The Beat Around') wrapped up in a catchy chorus. The producers repeated this winning formula in 1977 with the 'Discomania' 12-incher by The Lovers.

The two remaining Ritchie Family essentials both appeared in 1977. *Life Is Music* is irresistible chocolate-box disco with romantic melodies and ornate arrangements. Winning cuts include 'Long Distance Romance' with its sexy telephone call narrative and 'Lady Luck', a sophisticated entrée into disco *Casino Royale* bouncy Bond style.

African Queens introduced Nefertiti, Cleopatra and the Queen of Sheba in a not-exactly-heartfelt effort to recapture three slices of African history. The full-length album cut moves slightly away from the usual lush Ritchie sound as it is based on a relentless Euro-style snare-drum beat by the rhythm section Gypsy Lane Inc. However, the album did spawn one of the paradigms of the whole disco genre, a resplendent version of the Martin Denny tiki-tiki smash 'Quiet Village'. The album version evokes all the languorous images of moonlit jungles and wave-washed beaches of the original classic but puts it in disco Cinemascope with a commanding drum beat.

The following year Jacques Morali and Henri Belolo further

displayed their flair for novelty in one of their fluffiest and most fabulously kitschy creations. The soundtrack to the French comedy film *Je Te Tiens, Tu Me Tiens Par La Barbichette* flies dancers first class to Paris with the high-kicking cancan title track 'La Barbichette'. As the string section fiddles frantically, the vocalists get completely carried away by the spirit of excitement sweeping into the mix and break into ear-piercing upper-register whoops during the song's grand finale. 'Forever Dancing' continues in the same highly animated mood, presenting a rousing version of Marc Anthony Charpentier's '*Te Deum*', a fanfare of a tune familiar to most Continentals from the opening ceremonies of the Eurovision Song Contest.

In the wake of all things *Saturday Night Fever*, producers preferred a heavier beat with a poppier edge mainly because the public wanted such accessible product with stronger hook-lines. Not only did the next Ritchie Family release reflect that trend but the album sleeve design was attuned to the radical change in the texture of the music. Gone were the mock-historical head-dresses and all the feathers, furs and chiffon outfits. The new look was sporty Americana with the girls in leg-warmers and revealing red, white and blue bikinis. The *American Generation* album kicked off with a bubbling Surf's Up song for the summer of '78, perfectly in tune with the sleeve. What followed, however, did not live up to the Beach Boys disco opening and sounded like leftovers from a stagnant Belolo/Morali recording session.

Bad Reputation in 1979 was better, if many dance steps away from the charm of the early orchestral wonders – in terms of arrangements it was a much simpler album. However, the Ritchie Family had turned into a female version of The Village People with a similarly constructed and sounding set. True to this tailoring, the record boasted an eye-popping sleeve with the girls in full leather regalia atop a shiny motorcycle, surrounded by a Doberman Pincher and five enormous musclemen flexing their pecs, including Mr World, Peter Grymkowski.

The songs were reasonably catchy nudge-nudge sing-along numbers like 'Where Are The Men?' and 'Sexy Man' delivered with suitably emoting drama-queen vocals. The standout cut was 'Put Your Feet to the Beat' which bangs out stomping rhythms and barked instructions to march into a severe dance workout. The same year saw the release of their final bona fide disco album centred around the popular 'Give Me A Break', which is also heard on the *Can't Stop The Music* soundtrack.

DISCO FACT!
As the disco took off among the adult population, adolescents wanted to get in on the act too. To keep them happy, Disco-Tots opened at 111 Hudson in New York, and Dingbats followed suit in Chicago.

DISCO FACT!
Janet Cutting and Alphonse Robles of Boston were the grand prize-winners of the first disco dance contest sponsored by Casablanca Filmworks and *Nightfall* magazine.

Haven't Been Funked Enough

JAZZ FREAKS AND SLOW-BURN TEMPI

You may know how to make the Funk Sign – form a U shape by clenching your hand into a fist and stick out your index finger and pinky. But do you know what the word itself means? What is it to 'funk' and get downright 'funky'? Is it playing hard on the beat and scratching that itch for something basic, something to do with going back to the roots of the black music experience? Is it an attitude?

Yes, it's all that, but in the ghetto slang of the early-'50s, the term 'funk' meant a bit more. It referred to the sights, sensations and smells of sweaty sex – the sticky sounds and musky odours that bodies create during an especially heated groping session. So, in musical terms, making it 'funky' meant returning to the raw powerful expression of rhythmic thrust with none of the streamlined 'cool' developed by West Coast boppers and other jazz intellectuals.

During the '50s and early-'60s, musicians like Horace Silver began to incorporate these gritty, bluesy cadences into their recordings and to use the word in a musical context. The term 'funk' entered mainstream vocabularies through black artists some years later and, by 1972, Wilson Pickett had stepped out on to 'Funky Broadway', Clarence Carter had done the 'Funky Walk' and James Brown had simply barked the order to 'Make

It Funky'. All raw, all very tight and very together. Producer Norman Whitfield also directed The Temptations towards hits like 'Papa Was A Rolling Stone' which ended up at No. 1 in the American charts in 1972, got the world tapping its feet to more orchestrated funk and thus helped usher in the dancing era.

As the first rumblings of disco started to emerge from the streets, funk rock combos like The Incredible Bongo Band, and funk bands proper like The Isley Brothers, Kool and the Gang and The Ohio Players, provided dancers with hard-edged boogie tunes that have deservedly become party classics. They have also been repeatedly recycled by the likes of the cooler-than-thou Quentin Tarantino brigade for various multi-media Pulp Fiction entertainments. The Isley Brothers, who hit big with 'Fight The Power', had carved their name in music history in 1962 with 'Twist And Shout', covered by The Beatles on one of their earliest albums. They would do it again with 'It's A Disco Night (Rock Don't Stop)' in 1979.

The Ohio Players were already making music as a group in 1959, but for them a taste of real success took ages as their first hit album, *Pain*, only arrived a decade later. *Pleasure, Ecstasy* and *Skin Tight* followed, enjoying considerable R&B sales due to more than just the music. All the gatefold-sleeve album covers featured strikingly photographed art, with statuesque models in suggestive poses handling whips, chains and phallic fire hoses. They quickly became essential wall-decoration in colleges worldwide and have now become much-sought-after collector's items. The most infamous image graced the sleeve of *Honey*, which naturally depicted a naked woman completely covered with the dripping confectionery. For dancers, each release offered raunchy, bass-heavy jams spiced with vocal innuendo like 'Fire', influencing such later disco favourites as The Fatback Band with strong, sparse and repetitively grooving rhythm tracks.

Also from Ohio came one of the living legends of black music and the founder of the famed P Funk collective. George Clinton had formed his first music organisation, Parliament, as early as 1956. After a series of unsuccessful recordings for several labels, including Tamla Motown, he finally scored an aggressive hit single during the crazed psychedelic heyday of 1967 with '(I Wanna) Testify'. Completely transformed by cosmic vibrations, Clinton began to develop his musical ideas into a bizarre tongue-in-cheek philosophy with funk as the elixir of life, a universal healing force and the answer to all the world's most pressing problems. Parliament then mutated into The Funkadelic, further preaching the funk and fusing psychedelia with rock and soul in ironic and zany albums like *Free Your Mind And Your Ass Will Follow*.

Meanwhile, another Ohio artist named William 'Bootsy' Collins (born Cincinnati, 1951) had formed his Pacemakers group. The Pacemakers operated during the late-'60s as a backing band for the raspy-voiced crooner Arthur Prysock (who would surprisingly deliver the beautifully accomplished disco 12-inch single 'When Love Is New' in 1977) and, later, as The New JBs for the Godfather of Soul himself, James Brown. Collins then met George Clinton in 1972 and the two instantly connected. The resulting Funkadelic album, *America Eats Its Young*, was the start of a lasting and extremely productive musical relationship.

The duo subsequently introduced a strange and colourful cast of P Funk characters in cartoon space costumes like Bootzilla, Bootsy's Rubber Band, The Horny Horns and The Brides of Funkenstein. In 1978 they brought on the original Funkadelic battalion and had a huge club and chart hit with the defining 'One Nation Under A Groove'. This anthemic monster is highly respected by old-school B-Boys and rappers; it was also erroneously featured in Isaac Julien's film *Young Soul Rebels*, a story set a year before the record had even been released.

The summer of 1978 also saw Rick James, a disciple of both Collins and Clinton, in ultra-tight leather pants, braided Masai hair and the requisite platform boots, burst onto the scene with a funky club smash 'You And I'. Described as a new-wave punk funker, James enjoyed a few years of international success as a recording artist for Tamla Motown and clearly set the stage for Prince with his overall look and stylistic manoeuvres before fading down the fast lane in a puff of dope smoke. During the '80s, Clinton and Collins renamed their collective The P Funk All-Stars, heightening or diminishing – according to one's taste – the power of their funk with harsh metallic break-beats.

Although funk is an ingredient of disco, and funkers did their thing in clubs, the sound was not really disco music. It was funk pure and simple. However, during the early disco years, a considerable number of dance hits could be classified as both, especially when bands like Brass Construction put their feet firmly on the dance floor with 'Movin'' and 'Ha Cha Cha'. Take the cut 'Do You Wanna Get Funky With Me' by Peter Brown. It is built with gradually intensifying segments, vocal phrases and percussive instrumental breaks just like any traditionally orchestrated disco record. But like the Rick James hit 'You And I', it was disco funk.

Many legendary names associated with funk saw the dance craze as a sign of the changing times to be dealt with, and many did just that with no compromise to their roots. Denise LaSalle, a voluptuous, full-bodied and earthy vocalist, delivered a hollering good-time party song 'Freedom To Express Yourself' which found fans in both camps of clubbers. Other funk and soul singers turning out the odd Terpsichorean delight included Chaka Khan and Candi Staton, who declared their independence in 'I'm Every Woman' and 'Young Hearts Run Free' respectively. Both women struck similar notes and communication chords as their voices soared commandingly over large orchestras, crossing over into the pop charts as well. Several trusted soul harmony groups like The Detroit Emeralds ('Feel The Need In Me', 'Turn On Lady'), The Originals ('Down To Love Town') and Archie Bell and the Drells ('Soul City

Walk') revitalised their careers by injecting dance stylings into their recordings or switched into disco full time. Archie Bell and the Drells shamelessly cashed in on the dance craze with 'Disco Showdown', 'Tighten Up At The Disco', 'I Bet I Can Do That Dance You're Doing', 'Dancin' Man', 'Show Me How To Dance' and 'We Got 'Em Dancin''. Besides funk and soul musicians, noted jazz names started to experiment with the possibilities of the 'Thumpus Uninterruptus' as *Newsweek* magazine named the music in their 1979 cover story 'Disco Takes Over'.

It's now filed under acid jazz, groove or jazz funk, but in the beginning it was called fusion – the merging together of several distinct styles: rock, jazz, Latin and funk. The phrase was coined by producer Dennis Preston during the mid-'60s when he introduced Indian-born musicians into a jazz quintet and called the resulting sounds 'Indo-jazz Fusion'. Later, 'alien' influences were steadily being accepted into modern jazz, especially on the American East Coast, thanks to innovators with sufficient credibility as Miles Davis. By the early-'70s, jazz recordings incorporating various rhythms were seen as the norm. America embraced the rock-tinged side to a degree, while in Great Britain the funkier end of the spectrum became very popular, growing into a club scene of its own and known simply as jazz funk.

The bittersweet sound was adopted not only by neo-Bohemians in berets and Juliette Greco wannabes in smoke-filled basement clubs. It was also making nodding dogs nod madly and furry dice shake furiously in Ford Cortinas heading for special all-dayers or weekenders held at big dance venues and introducing jazz to a brand-new club audience. The scene rewarded veteran artists like The Crusaders, Donald Byrd, Freddie Hubbard and Herbie Hancock with surprising chart entries undreamt of in their homeland of America. Some of these imported recordings had found fame at hardcore discos as well – the relentless nine-minute drum-break orgy of the 1975

'Caravan/Watusi' medley by the Brazilian instrumentalist Eumir Deodato being one of the earliest examples.

'The Chicago Theme' by Hubert Laws, a seasoned flautist recording for the CTI label, was another prime standard. Laws was one of the first jazzers to come up with a real disco arrangement as opposed to just laying a tune over danceable drumming. He had studied classical flute at Texas Southern University in Houston and had played with Mongo Santamaria as well as an early incarnation of The Crusaders. His contribution to the genre shows him completely at his ease and in command of his art, silencing the purists who doubted his judgement at entering the disco fray. The piece gets under way with a gently throbbing rhythm, creating a wide-screen soft-focus illusion of a night-time ride through the rainy streets of the Windy City. Laws' flute eases in and out of the beat with a cool, sinuous slide and sophisticated expertise. The performer is complemented by the cream of the CTI house musicians, Eric Gale on guitar, Bob James on keyboards and Steve Gadd on drums.

These same experts returned with another similar-sounding winner in 1976. Lalo Schifrin's 'Jaws' was loosely based on the suspenseful John Williams-composed chords heard during the shark attack scenes in Steven Spielberg's summer blockbuster. Instead of the expected orchestral workout in the fashionable Love Unlimited Orchestra vein, the Argentinian composer-cum-keyboardist presented a killer jazz galloper with menacing strings and an icy flute melody. Schifrin was no beginner in dabbling with celluloid themes. He had scored over seventy movies himself, including *Dirty Harry*, *Bullitt* and *Enter The Dragon*, plus music to such cult television shows as *Mission Impossible* and *Starsky And Hutch*. How much cooler could you get?

All this sense of drama and the audio-visual was there in his splendid 'Jaws' treatment as the rolling bass-lines slowly built the momentum towards the staccato shrieks of the climactic

Hubert Laws flute attack. The follow-up to this disco thriller, the 1977 *Towering Toccata* album, contained more cinematic head trips in the jazz funk mode, and several underground dance gems like the lurking 'Most Wanted Theme' and the title track, a weird take on Bach's classical plum 'D Minor Toccata And Fugue For Organ'.

For a while everyone from Gato (*Last Tango In Paris*) Barbieri to Chuck Mangione seemed to be slipping danceable tracks into their fusion albums. One of the most eccentric entries was 'Howduz Disco' by Arni Egilsson, an Icelandic bassist who recorded in Hollywood. This 1980 mutation featured distorted solo playing and whole bass ensembles pizzicato-ing madly over a pumping backtrack and is arguably the first acid jazz disco cut.

174

Boogie Wonderland

FOUR FACES OF DISCO AMERICANA

Chic

It was an immediate sensation from beat one – an unheard-of rumble of bass recorded way below the customary hertz level, a ferocious sound making your heart skip and the speakers shake. Over this relentless new drive a cool fluorescent voice appeared, exhorting you to rhumba, tango and Latin hustle the night away, to go even wilder and dance, dance, dance some more. Then a ringleader voice screamed in your ear: Yowsah, Yowsah, Yowsah!

Originating from the cotton fields of the old South and bellowed through the delirious *They Shoot Horses Don't They?* dance marathons of the '20s to coax the stumbling couples on, this manic 'Yes, Sir!' chant became a catchphrase during late-1977 as the unknown track began to set New York dance floors on fire. Finally released through the Atlantic label, 'Dance, Dance, Dance' by the studio band Chic not only topped the disco charts but also became a major pop hit the world over, selling over a million copies in its first month alone.

Masterminded by the producer/songwriter team of Nile Rodgers and Bernard Edwards, and inspired by Roxy Music's stage act mixing smart-looking men with sophisticated ladies, Chic emerged as the most successful and musically qualified disco band of the era. Like an expensive, silky evening garment, their music seduced you with sensuous, luxurious layers, all cunningly designed and carefully arranged. A bit of Chic on your car sound-system or during a late-night smooching session back home signalled not only style awareness but also street credibility. It was the perfect mating soundtrack for the economically optimistic and pan-sexual late-'70s as the Chic production would often be as stripped bare as your date ended up after a night out dancing.

Edwards was born in Greenville, North Carolina, and moved to New York at the age of ten. There he attended the High School for Performing Arts (immortalised in the movie *Fame*) and gained extensive experience as a musician while performing backing vocals. It was while earning pocket money as a postal worker that he met Nile Rodgers – the latter's girlfriend's mother worked at the same post office. Rodgers was born on the Triboro Bridge, en route to Queens General Hospital, and had grown up in Greenwich Village and Hollywood. Musically he had moved from hard rock guitar through classical studies to jazz when he first met Edwards, who quickly turned him on to rhythm and blues and the more contemporary sounds of the day.

The duo's friendship resulted in them both supplying backing vocals for the group New York City (who had a 1972 hit with 'I'm Doin' Fine Now') and also gigging with Carol ('Doctor's Orders') Douglas. Dubbing themselves The Big Apple Band, Rodgers and Edwards became a focal point of the back-up touring group until New York City split up. It was then that the two men decided to take control of their destiny and go it alone. Auditioning for new Big Apple Band members, the duo put together drummer Tony Thompson from Labelle, and piano players Rob Sabino and Raymond Jones.

Featured female vocalist Norma Jean Wright joined the group in 1976 after working extensively with bands like The Spinners. But Walter Murphy (of 'A Fifth Of Beethoven' fame) was also calling his backing group The Big Apple Band. So Rodgers and Edwards thought long and hard to find a name that would convey class and sophistication in a one-syllable, easy-to-remember word. Chic it was.

Rodgers and Edwards followed 'Dance, Dance, Dance' with the breezy 'Everybody Dance', another smash hit. The first album was simply called *Chic* and the cover featured a bland duo of blond models, instead of the lead vocalist Wright and Alfa Anderson. Ohio-born Wright left the group for a solo career soon after and the anonymous studio band feel was shed with the following releases. The look now conveyed high musicianship as well as visual elegance. Replaced by vocalist Luci Martin, and enjoying only moderate success with her 'Saturday' outing, Wright probably wished she had stayed in the group as 'Le Freak' turned out to be one of the biggest-selling hits of 1978.

In the beginning, the song was ironically penned by Rodgers and Edwards as something quite different, as it resulted from one of those typical incidents at the door of Studio 54. Grace Jones had invited the duo over to the club to discuss a possible producing deal, but as the doorman had misplaced their names from the guest-list, they were unceremoniously turned away. Enraged, they quickly wrote the future hit as a bitchy paean to the snobby club, complete with an *Aaah . . . Fuck Off!* refrain. For Rodgers and Edwards revenge would be sweet: the song, its swearing sanitised to *Freak Out!* to cash in on the latest dance craze to sweep New York's clubland, was to sell in excess of six million copies in the United States alone.

The next year, Chic hit immortality with a cut taken from their *Risqué* album. 'Good Times' was to become one of the most celebrated dance music anthems ever, endlessly remixed, illegally sampled and circulated through the next decade of rap music. After the release of 'Good Times', the seemingly simple Rodgers and Edwards formula, with its instantly recognisable trademark bass-lines, was soon copied by funkers and rockers alike, sometimes to even greater success. Their familiar riffs boomed through Queen's 'Another One Bites The Dust' and Sugarhill Gang's 'Rapper's Delight', making Chic an integral part of rap's sound iconography.

After 'Good Times', the hits dried up. But the producers enjoyed further success, writing, producing and jump-starting the careers of Diana Ross and Sister Sledge. For Ross, with whom they had a volcanically explosive relationship, they penned the acclaimed 'Upside Down' and 'I'm Coming Out'. For Sister Sledge, they produced the *We Are Family* album which became an all-time classic disco must-have because of the ever-popular title track as well as 'He's The Greatest Dancer' and 'Lost In Music'.

Rodgers and Edwards made their presence felt throughout the 1980s too. The former played for artists such as David Bowie, Madonna and Mick Jagger, while the latter worked with Robert Palmer and soul diva Jody Watley. During the height of Chic's popularity the late Edwards said, 'We're not trying to deliver any heavy message, just entertainment. When you're off from work, come and see us and have a good time. No moral issues, no heavy problems – you just come and see us, have a good time, and split – that's it!'

Yowsah, Yowsah, Yowsah!

D.C. LaRue

There were few songwriters who presented a distinctly non-neutralised, exaggerated soap-opera stylisation of sexual mores during the disco era. But one of them was D. C. LaRue whose best known club hit 'Ca-The-Drals' had first appropriated the scene in June 1976. Moving out of the gay disco environment where the track first broke, it became one of the most danceable records of the year. Superficially condemning the loose '70s way of conducting relationships through promiscuous sexual activity, it naturally only emphasised the picture of sexually dominant lifestyles with its pumping bass and shimmering sexy vocals.

LaRue was born David Charles L'Heureux on 26 April 1949 in New Haven, Connecticut, and, after studying graphic design at college, he entered the record industry as an album-sleeve designer for such acts as John Lennon, Bruce Springsteen, Jim Croce, John Sebastian and Janis Ian. LaRue always saw design as a way to get into the industry through the back door because his ambition was to become a singer. He won two prestigious Paul Revere Awards for his sleeve work before deciding to take the giant step into the disco limelight, signing a deal with Pyramid Records.

'Ca-The-Drals' was written as a result of a breakup between LaRue and a girlfriend and the personal antagonism he felt towards the promiscuity inherent in disco culture at the time. But he was back the next year with a more appropriately disco-friendly celebration of the party idiom. *The Tea Dance* was constructed as a kind of soundtrack to a '30s musical or a stage revue with a tinny gramophone intro and an 'Overture (All We Need Is Love)', and the chugging mid-tempo cut contained yet another vague plea for understanding and universal love. Delivered with LaRue's slightly nasal but not unappealing light vocal style, the old Brazilian samba 'O Ba Ba' was transformed into a voluptuous, exotic artifice with an opening percussive passage leading into well-established tropical imagery of magical sunsets and lush palatial gardens. 'Don't Keep It In The Shadows' featured a guest vocal spot by Lou ('Lightnin' Strikes') Christie.

After supplying the song 'Do You Want The Real Thing' for the *Thank God It's Friday* soundtrack, LaRue put more 'messages' in his music. Anxiety attacks were promoted in 'I'll Wake Up Screaming In The Middle Of The Night' from the *Confessions* album and the title cut from the *Forces Of The Night* album. The latter found the composer/singer diversifying his disco sound with a more rock 'n' roll bent while penning less abrasive lyrics. All of LaRue's work was produced by Bob Esty as a structured musical form, and the 'Dancing With Strangers' cut, describing clubbers as sinister nocturnal creatures, was another effective merging of both the synthesised and acoustic aspects of disco while retaining the dance rhythms.

The Trammps

The Trammps did more to fan the flames of the disco inferno than practically anyone. Their storming eleven-minute track 'Disco Inferno', entered club consciousness in 1976 but didn't begin its meteoric climb to classic status until it was included in *Saturday Night Fever* and subsequently hit the charts twice in 1977. The group's inclusion on the soundtrack was down to fate in many ways because the Odyssey 2001 club in Bay Ridge, Brooklyn, where the film was shot, was their second home. The Trammps played gigs there at least once a month.

The Trammps' career is split into four major parts. The five-man group was an amalgam of two local Philadelphia acts in the '60s, The Volcanoes and The Exceptions. Leader Earl Young chose their new name because people kept telling them 'All you'll ever be is a bunch of tramps' as they hung around street corners, and because he loved silent-movie star Charlie Chaplin. The extra 'm' was added to make them superior tramps! The group actually used to go on stage wearing denim dungarees as part of their folksy image. But as they grew more famous, this 'working on the chain-gang' look was replaced by the more '70s-friendly fashion of velvet flared suits and matching frilly shirts.

They first made an impact in the clubs and on the charts in 1974 with 'Penguin At The Big Apple/Zing Went The Strings Of My Heart', its beautifully melodic intro written by Young, Ronnie Baker and Norman Harris segueing into a stunning adaptation of Judy Garland's 1943 American hit. This release on the Buddah label was followed by 'Sixty-Minute Man' and 'Hold Back The Night', their most popular song until 'Disco Inferno'. After a move back to Philadelphia, their spiritual home, they appeared on their own Philadelphia International record label off-shoot Golden Fleece for a while. But the peak of their achievement was to be for Atlantic Records after the crowd-pleasers 'That's Where The Happy People Go' and 'Soul Searchin' Time'. 'Disco Inferno' really did burn up the dance floor, and their disco immortality has been assured ever since.

Although The Trammps released many more records -'Here We Go Again', 'Where Do We Go From Here', 'People Of The World' – they never could match the success of 'Disco Inferno'. But Young, Baker and Harris were already diversifying into the production side of the business. They produced material for the Salsoul Orchestra, Loleatta Holloway, First Choice, Love Committee and The Temptations' debut album for Atlantic. Under the name BHY & Company, the initials taken from their own surnames, they also produced an instrumental album – a little like MFSB – with Trammps vocal sections featuring on some of the tunes.

.But 1977 was the main year for The Trammps. For the third year in a row they were voted Top Disco Group by *Billboard* magazine and in the early spring of 1977 they played a sold-out gig at New York's Roseland Ballroom. Over three thousand people turned up to witness a miraculous five-hour dance celebration that became known as one of the legendary happenings of the disco era.

Earth Wind And Fire

Earth Wind and Fire sang the companion song to 'Disco Inferno', their 1979 worldwide hit 'Boogie Wonderland' stunningly encapsulating the disco experience and putting it into user-friendly dance terminology. With over seven gold albums to their credit, there were few weeks throughout 1978 and 1979 that Earth Wind and Fire weren't in the charts with one fabulous foot-tapper or another. 'Fantasy', 'September', 'After The Love Has Gone', 'All 'n' All' and 'Let's Groove' compounded their impact on the club scene as they became one of the most successful recording acts of all time.

The driving force behind the group was Maurice White who was born in Memphis, home of Isaac Hayes and Booker T. Jones of the MGs. Before joining his brother Verdine at the age of sixteen in Chicago, Maurice gained musical experience playing with numerous blues bands. Soon after arriving in the Windy City he got a studio gig with the Chess Records label and it was this training, where he played every instrument and on everybody's records, which gave White a complete all-round experience in the music business.

Then he joined the Ramsey Lewis Trio, along with Cleaveland Eaton, with whom he cut ten albums for Chess. But it was touring through the Orient with Ramsey Lewis and the higher consciousness he felt in the East which put White on the track of forming his own group. Because he was very into Egyptology and astrology at the time, he decided to go for a band name from his favourite star charts. After first thinking Fire was suitable, he finally added another two elements and eventually conjured up Earth Wind and Fire.

The initial group line-up was Maurice, Verdine, Wade Flemons, Don Whitehead, Jacob Ben Israel, Clint Washington, Michael Bill, Leslie Drayton and Alex Thomas. Signing with Warner Bros Records for their first two pop-influenced albums, the group moved to Columbia in the early-'70s with numerous personnel changes. Ronnie Laws, Phillip Bailey, Jessica Cleaves, Ronald Bautista, Larry Dunn and Ralph Johnson replaced the original line-up who all felt the need to move into musical areas other than the aggressively commercial one envisaged by White.

White himself called the early incarnation of Earth Wind and Fire's music too advanced for the time. Extraordinarily, too, the group were being perceived as white. But the name did create an entity and an underground cult formed around the music. It was this influence which eventually pulled Earth Wind and Fire into the disco arena. White chose to sign with Columbia because he was impressed with the way head honcho

Clive Davis had pushed Sly and the Family Stone into the chart limelight.

It was in 1974 that Maurice formed his own production company Kalimba which started producing records for Ramsey Lewis, The Emotions ('Best Of My Love'), Deniece Williams ('Free', 'That's What Friends Are For'), Pockets and D.J. Rogers. Deniece Williams had brought songs she had expressly written for The Emotions to White, but when he heard her sing on the demo tapes, he immediately took her into the recording studio with the material. Williams had a huge hit in 1978 with another CBS artist, Johnny Mathis, and the song 'Too Much Too Little Too Late'.

It was The Emotions who joined Earth Wind and Fire for their mega-dance smash 'Boogie Wonderland', a lilting anthem with the oh-so-catchy chorus that quickly became a disco staple. The group's stage shows became legendary, too, as White considered music and theatre to be one spectacular entity. Based on the old vaudeville shows his father used to take him to see, except at a mid-'70s cost of $250,000, Earth Wind and Fire put on amazing concerts packed with showbiz razzle-dazzle and pizzazz. And that's precisely why 'Boogie Wonderland' has endured. Because of White's theatrical influences, the song conjures up a proscenium arch around its disco sound and presents it as a timeless mystical fantasy to be vicariously enjoyed for all eternity. After all, it always was Maurice White's wish to perform next to the pyramids in Egypt.

One of the cuts on the *All 'n' All* album was entitled 'Serpentine Fire'. The song referred to the magic fluid in the spine that, in Indian mythology, transferred energy from the brain to the genital area – and vice versa – and was reactivated by vigorous yoga exercise. No one ever came up with a more cabbalistic explanation for the disco lifestyle.

183

Hollywood Hot

SATURDAY NIGHT FEVER

'Vincent was the best dancer in Bay Ridge . . .'

So began the magazine feature 'Tribal Rites of the New Saturday Night' by rock commentator Nik Cohn which led directly to the disco craze being absorbed into popular mainstream culture. Born in 1946, Cohn grew up in Ireland before moving to England at the age of fifteen. He left school a year after that and immediately started writing professionally, publishing a number of novels including *King Death* and *Teenage Pinball Queen*. He published a history of rock 'n' roll entitled *Rock From The Beginning*, wrote the text for the classic artwork book *Rock Dreams*, and contributed many features to such high-profile magazines as *Playboy*, *Esquire* and *Rolling Stone*.

'Tribal Rites' was written for the June 1976 issue of *New York Magazine*. Although the writer confessed in the '90s that he'd made up most of the article, at the time Cohn said he'd spent many nights and weekends in Brooklyn exploring the suburban disco lifestyle. In the introduction to his feature, he stated that all the events were factual, most he had participated in, and only the names had been changed.

Colin's article focused on a clique of friends, dubbed 'The Faces', living in the Bay Ridge area who couldn't wait for the weekend so they could dance the night away at the local disco and forget their mundane jobs and family problems. Vincent was the lead character of Cohn's feature, an ordinary Italo-American who found his release and identity on the flashing floor as his spectacular dancing technique shot him to local stardom. Vincent may have been a composite character but the sketch used to illustrate Cohn's feature was based on a photograph of the unmistakable face of eighteen-year-old Eugene Robinson, highschool drop-out, paint store delivery boy and weekend disco king.

The feature caught the eye of producer Robert Stigwood who saw the aspiring Everyman potential of the stimulating story given a contemporary disco spin, and promptly bought the screen rights. A native of Australia, Stigwood arrived in London in 1957 to become one of the most famous show-business tycoons of all time. He launched the careers of The Bee Gees, Cream and Blind Faith, produced such landmark stage shows as *Hair*, *Jesus Christ Superstar* and *Oh! Calcutta*, was directly responsible for launching the classic TV sitcoms *Till Death Us Do Part* and *Steptoe And Son*, and produced the films *Jesus Christ Superstar* (1973), *Tommy* (1975) and *Survive!* (1977, co-produced with *Can't Stop The Music*'s Allan Carr). Stigwood formed RSO Records in 1973 and signed up Smokie, Eric Clapton and, most significantly, The Bee Gees, whom he brought back into his management fold.

After hiring writer Norman Wexler, two-time Oscar nominee for the screenplays of *Joe* (1971) and *Serpico* (1974), to turn Cohn's article into a workable script, Stigwood engaged director John Badham, who only had *The Bingo Long Travelling All-Stars and Motor Kings* (1976) to his credit, to take control of the project. (Stigwood originally hired *Rocky* director John G. Avildsen, but fired him after he wanted to rewrite the script.) To headline the Paramount Pictures release, Stigwood looked no further than the twenty-three-year-old actor he had just signed to a three-picture deal based on his wild success in the

TV show *Welcome Back Kotter* after a credible career on the stage (in The Andrews Sisters' Broadway musical *Over Here!*) and the photogenic qualities he exuded in his film debut, Carrie (1977).

The youngest of six children, John Travolta was born on 18 February 1954 in Englewood, New Jersey, and was inspired by his drama-coach mother Helen to take dancing lessons at the age of six with Gene Kelly's brother, Fred. The two other pictures he would make for Stigwood after the enormous success of *Saturday Night Fever* would be the equally blockbusting *Grease* (1978) and the legendary romantic disaster *Moment By Moment* (1978) which would send Travolta's career into a sharp nose-dive.

Because Travolta played a character named Vinnie (Barbarino) in *Welcome Back Kotter*, Wexler changed the name of Cohn's Vincent to Tony Manero in order not to confuse the rising star's core audience. Nineteen-year-old Tony lives for the Saturday nights he spends with his old school pals Bobby C (Barry Miller), Joey (Joseph Cali), Double J (Paul Pape) and Gus (Bruce Ornstein) in the 2001 Odyssey disco where he is the acknowledged King of Dance. Belittled by his bitter, unemployed father (Val Bisoglio), especially when he receives a paltry raise at the Bay Ridge paint store where he works, and constantly being unfavourably compared by his mother (Julie Bavasso) to his elder brother Frank Junior (Martin Shakar), who is studying for the priesthood, Tony stops feeling so undermined when Frank turns up out of the blue having given up his vocation. 'Maybe if you ain't so good,' says Tony to his brother, 'I ain't so bad.'

Although constantly stalked by Annette (Donna Pescow) as husband material throughout his disco downtime, Tony becomes smitten with New Dancer on the Block Stephanie (Karen Lynn Gorney) when she turns up with her apparent boyfriend at 2001 and wipes the floor with all his other disco partners. Finally getting the chance to talk to Stephanie at the dance studio where he practises, she scorns Tony's limited aspirations and boasts of her own job in show-business public relations (meeting stars like Sir Laurence Olivier) and her intention to leave Brooklyn behind for the bright lights and opportunities of Manhattan. But while she refuses point blank to have any romantic attachment with Tony, she does agree to partner him for the upcoming disco dance contest at 2001. As a result, he dumps Annette, much to her resigned annoyance.

As Tony and Stephanie practise their hustle moves, Bay Ridge life goes on: Frank junior leaves to start a new life; Gus is beaten up by a rival Puerto Rican gang – or so he thinks; Bobby anguishes over being forced to marry his pregnant girlfriend; Annette starts looking into birth control in the hope that giving up her virginity to Tony will seal their one-sided love affair.

Tony finally sees how hollow, hypocritical and pathetic his whole life truly is during the night of the dance contest. Firstly, he joins his friends in a mistaken attack on the Barracudas who turn out not to be responsible for Gus's hospitalisation. Secondly, he and Stephanie win the contest because the judges show clear racism towards the better Puerto Rican couple and in a rage Tony presents them with the prize money instead. Then, after clumsily making advances towards Stephanie, he joins his friends to witness them gang-rape a drunk Annette and watches in horror as Bobby C falls to his death from the Verazzano Bridge. In shock, and after a long subway journey where he ruminates on the meaning of life, Tony contritely arrives at Stephanie's new Manhattan apartment, says he too is leaving Brooklyn, and begs her to be his friend.

Shot on location in the Bay Ridge area (2001 was an actual club and still has the famous flashing floor in place – Paramount left it behind to cover any hidden expenses incurred), it was the film's theme that every person has the talent to make it somehow which propelled *Saturday Night Fever* into the box-office stratosphere. You too could escape the neighbourhood you grew up in, where there were no opportunities, so long as you had the drive and the determination. That message massaged to the disco beat of the street meant director John Badham's vicarious *Pilgrim's Progress* through the urban jungle of sex-crazed and thrill-hungry youth hit pay-dirt. Basically nothing more than a refitted juvenile delinquent flick from the attitude-heavy '50s, dancing was seen as the only self-fulfilment worth striving for in such confusing times.

Badham's frenetic and exaggerated direction instantly lifted the dancing and the star to iconic status. The effects were two-fold. There was an explosion of new applicants in dance classes all over the world as everyone who wasn't clued in finally got the disco feeling. And John Travolta became a superstar. He is electrifying whether getting dressed in his room (and Badham explored Travolta's pan-sexual appeal in remarkably erotic ways using low-angle underwear shots), wiggling down the street (in fact, Travolta's stand-in Jeff Zinn did most of the celebrated walking in the opening credits), stumbling over his true feelings and, of course, putting on the amazing display of disco virtuosity in the 2001 environs wearing that famous white suit.

Saturday Night Fever was everything a social consciousness-raising pop-culture phenomenon should be. It was remarkably gritty for its time, too. Liberally peppered with the words 'fuck' and 'cunt', and not holding back on the more distressing elements of dysfunctional families, gang mentality, ethnic rivalry and macho posturing, Paramount finally had to issue a softer version for the teenybopper market anxious to see what all the fuss was about. The original 119-minute movie was sanitised and cut down to 106 minutes as a result. Unfortunately it was this 'family' version which the media picked up on after the event, giving rise to the misconception it was originally made for that market.

Perhaps the most important part of the *Saturday Night Fever* package was the music. Although the soundtrack utilised such tried and tested favourites as 'Disco Inferno' by The Trammps, 'Boogie Shoes' by KC and The Sunshine Band, 'Open Sesame' by Kool and the Gang, 'Disco Duck' by Rick Dees and 'A Fifth Of Beethoven' by Walter Murphy, and David Shire would compose the incidental tracks 'Manhattan Skyline', 'Barracuda Hangout', 'Salsation' and 'Night On Disco Mountain' (many of which would appear on the accompanying album), Stigwood wanted five extra solid gold hits to sandwich between those two extremes and asked The Bee Gees to supply them.

The Bee Gees, three Australian brothers, Barry, Robin and Maurice Gibb, had already had a steady stream of hits since being signed up for the first time by Stigwood in 1967. 'I Can't See Nobody', 'World' and 'I Gotta Get A Message To You' were just three of their classic back catalogue chart entries and at the time of Stigwood's request for material with soundtrack potential, the group were recording a new album at the Chateau d'Heronville Studios in Paris. They had already written 'How Deep Is Your Love', 'If I Can't Have You' and 'Stayin' Alive' for the album they were working on and Stigwood immediately appropriated them for his film project, at that early stage sporting the working title *Saturday Night*.

'How Deep Is Your Love' had been written as a possible song for American *Hair* star Yvonne Elliman to record, but when Stigwood insisted the boys sing it on the soundtrack, they gave her 'If I Can't Have You' instead. A further track, 'More Than A Woman', was recorded by both the trio and soulsters Tavares of 'Heaven Must Be Missing An Angel' fame, and both versions were included on the soundtrack. Their 1975 and 1976 hits 'Jive Talkin'' and 'You Should Be Dancing' were purloined for inclusion too and when the group composed their 'Night Fever' song specifically for the movie, it impacted on the film's eventual title.

While the movie was released in America in 1977, the double soundtrack album wasn't issued until early-1978. But it immediately became a chart-topper, spawned a continuous succession of Top 10 hits, and would go on to sell in excess of thirty million copies worldwide. It also meant that for six solid months the songs were played incessantly in suburban clubs and on the radio and consequently got on everyone's nerves, certain radio stations actively promoting 'Bee Gee-Free' zones. It was this cumulative effect which mainly got the trio blamed for killing off disco after supposedly starting it in the first place. Erroneous assumptions on both counts.

In fairness, The Bee Gees were never a disco group to begin with. They were more influenced by classical rock and hadn't even written the main body of their songs with the disco outlet in mind. Radio stations might have been playing 'Night Fever' by The Bee Gees, but hipper club deejays were spinning the more up-tempo Carol Douglas cover version instead which better fitted the contours of hip disco. Yet such is the power of *Saturday Night Fever* that to this day The Bee Gees are synonymous with disco.

It is ridiculous to assume that the day before the December

premiere of *Saturday Night Fever* everyone stayed in and that immediately after the first public performance straight suburbia cottoned on to the movement, donned white polyester suits and sequinned boob tubes, and started taking hustle lessons. But that's precisely what most people think happened. Or that the movie was always considered a surefire hit. It wasn't.

Some members of the audience were not that impressed by what Tony Manero got up to on the dance floor – his hustle steps are rather slow for the era and the contest display slightly awkward to accommodate Gorney's lack of co-ordination. *Hey! I can do better than that! I'll show you*, thought the more inspired viewer and that was another reason for the disco boom. For the earnest clubber, though, all the film did was make the dance floors more crowded and cause deejay disgruntlement with annoying novices assuming they could request certain songs.

Apart from Travolta and The Bee Gees (currently the fifth biggest-selling act of all time and the only group to have No. 1 singles in each of the last four decades), very few people attached to *Saturday Night Fever* went the distance. Karen Lynn Gorney, for example, returned to daytime soap-opera glory and Barry Miller claimed a leading role in *Fame* before vanishing into obscurity. The rest of the cast did likewise – apart from the eighteenth-billed actress who played Connie. Fran Drescher would endure to become the popular star of the sitcom *The Nanny* and in one memorable episode taught the cast how to do the hustle. Behind the camera, John Badham went on to direct numerous Hollywood blockbusters including *WarGames* and *Short Circuit*; production manager John Nicolella turned director and changed the face of series television with *Miami Vice*; and location executive Lloyd Kaufman formed Troma Films and distributed an endless array of schlocky horror exploiters throughout the '80s including the *Toxic Avenger* series.

The *Saturday Night Fever* saga was picked up again in the limp 1983 sequel *Staying Alive* with Tony Manero deserting the discos of Brooklyn for the bright lights of the Broadway stage. The hungry atmosphere of the original was missing, however, and misguided direction by Sylvester Stallone doomed it to dullness. Travolta reprised his role with support from Cynthia Rhodes, Finola Hughes and Steve Inwood.

Just how quickly Travolta's famous dancing was absorbed into popular culture was shown by the 1980 spoof *Airplane!* which delightfully sent up the whole agile sequence.

Of far greater importance is the *Saturday Night Fever* stage musical which opened in London at the Palladium theatre on 5 May 1998. Produced by Robert Stigwood, Paul Nicholas and David Ian (the same team which brought back the revamped *Grease* to the London stage), directed and choreographed by Arlene Phillips (of *Can't Stop The Music* fame), and starring Adam Garcia, Anita Louise Combe, Tara Wilkinson and Simon

Greiff, the lavishly mounted £4 million transfer cannily redefined the story and music for a nostalgic '90s audience. With the addition of The Bee Gees' 1979 No. 1 hit 'Tragedy', and songs specifically written for the show ('Immortality', 'First And Last', 'What Kind Of Fool', 'It's My Neighbourhood'), once you get past the fact that what was initially meant to be background music is now sung by the cast (with 'If I Can't Have You' turned into a big ballad for Annette), *Saturday Night Fever* ensures the disco era, with its sights, sounds and ambience, will continue to live beyond the millennium in yet another medium.

DISCO FACT!
Writer Truman Capote: 'Disco is the best floor show in town. It's very democratic; boys with boys, girls with girls, girls with boys, blacks with whites, capitalists with Marxists, Chinese and everything else. All one big mix.'

DISCO FACT!
The best disco speakers? Klipschorns, designed in the 1920s by Paul Klipsch, because the inventor was upset there wasn't an amplifier decent enough to run a speaker. So he invented a speaker that would require a small amount of power but which would sound like it had a massive amount driving it. The Loft and Michael Brody's club at 143 Reade Street, New York, were the first clubs to install them.

Boogie Nights

DISCO MOVIES

In the wake of *Saturday Night Fever*, every single film industry in the world copied the disco lads/dance competition formula for their own cultural needs. Brazil's *Vamos Cantar Disco Baby* (1979), India's *Qurbani* (1980), Argentina's *La Discoteca Del Amor* (1980), Uruguay's *Sabado Disco* (1981) and Yugoslavia's *Disco* (1984) are just a few of the titles to cash in on the trend. Here, in chronological order, are the good, the bad, the ugliest and newest to use the disco craze, the music or an authentic club setting to tell their story.

CAR WASH (1976)
An unpretentious, funky and uproariously funny semi-musical about the mixed bag of people working in an LA car wash. Epitomising different personalities, lifestyles and sexualities without resorting to stereotype, director Michael Schultz's super-smart scenario is clearly influenced by *Nashville* with its free-form parallel storylines. A massive hit with black, white, straight and gay audiences (queen Antonio Fargas has the best line: 'I'm more of a man than you'll ever be and more woman than you'll ever get!'), the soundtrack was produced by Norman Whitfield and featured Rose Royce and The Pointer Sisters singing such gems as the title song, 'I Wanna Get Next

To You', 'Yo Yo', 'Keep On Keepin' On' and 'Put Your Money Where Your Mouth Is'.

Car Wash: Producers: Art Linson and Gary Stromberg. Director: Michael Schultz. Writer: Joel Schumaker. Starring Franklyn Ajaye, George Carlin, Irwin Corey, Ivan Dixon, Bill Duke, Antonio Fargas, Melanie Mayron and Richard Pryor. 97 minutes.

LOOKING FOR MR GOODBAR (1977)

Jekyll and Hyde goes disco in the screen adaptation of Judith Rossner's best-selling airport novel. Diane Keaton is a teacher of deaf children who cruises singles bars and clubs at night for exciting high-risk sexual adventures. En route she meets Richard Gere as the self-styled 'greatest fuck of your whole life' who turns her on with sadistic mind games and, ultimately, bisexual psychopath Tom Berenger. The issues may be fudged (The desperate search for personal identity in a world of self-obsession, music, sex and dope is delineated in a too-obvious manner) but the disco ambience is spot-on. Donna Summer sings 'Try Me I Know We Can Make It' and 'Could It Be Magic', The Commodores offer 'Machine Gun', Thelma Houston warbles 'Don't Leave Me This Way', Diana Ross has a 'Love Hangover' and The O'Jays deal with those 'Backstabbers' again. Both the line hustle and the New York hustle are shown in full action.

Looking For Mr Goodbar: Producer: Freddie Fields. Director and writer: Richard Brooks. Starring Diane Keaton, Tuesday Weld, William Atherton, Richard Kiley, Richard Gere and Tom Berenger. 135 minutes.

THE STUD (1978)

Fontaine (Joan Collins), the wife of millionaire Ben Khaled (Walter Gotell), gets her hooks into handsome Tony Blake (Oliver Tobias) whom she hires to manage her glossily fashionable London disco, The Hobo, in this tawdry *Top Of The Pops* version of Jackie Collins's sex-and-shopping bestseller.

194

Although unmitigated softcore trash, and acted histrionically by La Collins, *The Stud* is hilarious porno tongue-in-chic featuring a fabulously naff all-starlet cast including Sue Lloyd, Mark Burns, Chris Jagger and Minah Bird. Directed by Quentin Masters on disco dementia overdrive, the Brent Walker production was a huge hit, re-establishing Joan Collins' fading star, and supplying Ronco Records with a heavily TV-advertised soundtrack composed by Biddu and packed with contemporary dance hits. It includes Hot Chocolate's 'Every One's A Winner', The Real Thing's 'Let's Go Disco', Baccara's 'Sorry, I'm A Lady', Odyssey's 'Native New Yorker', KC and The Sunshine Band's 'That's The Way (I Like It)', Space's 'Deliverance', Rose Royce's 'Car Wash' and Biddu protégée Tina Charles's 'Fire Down Below`.

The Stud: Producer: Ronald S. Kass. Director: Quentin Masters. Writer: Jackie Collins. Starring Joan Collins, Oliver Tobias, Sue Lloyd, Mark Burns, Doug Fisher, Walter Gotell, Tony Allyn, Emma Jacobs, Peter Lukas, Guy Ward and Sarah Lawson. 90 minutes.

THANK GOD IT'S FRIDAY (1978)

The fabulous LA disco The Zoo is holding a big dance contest and the event attracts a diverse crowd of revellers. There's a young couple (Mark Lonow and Andrea Howard) from the suburban San Fernando Valley wondering what all the fuss is about who decide to take their first hesitant steps into the seductive world of disco. There are two fifteen-year-old girls (Valerie Landsberg and Terri Nunn) who hitchhike to the club and sneak in wanting to see The Commodores live on stage and hoping to win the prize money so they can attend a special Kiss concert. There are two office girls (Debra Winger and Robin Menken) looking for Mr Right. And there's Nicole Sims (Donna Summer) determined to break into stardom by crashing the live radio broadcast hosted by deejay Bobby Speed (Ray Vitte). Naturally everyone gets what they want in Casablanca's slice-of-disco-life special that dwells on the fantasy aspects of night fever for the best possible feelgood return. Despite the story doing nothing more than updating old '50s teen exploitation stand-bys, *TGIF* – as all the freebie merchandise was labelled – was as sweet and light as chocolate mousse with an equally soft centre. Drugs, sex and heartbreak were all given an easily digestible candy coating by director Robert Klane as he served up one Judy Garland/*Valley Of The Dolls*/*42nd Street* sequin-studded cliché after another. The virtually non-stop disco soundtrack featured an eclectic range of Casablanca and Tamla Motown artists singing or playing their hits, including 'Love Masterpiece' by Thelma Houston, 'From Here To Eternity' by Giorgio Moroder, 'Hollywood' by The Village People and 'After Dark' by Pattie Brooks. New songs included the Love and Kisses title track, 'Trapped In A Stairway' by Paul Jabara and the Oscar-winning song 'Last Dance' by Donna Summer. Filmed entirely on location at Osko's disco (on Third and La Cienega Boulevard in LA), *Thank God It's Friday* didn't pretend to carry a message like *Saturday Night Fever*. Nor did it revolve around a gimmick like *Roller Boogie*. What it did, and did very well, was place the audience in an exciting, buzzy, up and happening disco environment, and communicated the whole joy-sharing attitude of the musical movement extremely effectively. This was the nearest any audience got to an authentic Studio 54-type experience.

Thank God It's Friday: Producer: Rob Cohen. Executive producer: Neil Bogart. Director: Robert Klane. Writer: Barry Armyan Bernstein. Starring Valerie Landsburg, Terri Nunn, Chick Vennera, Donna Summer, Ray Vitte, Mark Lonow, Andrea Howard, Jeff Goldblum, Robin Menken, Debra Winger, Paul Jabara, The Commodores. 89 minutes.

THE BITCH (1979)
The further adventures of Fontaine Khaled (Joan Collins) – see *The Stud*. This time La Collins is up to her arched eyebrows in

financial woes due to a messy divorce and the fact that her celebrity disco, The Hobo, isn't the hot-spot for the in-crowd any more. So she decides to investigate other straight and gay establishments to see how she can improve things for her clientèle. Add a jewel robbery, handsome conmen, horseracing and glamorous disco party scenes, and *The Stud* sequel is the usual Jackie Collins cocktail of sexy sleaze and potboiling hysterics revolving around her movie star sister's mindboggling all fur-coat and no-knickers demon diva performance. Once again the heavily TV-advertised soundtrack of this Collins family affair (the sisters' husbands were the executive producers) was a veritable cornucopia of disco hits and muzak misses (including the title theme song by The Olympic Runners, 'Turn The Music Up' by The Players Association, 'Giving Up, Giving In' by The Three Degrees, 'I Haven't Stopped Dancing Yet' by Gonzalez, 'Standing In The Shadows Of Love' by Deborah Washington and 'Cuba' by The Gibson Brothers).

The Bitch: Executive producers: Edward D. Simons, Ronald S. Kass and Oscar S. Lerman. Producer: John Quested. Director and writer: Gerry O'Hara. Story: Jackie Collins. Starring Joan Collins, Michael Coby, Kenneth Haigh, Ian Hendry, Carolyn Seymour, Sue Lloyd, Mark Burns, John Ratzenberger, Pamela Salem and Anthony Heaton. 90 minutes.

DISCO DELIRIO/DISCO MUSIC FEVER/THE DISCO KING (1979)

The Italian film industry has a long tradition of looking to American hits and then shamelessly ripping them off for Spaghetti-lite productions. Just as *The Deer Hunter* and *Dawn Of The Dead* launched a slew of copycat violent war epics and gory horror schlock in the '70s, so *Saturday Night Fever* had the same effect on the *cantarelli* genre. *Disco Delirio* was a virtual scene-for-scene duplicate of John Badham's original with Tino (Maurizio Micheletti), Patrizia (Alida Baglioni), Raf (Dario

Bramante) and Ornella (Ada Pometti) as two ballet-school couples entering a disco dance competition in Milan. A so-so disco tableau, the soundtrack featured 'Love Is In The Air' and 'The Day My Heart Caught Fire' by John Paul Young, 'Le Freak' by Chic, 'Think It Over' by Cissy Houston, 'Araxis Spaceship' by Araxis and 'SEX' by Idris Muhammad.

Other notable Italian knock-offs using virtually the same story are *American Fever* (1978), *I Ragazzi Della Discoteca* (*The Discothèque Boys*), *L'Anno Dei Gatti* (*The Year Of The Cats*) (1979), *John Travolto . . . Da Un Insolito Destino* (*John Travolto . . . By An Unusual Destiny*) (1979), and *La Discoteca* (*Discothèque*) (1983).

Disco Delirio: Production company: Consul International. Director and writer: Oscar Righini/Oscar Roy. Director of photography: Paolo Montalbano. Starring Alida Baglioni, Ada Pometti, Ambra Davy, Erminia Cristoforo, Luana Barbieri, Patrizia Levre, Ed Taylor, Maurizio Micheletti, Dario Bramante, Sergio Castellini, Raf Rabaioli and Warren Wallace. 89 minutes.

DISCO GODFATHER/THE AVENGING DISCO GODFATHER (1979)

One-man blaxploitation factory Rudy Ray Moore turned his sights on gyrating disco fever after producing and starring in the pseudo-classics *Dolemite*, *The Human Tornado* and *Petey Wheatstraw, The Devil's Son-In-Law*. The result is a demented cross between *Gordon's War* and *Can't Stop The Music* with Moore playing ex-cop Tucker Williams, the rapping owner and main attraction of the Blueberry Hill disco. Called back into police action when his nephew (Julius J. Carry III) gets hooked on Angel Dust, Williams and his 'gal Friday' Noel (Carol Speed, star of the black *Exorcist* rip-off *Abby*) declare war on super pusher Stinger (James H. Hawthorne) and his cronies using his club to peddle the PCP. Skid-row production meets hefty Moore's skin-tight studded disco ensembles to create a funky fiasco packed with roller-disco scenes, cheap psychedelic freak-outs (with zombies and skeletons), hilarious exorcisms to rid drug addicts of their evil spirits and jaw-droppingly awful kung fu choreography by martial arts champion Howard Jackson. No disco hits are featured on the soundtrack because of the cost, so original music was especially composed according to this convoluted credit: 'Produced by Bob Rooks, arranged and conducted by Ernie Fields Jr., theme suggested by Theodore Toney and Fred Williams'.

Disco Godfather: Producers: Rudy Ray Moore and Theodore Toney. Writer: Cliff Roquemore. Director: J. Robert Wagoner. Starring Rudy Ray Moore, Carol Speed, Julius J. Carry III, James H. Hawthorne, Jerry Jones and Lady Reed. 93 minutes.

FOXES (1979)

From the eventual producer of *Chariots Of Fire* and the director of *Fatal Attraction* comes a predictable pot-boiler about the adolescent problems faced by Jodie Foster and her San Fernando Valley friends. Pure teen soap, dragging in parental neglect, drug abuse and sexual awakening, this 'youth' drama (originally entitled *Twentieth-Century Foxes* until the film studio objected) was an odd mixture of awkward punk meets disco perceptiveness that became prevalent as both fads started being phased out of the mainstream. The presence of '60s British pop star Adam Faith, playing Foster's rock-concert-promoting father, only added to the weirdness. The Casablanca soundtrack featured music by Giorgio Moroder, 'Shake It' by Brooklyn Dreams, 'Greedy Man' by Munich Machine and 'Bad Love' by Cher, with Donna Summer's 'On The Radio' adopted as its haunting theme song.

Foxes: Producers: David Puttnam and Gerald Ayres. Director: Adrian Lyne. Writer: Ayres. Starring Jodie Foster, Cherie Currie, Sally Kellerman, Adam Faith, Scott Baio, Marilyn Kagan, Randy Quaid and Candice Stroh. 108 minutes.

LOVE AT FIRST BITE (1979)

Evicted from his Transylvanian home after seven hundred years of 'one-bite stands', Count Dracula (George Hamilton) moves himself and his coffin to New York City where he plans to search for true love. There he meets fashion model Cindy Sondheim (Susan Saint James) and heads for the disco floor to dance to 'I Love The Nightlife (Disco Round)' by Alicia Bridges. A hilarious vampire spoof that hit the social mores bull's-eye, the debonair Hamilton is perfect as the thickly accented, caped lounge lizard falling in 'lob' with the adorably ditzy James. The Dracula = disco formula was a popular one at the time because both lifestyles involved living at night, supposedly kinky sexual practices, hints of exotica and the 'tomorrow is another day' hedonistic credo. A huge box-office success because it captured the feeling and atmosphere of the disco years with affection and verisimilitude, the promised sequel *Love At Second Bite* sadly never materialised.

Love At First Bite: Producer: Joel Freedman. Director: Stan Dragoti. Writer: Robert Kaufman. Starring George Hamilton, Susan Saint James, Richard Benjamin, Dick Shawn, Arte Johnson and Michael Pataki. 96 minutes.

THE MUSIC MACHINE (1979)

Saturday Night Fever relocated to London's Camden Town but with a dismal plot (the usual dance competition), lacklustre music, second-division dancing from its third-rate headline cast (dreadful Travolta pose-alike Gerry Sundquist, stereotypical Patti Boulaye, future *Brookside* soaper David Easter) and awful production values (three fairylights if you're lucky!). Made by producers more used to the horror exploitation of *Expose* and *Vampyres: Daughters Of Dracula*, Boulaye sings 'Disco Dancer' (co-written by session singer supremo Madeline Bell), 'Ready For Love' and 'Get The Right Feel', while Music Machine (featuring Trevor Bastow, Paul Keogh, Harold Fisher, Frank Ricotti and Les Hurdle) contribute the forgettable tunes 'Let Me Feel Your Heartbeat', 'Music's My Thing' and 'The Dilly'.

The Music Machine: Producers: James Kenelm Clarke and Brian Smedley-Aston. Director: Ian Sharp. Screenplay: Clarke. Idea: Sharp. Starring Gerry Sundquist, Patti Boulaye, David Easter, Michael Fcast, Ferdy Mayne, Clarke Peters, Richard Parmentier, Billy McColl and Chrissy Wickham. 90 minutes.

NOCTURNA, GRANDDAUGHTER OF DRACULA (1979)

Trying to make ends meet, and sporting dentures instead of fangs, Dracula (John Carradine) turns his Transylvanian castle into a hotel-cum-disco complex. But when his rebellious granddaughter Nocturna (ex-belly dancer Nai Bonet) runs off to New York with a rock musician, he follows in hot pursuit. Yvonne De Carlo turns up as Jugulia in a parody of her Lily Munster role in this pathetic disco horror movie financed by Bonet herself and ex-actor/embezzler William Callahan who was slain in a gangland killing in 1981. Director Harry Tampa's crushed-velvet vampire sleaze epic may be the absolute pits yet it did provide two classic disco stormers in Gloria Gaynor's 'Love Is Just a Heartbeat Away (Nocturna's Theme)' and Vicki Sue Robinson's 'Nighttime Fantasy'. Other cuts on the MCA soundtrack are 'Watcha Gonna Do', 'Bitten By The Love Bug' and 'Chopin's Nocturne' by The Heaven 'N' Hell Orchestra, and 'Love At First Sight' and 'I'm Hopelessly In Love With You' by Moment of Truth.

Nocturna, Granddaughter Of Dracula: Producers: Nai Bonet and William Callahan. Director and writer: Harry Tampa. Starring Nai Bonet, John Carradine, Yvonne de Carlo. 83 minutes.

ROLLER BOOGIE (1979)

From Irwin Yablans, who became the producer of the hot horror hit *Halloween*, came the not-so-hot, horrific flop *Roller Boogie*. Poor little rich girl Terry Barkley (Linda Blair, in her first non-

Exorcist starring role in a feature film) runs away from her luxury lifestyle to become part of the Venice Beach roller-skating scene. There she falls for geeky roller maniac Bobby James (Jim Bray) and together they fight the mob (led by *Lost In Space* TV icon Mark Goddard) trying to close down their beloved disco rink on the eve of an eight-wheel dance contest. Despite the slick opening showing the fashion and mechanical preparations needed for a night out at the roller-disco, *Roller Boogie* is a hopeless time-warp farrago which *Babes In Arms* did better forty years before it. Directed by Mark Lester, whose sterling work with the exploitation gems *Truck Stop Women* and *Class Of 1984* led everyone to expect far more roller raunch and stylish pizzazz, the major flaw in the mindless movie is Blair herself. Here she turned other people's heads for being perhaps the worst roller-skater in history! Barely able to stagger to her camera cues and basically being held aloft by partner Bray during most of the competition finale, Blair did her erratic career no favours at all with this unimaginative foray into a craze few in front of the camera, and no one behind it, seemed to understand. Casablanca released a various artists double soundtrack with the inevitable 'Boogie Wonderland' by Earth Wind and Fire, the obvious 'Hell On Wheels' by Cher and numerous cuts by producer Bob Esty including 'Summer Love', 'Elektronix (Roller Dancin')', 'Cunga', 'Lord Is It Mine', 'Rollin' Up A Storm', 'The Roller Boogie' and 'Love Fire'.

Roller Boogie: Executive producer: Irwin Yablans. Producer: Bruce Cohn Curtis. Director: Mark Lester. Writer: Barry Schneider. Starring Linda Blair, Jim Bray, Beverly Garland, Roger Perry, James Van Patten, Kimberly Beck, Rick Sciacca, Sean McClory, Mark Goddard and Albert Insinnia. 103 minutes.

ROLLER MANIA (1979)

Director William Webb's documentary on roller-skating in all its varied forms from roller-derby to roller-disco is by turn fun to watch, ineptly inert and mercilessly stretched out. Centring on Venice, California – that late-'70s mecca for eight-wheeled sun-worshippers – 'Where it's all at!' as narrator Damien Evans says in his laid-back LA drawl, the film is a hastily assembled montage of snatched sports footage mixed with newsreel clips and lengthy roller routines by famous skaters. The old clips of skating in the '30s and '40s are of enormous interest but little effort goes into presenting them in a historical context and showing the development of the sport over the decades into the roller-disco phenomenon. There's a sequence on how to customise your roller-skate boots with hand-painting, but Webb, as he does throughout the entire ninety-minute running time, quickly dismisses this interesting segment in order to get back to Kerry Cavazzi, Fred Blood and Lynne Turner (who was skating consultant on the movie) twirling on the traffic-free Venice pathways. In the disco scenes the accent is very much on the floor space and lighting effects as the skaters limber up to do their thing. The *Roller Mania* soundtrack is one of its best aspects featuring Earth Wind and Fire, The Jones Girls, Citi, Dan Hartman, Bonnie Pointer, Celi Bee and the Buzzy Bunch and The Michael Zager Band, whose 'Life's A Party' is the anthem of the piece and accompanies some of the most spectacular figure-skating. But there's a limit to how much each holds the attention before becoming repetitive. Webb should have used his editing scissors to greater effect and reduced his full-length feature, which rarely got shown theatrically anyway, to a more dynamic and focused duration. However, as it stands, *Roller Mania* does show the reason why roller-disco and street-skating took off in the Sunshine State and will therefore always remain a shining artefact of the pop culture past.

Roller Mania: Producer and director: William Webb. Starring April Allen, Jack Cortney, Natalie Dunn, Kerry Cavazzi, Lynne Turner, Fred Blood, The Body Gliders, Michael Kirkpatrick, Duke Renny, Vecky Howe, C.C. Boots and Stephanie Starr. 90 minutes.

SKATETOWN USA (1979)

The first of the roller-disco exploitation movies featured great skating, a disco hit soundtrack and silly comedy schtick from a has-been cast. Set in a giant roller palace (owned by Flip Wilson and his supposed son Billy Barty) on one particular mythical night, the barely-there story pits blond street-skater Stan (Greg Bradford) against leather-clad bad boy Ace (Patrick Swayze making his debut) for the title of the rink's number-one champion. Hopelessly juvenile, with tiresome cardboard cut-outs posing as well-rounded characters, director William Levey (of *The Happy Hooker Goes To Washington* fame, so you knew what to expect!) wheels out his large cast of comedians to indulge in routines they've done a million times before in between the terrific skating by Bradford and Swayze. Superficially patched together by Nick Castle (co-writer of *Escape From New York* with his friend John Carpenter) and including the hits 'Shake Your Body' by The Jacksons, 'Boogie Wonderland' by Earth Wind and Fire, 'Born To Be Alive' by Patrick Hernandez, 'Roller Girl' by John Sebastian, 'Boogie Nights' by Heatwave, the original songs 'Feelin' Alright', 'I Fell In Love' and the title track by Dave Mason (playing himself in the movie), *Skatetown* USA is escapist fluff with lots of colour and roller action but little to engage the brain.

Skatetown USA: Producers: William Levey and Lorin Dreyfuss. Director: Levey. Starring Scott Baio, Flip Wilson, Ron Palillo, Ruth Buzzi, Dave Mason, Greg Bradford, Maureen McCormick, Patrick Swayze, Billy Barty, Kelly Lang, David Landsburg and Len Bari. 98 minutes.

STEPPIN' OUT (1979)

A look at London lifestyles in 1979 in which Lyndall Hobbs (future director of *Back To The Beach* and girlfriend of Al Pacino) investigates disco parties at the London hot-spots The Embassy and Blitz, participates in 'Mod Night' at Legends, captures a punk gathering outside the Vivienne Westwood store Seditionaries in the King's Road and hitches a ride with a coach-outing to a roller-disco in Dunstable, Bedfordshire. A patchy affair but an invaluable record of 'Swinging London' in the disco '70s even though Hobbs is not a pretty sight on roller-skates. Songs include 'Disco Roller' by Cynthia Woodard, 'Rock Around The Clock' by Telex and 'Stars' by Sylvester.

Steppin' Out: Producer, director and writer: Lyndall Hobbs. Starring Hobbs, Sponooch, The Roxy Rollers, The Merton Parkas, Secret Affair, Jeanette Charles and Marilyn. 26 minutes.

VAN NUYS BOULEVARD (1979)

What do you do down Van Nuys Boulevard on a hot Californian Saturday night? Cruise the freeways, go drag racing and hit the local nightclub in director William Sach's feeble exploitation flick aimed at disco-age teens. Virtually plotless, the soundtrack features 'Boogie On Down The Boulevard', 'Love Party', 'Discoliope', 'Mama's Car' and the main theme performed by Jump Start, Tere Mansfield and Ron Wright.

Van Nuys Boulevard: Director: William Sachs. Starring Bill Adler, Cynthia Wood, Dennis Bowen and Melissa Prophet. 93 minutes.

THE WORLD IS FULL OF MARRIED MEN (1979)

The wife of an advertising executive tries to pay him back in kind for his infidelity with a fame-whore mistress. Yes, it's just another Jackie Collins torn marriage manual made into a glitzy, ritzy superficial softcore melodrama complete with lashings of ludicrous lust – and all with a disco soundtrack, of course! Included on the Ronco record are 'Contact' by Edwin Starr, 'Heaven Must Be Missing An Angel' by Tavares, 'Woman In Love' by The Three Degrees, 'Now That We've Found Love' by Third World, 'Best Of My Love' by The Emotions, 'Shame' by Evelyn 'Champagne' King and 'Lovelines' by headliner Paul Nicholas.

The World Is Full Of Married Men: Producer: Adrienne

Fancy. Director: Robert Young. Writer: Jackie Collins. Starring Carroll Baker, Anthony Franciosa, Sherrie Cronn, Paul Nicholas, Gareth Hunt, Georgina Hale and Anthony Steel. 106 minutes.

YESTERDAY'S HERO (1979)

Okay, we know Oscar Lerman, the husband of best-selling writer Jackie Collins, owned London's poshest disco, Tramp. But did that give Collins the right virtually to corner the market in disco-orientated movies? Ian McShane is the George Best-inspired footballer aiming for a comeback after beating a booze problem. Will he make it to the Cup final? Paul Nicholas (as an Elton John-type rock star chairman) and Adam Faith (as his soccer manager) help him achieve his goal. The soundtrack album featured 'Ring My Bell' by Anita Ward, 'At Midnight' by T-Connection, 'Pick Me Up I'll Dance' by Melba Moore, 'Disco Music' by the JALN Band and US sitcom star Suzanne Somers singing the title song.

Yesterday's Hero: Producer: Elliott Kastner. Director: Neil Leifer. Writer: Jackie Collins. Starring Ian McShane, Suzanne Somers, Adam Faith, Paul Nicholas and Sam Kydd. 95 minutes.

THE APPLE/STAR-ROCK (1980)

A cut-price futuristic disco fantasy from Israeli wide-boys Menahem Golan and Yoram Globus, the owners of the now defunct Cannon International group. Rockers, hippies (led by Joss Ackland!), flashy discothèques, alien planets: it's all here in a tawdry glitter and tinsel *Top Of The Pops*-styled story about Alphie and Bibi, the winners of the 1994 Worldvision Song Contest, who pose too much of a threat to promoter Mr Boogalow (an enthusiastically camp Vladek Sheybal) and his duo, Dandi and Pandi. True love wins the day when Boogalow's attempts to split up Alphie and Bibi collapse as they are whisked off into space. Absolutely dreadful. George S. Clinton of the funkadelic band Parliament supplied the lyrics (along with Iris Recht) and adapted Coby Recht's music to the screen. Clinton also appears as Joe Pittman.

The Apple: Producers: Menahem Golan and Yoram Globus. Director and screenplay: Golan. Story: Coby Recht. Starring Catherine Mary Stewart, George Gilmour, Grace Kennedy, Joss Ackland, Allan Shell, Miriam Margoyles, Derek Deadman and Michael Logan. 94 minutes.

CAN'T STOP THE MUSIC (1980)

It was Christmas 1978, and the song you couldn't escape from during that holiday season was 'YMCA' by The Village People. The record sold over ten million copies worldwide and became the biggest hit single of the decade. Enough reason, then, for Allan Carr, the caftan-encased/floor-length-mink-coated producer of that summer's huge movie hit *Grease*, to announce the Six-Pack Sensation would be starring in their own big-budget musical entertainment *Discoland: Where The Music Never Ends!*. But whereas *Grease* got its '50s nostalgia timing exactly right, helped by the fact it starred *Saturday Night Fever*'s main attraction, John Travolta, Carr put his new $20 million extravaganza into production just as the disco craze was beginning to wane and a fickle public started wearing 'Disco Sucks' badges. By the time *Can't Stop The Music* (as the film was finally entitled, excising all reference to the dreaded disco word) was released in late-1979 it was far too expensive, far too coy, far too much and far too late. Even the Village People's hardcore gay audience hated it because it painted their 'Macho Man' heroes in heterosexual colours and, unless you could spot the arcane clues (a red handkerchief in the Leatherman's left pocket, gay code for fist fucking), or the double entendres in the dialogue ('It's your music that's bringing all these talented boys together – they ought to get down on their knees!') then, to all intents and purposes, the group had sold out to the female teenybopper crowd who embraced their music in the wake of 'Go West' and 'In The Navy'. Allan Carr and Bronte Woodard ('a teenaged Tennessee Williams', according to the larger-than-life mogul) wrote the screenplay (which the VPs loathed from the moment they read it) which centres around NYC composer Jack Morell, played by Steve Guttenberg (who left this movie off his list of credits for years), looking for that one elusive big break. The thinly veiled cypher of the VP's actual French producer Jacques Morali is aided in his goal by Samantha (Valerie Perrine), 'the Garbo of models', who wanders the streets of Manhattan rounding up her friends – a construction worker, a cowboy, a cop, a soldier, a leather-clad clone and an Indian! – to do justice to her friend's music. Model agency magnate Tammy Grimes (in OTT drag-queen mode), Jack's mother June Havoc (Gypsy Rose Lee's sister), and out-of-his-depth Olympic decathlon champion Bruce Jenner all eventually help the group become a wild success at a gala concert in San Francisco's Galleria. Directed by Nancy Walker (*Rhoda*'s mother) as a post-modern Busby Berkeley confection, complete with choreographed calisthenic gym exercises and rows of muscular Speedo-wearers diving in formation, *Can't Stop The Music* was a dishonest, tacky and hopeless mess as movie entertainment. But it had a great soundtrack featuring the evergreen title song, 'Liberation' (although from what is never made clear in the best example of the sexually fudged issues), 'Milkshake', 'Magic Night' and 'I Love You To Death' by The Village People. The Ritchie Family were drafted in to up the disco celebrity count with 'Give Me A Break' and 'Sophistication', while 'discovery' David London sang the opening number 'The Sound Of The City' (accompanying obvious Guttenberg body double Gary Kluger roller-skating through Greenwich Village) and the ode to Perrine's chirpy character, 'Samantha'. From a distance Carr's camp catastrophe is great nudge-nudge, wink-wink fun. it evokes the disco era and its surrounding 'Ready for the '80s' sensibilities extremely well and is the more playful flipside of the darker *Saturday Night Fever* coin. Contemporary reviews were devastating: 'It's

208

true – you really can't stop the music, no matter how much you want to, and at times you'll want to very, very much' (*New West*); 'The Village People should consider renaming themselves the Village Idiots' (*Los Angeles Magazine*); 'One doesn't watch *Can't Stop The Music*. One is attacked by it' (*New England Entertainment Digest*). Perhaps the most pertinent comment made about the whole débâcle, which placed all gay references on the periphery for commercial safety, came from Arthur Bell, founder of the Gay Activists Alliance. He called it 'a stupid gay movie for stupid straight people'. By trying to please everyone, Carr and company failed to please anyone, and *Can't Stop The Music* was an enormously embarrassing flop for all concerned. Only in Australia did the movie make money and that's where the producer established the annual 'Allan Carr Awards' at the Australian Film and Television School in gratitude. Of course, they had yet to see his *Grease II* and *Where the Boys Are '84* . . .

Can't Stop The Music: Producers: Allan Carr, Jacques Morali and Henri Belolo. Director: Nancy Walker, Screenplay: Carr and Bronte Woodard. Music composed and produced by Morali. Choreography: Arlene Phillips. Starring The Village People, Valerie Perrine, Bruce Jenner, Steve Guttenberg, Paul Sand, Tammy Grimes, June Havoc, Barbara Rush, Jack Weston and The Ritchie Family. 118 minutes.

CRUISING (1980)

The Exorcist/Boys In The Band director William Friedkin got everything hopelessly wrong in this disco delve into the seamy S&M side of gay life in Manhattan's Christopher Street area. Al Pacino is the NYPD cop assigned to go undercover to capture a gay serial killer and who becomes aware of his own homosexuality during the murder investigation. Debased by Sunday-supplement pop-psychobabble, ridiculously homophobic for a purportedly 'gay' movie, and extensively picketed on release, in fact the most offensive thing about Friedkin's fiasco was how badly Pacino danced in the disco scenes. While it features no real disco music, *Cruising* does offer a glimpse into the gay disco lifestyle suffused by Village People imagery as it takes the viewer on an almost documentary tour through The Mineshaft, one of the more notorious gay bars of the era, alongside The Anvil, The Eagle's Nest and The Toilet.

Cruising: Producer: Jerry Weintraub. Director and writer: William Friedkin. Based on the novel by Gerald Walker. Starring Al Pacino, Paul Sorvino, Karen Allen, Richard Cox and Don Scardino. 106 minutes.

DISCO-FIEBER/DISCO FEVER (1980)

A dreadful German exploitation disco movie which looks like it started out as a *Lemon Popsicle*-style inane teen sex comedy — fat youth, bumbling official, blonde in crisp white uniform — and on the tortuous way to a cinema release changed fashionable direction with hastily spliced-in footage of Eurodisco veterans Boney M, Eruption and La Bionda. Shot on video and including such terrible dialogue as 'She forgot to lock her bicycle again' — 'That's puberty for you', director Hubert Frank's abomination makes *The Music Machine* (see above) look like *The Sound Of Music*. Producer Dieter Geissler went on to package *The Neverending Story* series of fantasy movies. Songs performed are 'Rivers of Babylon', 'Rasputin', 'It's A Holi-Holiday' and 'Ribbons Of Blue' by Boney M; 'Leave A Light (In My Window)', 'Computer Love' and 'One Way Ticket' by Eruption; and 'Baby Make Love' and 'One For You, One For Me' by La Bionda. Other songs are performed by The Teens, Germany's answer to the Bay City Rollers, and headliner Tony Schneider.

Disco Fever: Producers: Hans Janisch and Dieter Geissler. Director: Hubert Frank. Script: Frank. Story: Karl Heinz Quade. Starring Tony Schneider, Hanna Sebek, Babsy May, Isabelle Dumas, Stefan Reber and Peter Lengauer. 86 minutes.

FAME (1980)

Four years in the lives of a group of teenagers attending Manhattan's High School for the Performing Arts are put under the microscope by director Alan Parker. It's a pacy and rich view of the microcosm that was disco New York, with Afro-Americans, Puerto Ricans, homosexuals, uptown and downtown individuals honing their talents (stand-up comedy, ballet, song-writing) to make it in the cut-throat world of showbiz. With an entertaining and gripping screenplay by Christopher Gore, and most songs composed by Michael Gore (brothers of 'It's My Party' hit-maker Lesley Gore), *Fame* includes visits to an audience participation night of *The Rocky Horror Picture Show* and puts one of the main characters, Leroy (Gene Anthony Ray), on roller-skates to dash between classes in the venerable academy The three stand-out disco cuts on the soundtrack are the Oscar-winning title song, now a perennial standard, 'Hot Lunch Jam' sung by shortlived diva Irene Cara (Coco in the movie), and 'Red Light' by Linda Clifford (who stormed dance floors in 1978 with 'If My Friends Could See Me Now').

Fame: Producers: David de Silva and Alan Marshall. Director: Alan Parker. Writer: Christopher Gore. Starring Irene Cara, Barry Miller, Paul McCrane, Lee Currei, Laura Dean, Gene Anthony Ray, Antonia Franchesi, Anne Meara and Eddie Barth. 134 minutes.

XANADU (1980)

Producer Allan Carr had first offered the Valerie Perrine role in *Can't Stop The Music* to Olivia Newton-John in the hope of attracting some of the *Grease* magic to this misbegotten project. But La Neutron Bomb turned him down to make another equally magnificent muzak mishap, which she saw as the perfect vehicle to reunite her with her *Grease* co-star, John Travolta. As it turned out, Travolta was waiting for an even lousier script before agreeing to team up with her again – the 1983 dog *Two*

Of A Kind. So Newton-John chose newcomer Michael Beck (after turning down Mel Gibson!) to take his place in this $20 million loose remake of *Down To Earth* (1947), the charming fantasy musical starring Rita Hayworth. *Xanadu* has fantasy in psychedelic spades. It's the charm that's missing in director Robert Greenwald's ludicrous pop pastiche where Newton-John plays the ancient Greek muse Terpsichore reincarnated from a mural – along with eight other goddesses – to help painter Beck and rich big-band clarinettist Gene Kelly open up a roller-disco. As the wispy story evaporates and is replaced by gaudy electric mayhem and one overblown musical number after another, *Xanadu* starts to resemble a series of early MTV videos in desperate search of a sensible plot. Animated cartoon sequences (by *Anastasia* artist Don Bluth), rock 'n' roll glitter and glitz and embarrassing tributes to dancer Kelly's illustrious past ('Singin' in the Rain' sung on skates, a *faux* '40s dream sequence and a musical Fiorucci fashion show situated in a pinball machine) jostle with Newton-John's leaden one-note performance for the disco kitsch supremo title. The climactic Battle of the Bands production number featuring the out-of-place punk group The Tubes is the neon icing on an impossibly rich day-glo cake. Visually *Xanadu* was an eye-popping frothy trash-fest supplying many Top 20 chart hits for Newton-John, Cliff Richard and Electric Light Orchestra. But the schlockathon couldn't fill the theatres and audiences stayed away in droves. 'Xanadu', 'All Over the World', 'Dancin'', 'I'm Alive', 'Suddenly' and 'Magic' are the songs that survive this gloriously bad movie. At one point Newton-John explains her character to Beck and says, 'We've been painted by Michelangelo, Shakespeare's written sonnets for us, Beethoven's played music for us.' Sadly none of those consummate artists was around when this stately pleasuredome concept was first suggested. Often lumped with *Can't Stop The Music* as the Dynamic Duo of Disco Disasters, *Xanadu* actually makes *Can't Stop The Music* look like . . . well, *Down To Earth*!

Xanadu: Producer: Lawrence Gordon. Director: Robert Greenwald. Writers: Richard Christian Danus and Marc Reid Rubel. Starring Olivia Newton-John, Gene Kelly, Michael Beck, Sandhal Bergman, Matt Latanzi, The Tubes and the voices of Wilfred Hyde-White and Coral Browne. 93 minutes.

PAUL RAYMOND'S EROTICA (1981)

Soho sex entrepreneur Paul Raymond entered the disco movie fray with a limp Strip-O-Rama set to fourth-grade boogie bump-and-grind starring legendary French hardcore queen Brigitte Lahaie. Written (!) and directed (!) by horror exploiter supremo Brian Smedley-Aston (producer of *Vampyres: Daughters Of Darkness* and *Expose*), Lahaie plays a French photo-journalist sent to London to do a spread on Paul Raymond's famous venue. Beginning with a sex romp in a Rolls-Royce and ending with a lesbian fantasy, the laughable drama-documentary takes in mixed saunas, Raymond relaxing at his country club and a nude disco in Smithfield meat market. As an assortment of bored models bare their flesh, Raymond's own daughter Debbie (soon to die of a drug overdose) warbled such forgettable disco trash as 'You And I', 'I'm On Fire' and 'Warm'. The tie-in soundtrack of 'sensual disco greats' included 'Use It Up And Wear It Out' by Odyssey, 'I Feel Love' by Donna Summer, 'Jingo' by Candido and 'Dancin' The Night Away' by Voggue. Future Capital Radio weather girl and Heart radio deejay Kara Noble contributed the cut 'Flesh'.

Paul Raymond's Erotica: Producer: Paul Raymond. Writer and director: Brian Smedley-Aston. Starring Diana Cochran, Brigitte Lahaie and Paul Raymond III. 86 minutes.

THE SPIRIT OF '76 (1991)

Rarely seen and highly underrated when it was, director Lucas Reiner's delightful comedy drama takes a simple idea and expands it brilliantly. Former *Partridge Family* member David Cassidy, former Bond Girl Olivia D'Abo and Geoff Hoyle enter

213

a time machine in 2176 in order to return to 1776 and find out exactly what the American Constitution was all about. Instead they end up by mistake in 1976 and get sucked into every deranged fad and fashion, including disco. Their guides to the taboo-breaking period are Jeff and Steve McDonald (from the group Red Kross) who lead them through the pleasures of eight-track tapes, Grand Funk, queues at petrol stations, Smile badges and the insane fashions of the day. Teen idol Leif Garrett (singer of the disco pop classic 'I Was Made For Dancin'') turns up as Eddie Trojan, 'The Bone Master', as do the Kipper Kids, playing comic CIA men, West Coast comedienne Julie (*Earth Girls Are Easy*) Brown and director Lucas Reiner's father Rob and grandfather Carl. Produced by Susie Landau (the daughter of Oscar-winning actor Martin Landau and his *Space 1999* wife Barbara Bain), *The Spirit of '76* perfectly captures the 'anything goes' atmosphere of the disco era with acerbic affection and knowing cliché all highlighted by the choice of such pop plums on the soundtrack as 'Love's Theme' by The Love Unlimited Orchestra, 'The Hustle' by Van McCoy, 'Kung Fu Fighting' by Carl Douglas, 'Rock The Boat' by The Hues Corporation, 'Boogie Fever' by The Sylvers and two cuts purloined from *Saturday Night Fever* – 'Disco Inferno' by The Trammps and 'A Fifth Of Beethoven' by Walter Murphy and the Big Apple Band.

The Spirit of '76: Producer: Susie Landau. Executive producers: Roman Coppola and Fred Fuchs. Director and writer: Lucas Reiner. Starring David Cassidy, Olivia D'Abo, Leif Garrett, Geoff Hoyle, Jeff McDonald, Steve McDonald, Liam O'Brien, Barbara Bain, Julie Brown, Tommy Chong, Devo, Iron Eyes Cody, The Kipper Kids, Don Novello, Carl Reiner, Rob Reiner and Moon Zappa. 90 minutes.

YOUNG SOUL REBELS (1991)
Oblique, difficult and ambitious, director Isaac Julien's look at the punk versus disco/soul movement is worthy of some

interest. Set in 1977, during the week of the Queen's Silver Jubilee, this coming-of-age saga focuses on Chris (Valentine Nonyela) and Caz (Mo Seasy), friends since childhood, who are deejays on a black pirate radio station called Soul Patrol which broadcasts its funk message from an east London garage. The story picks up speed when their friend TJ is murdered cruising in the local park and Chris realises a ghetto-blaster found by his little sister near the scene of the crime contains a recording of the killer's voice. The Soul Patrol play in The Crypt, a gay club, and that's where this muddled look at the roots of punk, racism and the sexual politics of dance culture holds the attention. 'Let's Get It Together' by El Coco, 'I'll Play The Fool For You' by Doctor Buzzard's Original Savannah Band, 'You Make Me Feel (Mighty Real)' by Sylvester and 'Message In Our Music' by The O'Jays are featured on the soundtrack along with Funkadelic and Parliament cuts.

Young Soul Rebels: Producer: Nadine Marsh-Edwards. Director: Isaac Julien. Writers: Julien, Paul Hallam, Derrick Saldaan McLintock. Starring Valentine Nonyela, Mo Sesay, Dorian Healy, Frances Barber and Jason Durr. 105 mins.

CARLITO'S WAY (1993)

Director Brian De Palma and his Scarface star Al Pacino resumed their gangster ways in this involving yarn taken from the best-selling novel by real-life judge Edwin Torres. Pacino is the legendary Puerto Rican hood Carlito Brigante who is just out of prison and determined to go straight, but who gets pulled inexorably back into a life of crime. Set in 1975, with Carlito living above a disco, much of the action takes place within the club confines and showcases the hustle being done on the dance floor and the songs 'Backstabbers' by The O'Jays, 'TSOP' by MFSB, 'Got To Be Real' by Cheryl Lynn, 'Lady Marmalade' by Labelle and 'Rock The Boat' by The Hues Corporation on the soundtrack.

Carlito's Way: Producers: Martin Bregman, Will Baer and

Michael S. Bregman. Director: Brian De Palma. Starring Al Pacino, Sean Penn, Penelope Ann Miller, Luis Guzman, Viggo Mortenson and John Leguizamo. 145 mins.

THE BIRDCAGE (1996)

The French drag farce *La Cage Aux Folles* (which spawned three successful French movies in 1979, 1980 and 1985) is relocated from St Tropez to Miami's South Beach with an equally mainstream dilution in charm and subtlety. Nathan Lane is the star attraction at the top transvestite nite-spot The Birdcage who must pretend to be a real woman when his lover's (Robin Williams) son turns up with the ultraconservative parents of his fiancée. Although set in contemporary Miami, disco songs on the soundtrack include 'Lady Marmalade' by LaBelle, 'She Works Hard For The Money' by Donna Summer and 'We Are Family' by Sister Sledge. One song it doesn't include is 'I Am What I Am' written by Jerry (*Hello Dolly*) Herman for the Broadway musical adaptation of *La Cage Aux Folles* (1983) and turned into a huge club hit by diva Gloria Gaynor. A cover version was recorded by La Cage. The show also provided a club hit for La Jetee with the title song.

The Birdcage: Producer and director: Mike Nicholls. Screenplay: Elaine May. The original *La Cage Aux Folles* story: Jean Poiret, Frances Verbier, Edouard Molinaro and Marcello Danon. Starring Robin Williams, Gene Hackman, Nathan Lane, Dianne Wiest, Dan Fetterman, Calista Flockhart, Hank Azaria and Christine Baranski. 119 minutes.

BOOGIE NIGHTS (1997)

Pornography, drugs and disco are the driving forces of director Paul Thomas Anderson's potent parable of the partying '70s. Spanning the height of the disco era, this Martin Scorsese/*Goodfellas*-influenced rags-to-bitches allegory is a visually stunning exploration of the American adult entertainment industry, centring on a hardcore movie outfit whose 'Things Go Better With Coke' members form a close-knit extended family under the watchful gaze of sleaze producer Jack Horner (Burt Reynolds in an Oscar-nominated supporting performance). Charting the rise and fall and rise again of busboy-turned-porn-star Eddie Adams/Dirk Diggler (Mark Wahlberg), the American Dream is screwed wide open by Anderson's playful vibrator, and disco is the lubricant on its sardonic shaft. Opening with a brilliant extended Steadicam shot through a nightclub as the main players come into focus, including Heather Graham as Rollergirl, the hustle is demonstrated halfway through Dirk's meteoric success story with songs including 'Best Of My Love' by The Emotions and 'Ain't No Stopping Us Now' by McFadden and Whitehead featured on the soundtrack.

Boogie Nights: Producers: Lloyd Levin, Paul Thomas Anderson, John Lyons and Joanne Sellar. Director and writer: Paul Thomas Anderson. Starring Mark Wahlberg, Burt Reynolds, Julianne Moore, John C. Reilly, Don Cheadle, Heather Graham, Luis Guzman, William H. Macy and Alfred Molina. 152 minutes.

FOREVER FEVER (1997)

Amusing, sentimental and touching, Glen Goei's Asian artefact is a highly engaging and affectionately nostalgic mixture of *Saturday Night Fever* sensibilities, *Strictly Ballroom* ambition and *The Purple Rose Of Cairo* fantasy. It's 1977 and Bruce Lee fan Ah Hok (Adrian Pang) is working in the Oriental Emporium, a Singapore supermarket, with no prospects, no girlfriend and an unhappy home life. Then he goes to see the thinly veiled *Saturday Night Fever* disco movie sensation *Forever Fever* (starring John Travolta lookalike Dominic Pace) and his life changes. Suitably inspired, he enrols at the Bonnie and Clyde Dance Studio to learn the hustle with Ah Mei (Medaline Tan), a barmaid he's keen on, and prepares for an upcoming dance contest at the Galaxy disco so he can win

$5,000 to buy a new motorbike. Whenever he feels down, Ah Hok heads back to the cinema to see reruns of *Forever Fever* where Pace steps out of the screen to give him advice on fashion, romance and disco. But the gorgeous and talented mover Julie (local Singapore deejay Anna Belle Francis) lures him away from Mei for the big night and her no-good ex-boyfriend Richard (Pierre Png) has him beaten up to sabotage their championship prospects. Bruised and bloody on the Galaxy disco floor, Ah Hok realises he's in love with Mei, beats the living daylights out of Richard and gives the prize-money to his alienated brother Leslie (Caleb Goh) to pay for his sex-change operation. Despite Goei virtually copying scenes frame by frame from *Saturday Night Fever* (the family dinner table exchanges being the most obvious), as well as the ragged edges and often crass humour, *Forever Fever* becomes its own unique East meets West entertainment with the addition of the cinema fantasy sequences, the transsexual sub-plot (a neat '90s twist on the priest dilemma in the Travolta original) and the use of Bruce Lee iconography. Ah Hok's disco mantra is 'Don't think, feel' – a line from *Enter The Dragon* – and the final kung fu battle is straight out of *Fists Of Fury*. Well choreographed by Zaki Ahmad, all the low-to-high energy dance routines are accompanied by reasonable cover versions of such disco classics as 'Instant Replay', 'Rock the Boat', 'Stayin' Alive', 'Jive Talkin'', 'You To Me Are Everything', 'How Deep Is Your Love', 'Souvenirs', and the inevitable 'Kung Fu Fighting'. Peculiarly enough, Ah Hok's motorbike fantasies are accompanied by the Nilsson song 'Everybody's Talkin''. Ah Hok walking into the Galaxy disco for the first time and gazing in wonderment at the bright flashing lights is a moment all disco lovers will cherish, as is the evocatively shot dance contest footage. (Originally entitled *Don't Call Me John Travolta*, Goei's film was re-edited and re-dubbed by Miramax Films for worldwide distribution.)

Forever Fever: Producers: Glen Goei, Jeffrey Chiang and Tan

Chin Chong. Writer and director: Goei. Starring Adrian Pang, Medaline Tan, Anna Belle Francis, Pierre Png, Dominic Pace, Caleb Goh, Steven Lim and Kumar. 95 minutes

54 (1998)

Strong on disco ambience and vividly capturing the Studio 54 atmosphere, director Mark Christopher's too ambitious chronicle of the notorious nightclub at its 1979 fashionable height is let down by a formulaic plot carved straight out of *Saturday Night Fever* by way of *Boogie Nights*. Completely naïve and wearing the wrong clothes, Shane O'Shea (Ryan Phillippe) leaves his drab New Jersey existence and crosses the bridge to glamorous Manhattan in order to get into the most exclusive disco in the world. Club owner Steve Rubell (Mike Myers) lets Shane cross the velvet ropes when he strips off in the queue, thus starting his fast rise from amateur busboy to hunky bartender and *Interview* magazine centrefold. Mirroring Mark Wahlberg's character in *Boogie Nights*, the club and its employees become Shane's surrogate family as he gets sucked into the decadent glitzy lifestyle, mixes with the Park Avenue set and becomes romantically involved with soap star Julie (Neve Campbell). The action takes place over ten nights, each illustrating a major theme as the disco devolves from a celestial paradise to a lost one awash with drug overdoses, tax investigations, Rubell's subsequent imprisonment, and Shane's rehabilitation as an NYU business student. Except for Myers, who is terrific as the club's zonked-out gay MC, and an appealing turn by Salma Hayek as the coat-check girl aspiring to be a disco singer, the cast is rather undistinguished. It's the colourful party-like circus mood evoked by Christopher that makes the movie a painless experience superbly cut to a brilliant array of disco numbers, including 'Lovin' Is Really My Game' by Brainstorm, 'Heaven Must Have Sent You' by Bonnie Pointer, 'I Need A Man' by Grace Jones, 'Move On Up' by Destination and 'Love Machine (Part 1)' by The Miracles and the usual assortment of Chic, Odyssey, Dan Hartman, Thelma Houston (who appears as herself singing a Christmas song) and Santa Esmeralda classics. Although acknowledging the enormous gay contribution to the disco scene, much of the homo-erotic gay subtext between Rubell and Shane was excised prior to release. Mark Christopher also directed the acclaimed short, *Dead Boys Cub* (1992), about a pair of magical shoes transporting a man back to the pre-Aids time of his dead gay uncle, clubbing at 12 West.

54: Producers: Richard N. Gladstein, Dolly Hall, Ira Deutchman. Executive producers: Bob Weinstein, Harvey Weinstein, Bobby Cohen and Don Carmody. Writer and director: Mark Christopher. Starring Ryan Phillippe, Salma Hayek, Neve Campbell, Mike Myers, Sela Ward, Breckin Meyer, Skipp Sudduth, Heather Matarazzo, Lauren Hutton and Michael York. 92 minutes.

THE LAST DAYS OF DISCO (1998)

Completing director Whit Stillman's trio of urban romantic comedies (and in the scheme of things fitting between *Metropolitan* and the Eurodisco-tinged *Barcelona*), this scintillating look at the yuppie disco experience is the best yet at capturing the etiquette and atmosphere of the era. This is how it was: the anxieties over getting past the velvet ropes, the thrill of hearing the muted disco beat from the cloakroom area; the flirty cruise through the elegant, flotsam-and-jetsam crowd checking out the talent; excitedly edging your way to the dance floor and letting the non-stop parade of current hits jerk you around like a pop puppet in the flashing lights. Although it's never named, the disco which college classmates Alice (Chloe Sevigny) and Charlotte (Kate Beckinsale, looking fabulous) frequent is clearly modelled on Studio 54 – club assistant manager Des (Chris Eigeman) is portrayed as a coke-sniffing playboy stashing bags of skimmed cash in the basement. Scripted with Stillman's trademark sophistication, this painfully funny look at the disco lifestyle highlights sexual identity, promiscuity and dysfunction while indulging in scalpel-sharp comments on an eclectic array of topics ranging from Disney's *The Lady And The Tramp* and using venereal disease as a dating device, to the bitchy truths only your best friend will tell you and a pertinent oration on why disco will never die. 'Doctor's Orders' by Carol Douglas starts off Stillman's strobing still-life in hyper-drive and the ending, choreographed to 'Love Train' by The O'Jays, will reduce any fervent disco lover to tears as everyone on the New York subway system suddenly bursts out dancing. 'More, More, More (Part1)' by Andrea True Connection, 'Knock On Wood' by Amii Stewart and 'Let's All Chant' by The Michael Zager Band feature prominently on the disco classics soundtrack. The former wonderfully underscores a hesitant seduction scene between Chloe Sevigny and Robert Sean Leonard as they hustle into his bedroom.

The Last Days Of Disco: Producer, writer, director: Whit Stillman. Starring Chloe Sevigny, Kate Beckinsale, Chris Eigeman, Matt Keeslar, Mackenzie Astin, Matthew Ross, Tara Subkoff, Robert Sean Leonard, Jennifer Beals and Jaid Barrymore. 113 minutes.

CHARLIE'S ANGELS (2000)

The trend for adapting popular '70s TV series into event movies with big stars meant a disco backdrop became de rigueur. This is the one that started the retro craze and yet it couldn't have been worse. Commercials director McG's McRomp might be brimful of gorgeous babes in skintight costumes, lightweight 007 action, *Matrix*-skewed stunts and slow-mo hair flips, but its pop culture patchwork misses the *Austin Powers* benchmark by miles. No post-millennium film ever cost so much yet looked so cheap as sexy super agents Natalie (Cameron Diaz), Dylan (Drew Barrymore) and Alex (Lucy Liu) are assigned to save the kidnapped genius behind

Knox Electronics (Sam Rockwell) and recover some stolen technology that mustn't fall into enemy hands. Shot like a series of shampoo commercials and aiming no higher in the self-referential camp stakes than the stars' plunging necklines, the best scene has disco Diaz dancing up a hustling storm to the classic Tavares track 'Heaven Must Be Missing An Angel'. Leo Sayer's 'You Make Me Feel Like Dancing' snuck in too. The even stupider sequel *Charlie's Angels: Full Throttle* (2003) featured Donna Summer's 'Last Dance', Natalie Cole's 'This Will Be' and Andy Gibb's 'I Just Want To Be Your Everything'. Best of all the cop shows-turned-box-office blockbusters is *Starsky & Hutch* (2004), with Ben Stiller and Owen Wilson as the title detectives, which has great fun with the fads and fashions of its '70s setting. Starsky facing a disco dance-off with a John Travolta wannabe to KC and The Sunshine Band's 'That's The Way I Like It' and his undercover disguise in *Easy Rider* biker drag being pure Village People hits the spot.

Charlie's Angels: Producers: Leonard Goldberg, Drew Barrymore and Nancy Juvonen. Director: McG. Writers: Ryan Rowe, Ed Solomon and John August based on the TV series created by Ivan Goff and Ben Roberts. Starring Cameron Diaz, Drew Barrymore, Lucy Liu, Bill Murray, Sam Rockwell, Tim Curry and John Forsythe. 98 minutes.

PODIUM (2004)

One of the biggest French-language box-office hits of all time is this absolutely delightful tribute to the sequinned disco spectacle that was Gallic pop phenomenon Claude François. The French Elvis, affectionately known as 'Clo-Clo' to his legions of fans, had numerous dance hits throughout the '70s until he accidentally electrocuted himself in 1978. 'Alexandrie Alexandra', 'Magnolias Forever', 'Disco Meteo', *'Laisse Une Chance à Notre Amour'* (co-written by Biddu) and *'Cette Année-Là'* (the French version of The Four Seasons hit 'Oh, What A Night') were just a few of his signature floor-fillers. He is most famous outside France for writing '*Comme D'Habitude*', which, with English lyrics by Paul Anka, became the global hymn 'My Way' for Frank Sinatra. His television specials were lavish, kitsch and glittering affairs featuring his own incredible choreography expertly mirrored by his equally famous backing dancers The Claudettes.

All this and more finds its way into Yann Moix's hilarious, witty, affectionate and moving homage in which dull bank clerk Bernard Frédéric (played by the brilliant Belgian comedian Benoît Poelvoorde) is acknowledged as the best Claude François lookalike working the nostalgia nightclub circuit. Although he promises his wife to hang up the sparkling satin outfits and tinsel tonsils, when a TV programme offers a 100,000 euro prize for the best François double, the low-rent showbiz lure proves irresistible and pretty soon he's auditioning (and screwing) Claudettes and acting like the star he thinks he's becoming. Egged on by his best friend, Couscous (Jean-Paul Rouve), himself an uproarious dead ringer for Michel Polnareff (composer of the disco soundtrack *Lipstick*), Bernard is seen singing every famous François song, plus '*Chanson Populaire*' and '*C'est Comme Ça Que L'On S'est Aimé*', before blowing the competition by crooning his wife's favourite Julien Clerc song in the enormously touching finale. Also featured on the soundtrack is Sheila's 'Spacer'. *Podium,* titled after the name of the François fanzine, is a visually perfect recreation of the François ethos, precisely summed up in the amazing opening credit sequence that gets its disco sensibility exactly right while offering much more than a knowing drenching in the era's camp glam excesses.

Podium: Producers: Olivier Delbosc and Marc Missonnier. Director: Yann Moix. Writers: Olivier Dazat, Arthur Emmanuel-Pierre and Yann Moix, based on Moix's novel. Starring Benoît Poelvoorde, Jean-Paul Rouve, Julie Depardieu, Marie Guillard and Anne Marivin. 95 minutes.

WHATEVER HAPPENED TO HAROLD SMITH? (1999)

From *Bill and Ted's Bogus Journey* director Peter Hewitt a very strange slice of dreamily imaginary disco fantasy. An unsuccessful attempt at merging a coming-of-age working-class romance with a whimsical supernatural mystery, the uneven result is heavy-handed comedy despite inspired upbeat moments. It's 1977 and *Saturday Night Fever* is all the rage in dreary Sheffield. Disco-loving teenager Vince Smith (Michael Legge) practices Travolta dance routines in his bedroom and lusts after office clerk Joanna (Laura Fraser). During the Christmas holiday Vince's eccentric father Harold (Tom Courtenay) surprises everyone with his Uri Geller-style psychic party piece and subsequently grabs tabloid headlines when a similar telekinetic display accidentally causes pacemakers to stop at an old folks home. Vince's law firm is appointed as Harold's defence counsel but that's the least of his problems. Joanna is a punk, so out goes The Bee Gees' 'Night Fever', Tina Charles's 'I Love To Love', Heatwave's 'Boogie Nights', Maxine Nightingale's 'Right Back Where You Started From' and The Real Thing's 'You To Me Are Everything' and in comes The Sex Pistols. Needless to say the clash between punk and disco tends to jar the story and exacerbate disjointed matters even further.

Whatever Happened To Harold Smith? Producers: David Brown and Ruth Jackson. Director: Peter Hewitt. Writer: Ben Steiner. Starring Tom Courtenay, Michael Legge, Laura Fraser, Stephen Fry, David Thewlis, Matthew Rhys, Lulu. 95 minutes.

We Got the Groove

THE BRITISH INVASION

Mods and rockers alike avidly watched the pop programme *Ready Steady Go* in the mid-'60s. The Independent Television network's trendy rival to the BBC's *Top Of The Pops* was the musical showcase for many emerging bands and sounds – none more so than that of Tamla Motown, then coming out of Detroit thanks to Berry Gordy's 'Hitsville USA' operation. Arguably, Motown would not have had the market penetration and chart success it did in the UK had not *Ready Steady Go* so effectively brought it to the Swinging '60s masses. Dusty Springfield was a huge Motown fan and she hosted two programmes devoted to the label's artists. Soon after, The Supremes, Martha Reeves and the Vandellas, The Four Tops, The Temptations and Little Stevie Wonder were featuring in the Top 10 with such classic songs as 'Baby Love', 'Dancing In The Streets', 'It's The Same Old Song', 'Beauty Is Only Skin Deep' and 'Uptight'.

Early fans of soul and R&B instantly adopted the uptown sophistication of Motown and, suitably inspired and fired up, looked elsewhere for similar music to excite their jaded palettes. The Stax and Atlantic labels quickly filled the gap but there came a time when mere chart hits weren't enough to satisfy the soul seekers' growing addiction. Devotees began to realise that the prominent soul labels only scratched the surface of the burgeoning genre. Lurking beneath every 'Stop In The Name Of Love' and 'Jimmy Mack' was a wealth of obscure material from cult artists produced on sniff-of-a-shoestring budgets by tiny independent record labels. And the fans couldn't wait to track them all down!

As interest in little-known and criminally ignored soul 45s became a hip epidemic, specialist venues started opening up to let the ardent fan listen to them in the company of like-minded groovers. Because the music of Sly and the Family Stone and James Brown dominated the early funk-centred commercial London scene, the clubs playing obscurities by Levi Jackson, Jimmy Thomas, P.P. Arnold and Paula Parfitt tended to be north of Watford. And so the name Northern Soul was coined.

Soon the music, the lifestyle, the look (polo shirts and flares) and the clubs became legendary. There was the Twisted Wheel in Manchester, the Golden Touch at Turnstall in Stoke-on-Trent, the Mecca Ballroom in Blackpool and, most famous of all, the Wigan Casino. At the height of Northern Soul's popularity in the early-'70s, the Casino, with its sprung wooden dance floor, boasted a membership of over a hundred thousand people. And they queued for ages to get in, all armed with insignia-covered sports bags containing the vital survival kit of towel, talcum powder and a spare top to change into for the journey home.

Deejays like Ian Levine and Simon Soussan would control the thousands of sweaty, amphetamine-fuelled, gyrating bodies doing acrobatic movements and elaborate spins with rediscovered singles from unknowns ('I'll Hold You' by Frankie and Johnny), fading '60s stars ('Stop And You Will Become Aware' by Helen Shapiro) and soul survivors ('Movin' Away' by Kenny Lynch). The common denominator in each single played on the Northern Soul circuit was the contagious 4/4 beat as promoted by the in-house Tamla Motown sound. In the mid-'70s, as the famous clubs began to close (usually having been busted for drugs), Northern Soul found itself allied to the emerging disco movement because the sound was practically identical. Many Northern Soul deejays and artists glided into disco precisely because of this serendipitous convergence.

One of the best Northern Soul songs ever was 'Baby I Don't Need Your Love' by The Chants, a galvanising late-'60s cut on the RCA label. Styling themselves on The Temptations, The Chants hailed from Liverpool and were fronted by brothers Chris and Eddie Amoo. But as their singles continually missed the charts, despite huge critical acclaim, they decided to disband the group, freshen up their satin-suit image, and start again from scratch. The result was The Real Thing with the Amoo brothers being joined by group members Ray Lake and Dave Smith. After making their initial appearance on the ITV talent show *Opportunity Knocks,* The Real Thing grabbed the attention of Tony Hall, a former Radio Luxembourg deejay, who quickly secured them a recording deal with the Pye label. 'You To Me Are Everything', their first single release, raced to the top of the British charts in June 1976 where it stayed for three weeks. Subsequent soft disco releases followed – 'Can't Get By Without You' and 'You'll Never Know What You're Missing' – until 'Let's Go Disco', 'Can You Feel The Force' and 'Boogie Down (Get Funky Now)' secured proper dance floor credibility for The Real Thing.

Another popular Northern Soul track was 'Serving A Sentence Of Life' by Carl Douglas. This 1968 B-side on the United Artists label had attracted attention and secured Douglas the job of singing on the soundtrack of the Richard Roundtree movie *Embassy* (1972) composed by soon-to-be disco guru Biddu. The Indian-born maestro was searching for a singer to record a new song written by Larry Weiss entitled 'I Want To Give You Everything' and remembered the Jamaican-born Douglas. They struck a lucrative deal. If Douglas sang the song, he would supply the B-side for the proposed single.

One of the six songs Douglas suggested to fit the B-side bill was 'Kung Fu Fighting', which was geared around motifs from the popular Bruce Lee martial arts Hong Kong movies that were cleaning up at the box office at that time. The song was recorded in ten minutes, Pye loved it, flipped it to the A-side and, thanks to extensive disco promotion, the single hit No. 1 in the British charts in October 1974. It became an American No. 1 in December the same year. 'Dance The Kung Fu' was the next release from Douglas but the identikit cash-in failed to match the chart or disco success of his first sterling effort and the singer's one-hit-wonder status was assured.

Biddu would revive the careers of many other Northern Soul artists through disco reorientation. Jimmy James and the Vagabonds, who had a 1968 hit with 'Red Red Wine', resurfaced courtesy of Biddu, firstly in 1972 with the flop 'A Man Like Me', then more successfully in 1976 with the disco smashes 'I'll Go Where Your Music Takes Me' and 'Now Is The Time'.

But the biggest disco star Biddu created was British diva Tina Charles. The diminutive songstress had been plucked from the lineup of 5000 Volts after they had scored a Top 10 hit with 'I'm On Fire'. Without Charles, the session group had a further chart hit, 'Dr Kiss Kiss'. Biddu had just had a major disco instrumental hit with 'Summer of '42' when he produced 'You Set My Heart On Fire' for Charles. Despite gaining a great deal of play on Britain's gay disco circuit, the track failed to ignite popular interest. It was their next collaboration, 'I Love To Love (But My Baby Just Loves to Dance)', which hit the disco target. The 100bpm shuffler, written by James Bolden and Jack Robinson, took off like a rocket and stormed to the top of the British charts. It has since become one of the most familiar British disco hits thanks to endless remixes and reissues.

Charles's cut-glass voice, backed by Biddu's perky production, continued to set dance floors alight with 'Love Me Like A Lover', 'Dance Little Lady Dance', 'Dr Love', 'Love Bug

– Sweets For My Sweet' and her version of the Jimmy James hit 'I'll Go Where Your Music Takes Me'. 'Disco Love' and 'Halfway To Paradise' stretched the Biddu formula to breaking point but Charles's vocal punch was unmistakable and she worked hard on each song. It was her commitment to the melody of 'I Love To Love' that made it such a disco evergreen. The only other female singer to challenge Charles for the Queen of British Disco crown was Kelly Marie, whose 1980 No. 1 hit 'Feels Like I'm In Love' is another standard from the era which refuses to die.

Ian Levine was one of the most visible Northern Soul deejays. Although it would be in the '80s that Levine (with his partner Fiachra Trench) would make his strongest musical impact by virtually creating the HI-NRG genre with the Evelyn Thomas anthem 'High Energy', he did make an indelible mark on disco. His greatest disco achievement was with Barbara Pennington's 'Twenty Four Hours A Day', a brilliantly crafted paean to hot-and-heavy romance '70s-style. Levine also hit the spot with 'Cloudburst' and 'Never Let Go' by Eastbound Expressway, and 'Midnight In Manhattan' and 'New York's On Fire' by Seventh Avenue. He would loyally propel each of his disco acts into the HI-NRG boom years with varying degrees of success. Cult singer James Wells also found himself the recipient of major disco attention with his Levine-produced album, *My Claim To Fame*.

One of the artists Levine would victoriously turn into a gay diva in the '80s was Miquel Brown, singer of the infamous cruise cut 'So Many Men, So Little Time'. Brown, the mother of Sinitta ('So Macho'), had a brief taste of disco fame with her 12-inch release 'Symphony Of Love' and 'The Night They Invented Disco'. Fifteen minutes of British disco fame were also awarded to Gonzalez with 'I Haven't Stopped Dancing Yet', The Dooleys with 'Wanted', Liquid Gold with 'Dance Yourself Dizzy' and the American favourite 'My Baby's Baby', Dance People with 'Dance The Night Away', Family Tree with 'The

Caves', Gene Farrow with 'Move Your Body/Hey You Should Be Dancing', Rokotto with their *Boogie On Up* album, The Nolans with 'I'm In The Mood For Dancing' and The Players Association with their jazz-funk-disco entries, produced by Chris Hill, 'Turn The Music Up', 'Born To Dance' and 'We Got The Groove'.

The British-based band Heatwave comprised three natives of Dayton, Ohio – Johnny Wilder, his brother Keith, and Billy Jones – alongside Roy Carter and Rod Temperton from England, Mario Montese from Spain and Ernest Berger from Czechoslovakia. After releasing two so-so singles in Britain ('Ain't No Half Stepping' and 'Super Soul Sister'), their American record label Epic heard 'Boogie Nights' and decided it could go the disco distance. Which is precisely what it did on both sides of the Atlantic. The soul ballad 'Always And Forever' followed that smash hit in America only. In Britain, Heatwave continued to release dance-orientated material and scored again with 'Too Hot To Handle/Slip Your Disc To This', 'The Groove Line' and 'Mind Blowing Decisions'. The latter was then remixed with 'Always And Forever' for a British Top 10 hit in 1978.

The most popular British disco group was Hot Chocolate who enjoyed eleven Top 10 hits, twenty-one Top 30 entries and enormous disco exposure during their lifespan. Originally formed in 1969, it wasn't until bald Jamaican-born lead singer Errol Brown was drafted in, quitting his mundane job at the Treasury, that The Hot Chocolate Band began their rapid rise to the top. Their first single was on The Beatles' Apple label, a reggae version of 'Give Peace A Chance', but their chart success didn't begin properly until prolific producer Mickie Most took control of their career. He shortened the group's name to Hot Chocolate and released 'Love Is Life' in 1970, which reached No. 6.

Their first stab at dance music was 'Disco Queen' in 1975, followed by the ever-popular 'You Sexy Thing', 'So You Win Again', 'Every 1's A Winner', 'Mindless Boogie', 'No Doubt

About It' and 'Girl Crazy'. The distinctive Hot Chocolate formula of smooth, stylish, mid-tempo soul, sung with flair and pepped up with imaginative lyrics, ensured a massive and mixed following for the group, who continue to sell greatest hits albums today, thanks to the inclusion of 'You Sexy Thing' on the soundtrack of *The Full Monty* (1997).

British disco was a more precise sound than the one emanating from America. It got straight to the point, the beat was sharper and the lyrics were more hard-edged soap-opera-orientated than the bubblegum brand typified by Eurodisco. Some fitted the Eurodisco mood more than the British one, though – a perfect example being Sarah Brightman, a future Mrs Andrew Lloyd Webber, with her space-cum-*Barbarella* kitsch-fest 'I Lost My Heart To A Starship Trooper' backed by the dance troupe Hot Gossip.

Other pure pop disco entries failed to make the charts but did cause a certain flurry on British dance floors. The Pearls consisted of two '50s survivors, original members of the famed Vernons Girls. Lynn Cornell and Ann Simmons cut several bouncy sub-disco tracks including revivals of Martha Reeves and the Vandellas' 'Third Finger Left Hand', The Ronettes' 'You Came, You Saw, You Conquered' and the fine original, 'Guilty'. Their one stab at disco glory was a driving dance version of the Gus Kahn classic 'I'll See You In My Dreams'.

Polly Browne, one-time lead singer of Pickettywitch ('That Same Old Feeling'), had already had a disco flop with the Biddu composition 'Love Bug'. She also recorded the first version of 'Dance Little Lady Dance', which her record label hated, so Biddu re-recorded it with Tina Charles instead, gaining the singer a No. 6 hit. It was then that she decided to trust her own instincts and take virtually the same route as The Pearls with her disco version of the Rodgers and Hart song 'Bewitched, Bothered And Bewildered' from the musical *Pal Joey*. Released as simply 'Bewitched', Browne's gorgeously lush and silky track is the most underrated British disco record of them all.

A GUIDE TO DISCO DRUGS by Alan Jones

ACID: A full white blotter for that 'I'm entering the *Close Encounters* mothership and going through the *2001: Space Odyssey* ' feeling. Paranoia a definite possibility on the crowded dancefloor, though. **Mescaline** was even stronger.

COCAINE: A gram of white powder for that 'I Could Have Danced All Night' isolated feeling-cum-energy buzz. God knows what you'd be snorting lines up after cutting them out with credit cards in dirty toilet facilities. Nostril burn and dripping nose a dead giveaway.

MANDRAX: I'm Mandy, Fly Me! white pills. The ultimate *Valley Of The Dolls* downer for that 'Are my legs cemented to this dance floor or what?' feeling. **Quaaludes** were the American equivalent.

TUINAL: Similar to mandrax but a light-blue and reddish-orange capsule. The Tuinal Two-Step was a very lethal manoeuvre to contemplate if you were carrying drinks from the bar.

SPEED: Cocaine's poor white powder relation for that 'I Haven't Stopped Dancing Yet' feeling. The rush won't go away, however, putting a strain on nerves, and there was no point taking the amphetamine if the disco provided free snacks.

POPPERS: Break the glass capsule in your handkerchief, or open the more economical bottled version, sniff hard, experience a light-headed feeling for ten seconds, then back to normal – except you smelt like old socks for hours after! Nostril-burn warning, but the Viagra of the '70s because it was great for quick sex in the club toilets.

ANGEL DUST: Animal tranquiliser or ketamine powder. Carries such a knockout effect, you'd be rolling around on the floor for hours assuming you were still dancing upright.

MDA: Mandrax, Dexedrine and Acid mixed together in one convenient pill. The forerunner of **Ecstasy** for those special occasions and New Year's Eve disco parties where you wanted every high imaginable despite the next day's migraine-inducing low.

MARIJUANA/HASHISH: 'No, it's not the joint I'm smoking. Ottawan's "Hands Up (Give Me Your Heart)" really does have the best disco sound effects ever!'

ALCOHOL: 'A Strawberry Daiquiri, a Blue Angel and a Tom Collins, please. Don't forget the maraschino cherry and umbrella!' Anything sweet, naff and horrible was drunk in the disco era.

DISCO FACT!
Apart from Studio 54, the most exclusive, hard-to-get-into discos were Zorine's (Chicago), Doubles (in the basement of the Sherry Netherlands Hotel in Manhattan), The Daisy (Hollywood), El Privado (Los Angeles), Mumms (San Francisco) and Tramp (London).

DISCO FACT!
Famed deejay François Kevorkian (The Loft, Paradise Garage) began his career fresh off the boat from France drumming along to deejay Walter Gibbons's live mixing at Galaxy 21 in 1976. He went on to studio blend 'In The Bush' by Musique, 'Disco Circus' by Martin Circus and 'Let's Start The Dance III' by Hamilton Bohannon.

233

Fashion Pack

HAUTE AND LOW COUTURE TO LOOK THE PART

In the beginning, there really was polyester! Shiny floral shirts soaked with Hai-Karate aftershave were open to the waist, the surfaces catching and reflecting the revolving lights. Vinyl lime-coloured maxi-coats were shed to reveal electric-blue body-stockings or shoulder-baring dresses split up to the crotch. 'The Decade That Taste Forgot' was just that, at least during the liberating anti-fashion mid-'70s phase following the earlier Funky Chic and androgynous Glam Rock period.

'Wear what you want, where and when you want it, and do it all with maximum impact' was the order of the day. Exactly how much was too much glitter dust in the hair? How much stage blood should show through your Vivienne Westwood Sex sheer see-through black nylon T-shirt? In the pages of *Elle* and *Vogue*, glitz and nudity were acceptable. The Women's Liberation Movement might have made the miniskirt unacceptable but it did not clamp down on other displays of vulgar, often near-pornographic, dress sense.

But while the ultra-wide pointy lapels, bell-bottom jeans and other fashion violations which we now find charming and hip were certainly diffused throughout society, the burgundy pant-suit or wet-look avocado-green halter-tops were actually worn by the wilder movers and shakers only. The crowd at any

234

happening disco *circa* 1976 was a democratic mixture of show-offs, bland Annie Hall lookalikes, ethnically influenced or late-'60s counterculture types or just plain denim-wearing casuals.

From 1976 onwards club fashions became more distinct. The Peace and Love ethos was dropped as street styles gravitated towards violent punk. 'No Hope', 'Anarchy' and 'Hate' were the anti-establishment slogans now, worn on torn T-shirts with safety pins, dog collars, used tampons and visual accoutrements nicked from Naziism and sadomasochism. The world of high fashion took notice immediately. Vivienne Westwood built on her predilection for sexual fetishism as evening wear. 'Terrorist Chic' was introduced by Zandra Rhodes. The Village People made uniforms of all types de rigueur for the gay crowd. Art films like *Maîtresse* contributed to the vogue of mock-hostility and kinkiness, while fashion photographers Helmut Newton and Guy Bourdin shot portfolios of blindfolded, bound and brutalised top models in anonymous bedrooms and empty white-tiled swimming pools. Newton was hired as a consultant for the 1978 murder mystery movie *The Eyes of Laura Mars* where models in underwear pulled at each other's hair and posed to the 'whoop whoop' sounds of 'Lets All Chant' by The Michael Zager Band. The latent violence of fashion was now brought into the open and seen as liberating and subversive.

Gleaming white interiors, hi-tech living in spacious lofts and a new clean-cut modernism in clothes came into style around 1977. *Less* was definitely *more*. 'Lifestyle' was born as a catchword and the first mass-produced designer artefacts, such as Jordache and Gloria Vanderbilt jeans, became objects of desire. The name on every elegant minimalist's lips was Halston, the American designer. A permanent fixture at Studio 54 and the darling of influential magazines like *Women's Wear Daily*, he dressed well-heeled disco darlings in jersey halter-neck dresses and flowing silk caftans.

While the luminescent creations of Yves Saint Laurent or

Perry Ellis expensively exploited the eroticism of sexual ambiguity, the hardcore clubbers rubbed on musk oil and wore their jeans with Bryan Ferry-inspired plastic sandals, tennis shoes or comfortable penny loafers. Few actually heeded the advice of Sister Sledge to boogie in Halston, Gucci, Fiorucci, though the stage was already set for the Dress-for-Success uniformity of the '80s with the Fiorucci flagship store in New York's Upper East Side. The place did great business while non-stop disco music blared through two floors courtesy of the top-rated disco radio stations WBLS and WKTU. Fiorucci excelled in multi-coloured satin tube tops, blue jeans and glitter trainers.

The summer of 1978 saw everyone geared up in disco togs from head to toe – even 'Superstar Barbie' in sexy evening dress and 'Superstar Ken' in cool shades. Disco, after all, was a pure flight of fantasy, and exaggerated disco fashion was the passport to another personality altogether, if that's what you wanted. While the fashion magazines announced the safest disco look to be a navy blazer with khaki trousers for a man and a flimsy blouse with a big skirt for a woman, few settled on the better-safe-than-sorry option.

Fun was what you wanted to have and that was going to be reflected in your dress sense. Most outré of all was designer Norma Kamali''s 'diaper dresses' in either silk or terry towelling which freed the dancer's legs like a swimsuit. The casual sportswear vogue was also born during this time. Separates were cheap enough to ring the changes every day of the disco week if that was your thing, and they were lightweight and cool as you worked up a sweat. Polyester retained perspiration so cotton was the best choice. And you had to avoid leg-warmers unless your calves were slim. If you were serious about cooling down fast, the must-have gay disco prop was a fan – and the bigger the better as long as it didn't get in the way of your tambourine and whistle.

Drag was rarely seen even in the gay disco environment. If

you did dare to risk the constant stares, you knew you'd be completely ostracised by the mustachioed Village People clones who failed to see what *they* were wearing could also be termed drag of another kind. One popular gay look, mainly seen in San Francisco (where else?), were holes cut out of the seats of denim jeans in appropriate places with real flowers placed inside and their petals protruding.

Fashion magazines and books of the day fell over themselves to give their female readers disco dressing hints. Here are a few examples:

- Raid your mother's closet or the nearest charity shop for home-made disco chic. An art deco rayon scarf from the '20s is ideal.
- Head to the nearest army surplus stores for a wealth of military ideas.
- Pin cameos, brooches and war insignia on your socks. No more than six – that's bad taste.
- Take a string of beads, attach a small wallet for your money and keys, and sling it across your chest.
- Update a favourite outfit by attaching loads of multi-coloured scarves or handkerchiefs with safety pins.
- Thread coloured ribbons through your trouser bottoms and draw them in.
- Crochet your own disco bag. Why not crochet five for the all-important exaggerated look?
- Brighten up your trainers by dyeing the shoelaces.
- Wear a jacket four times too big and roll up the sleeves.
- Don't sport a baseball cap on that frizzy permed hair. A safari hat will set the style off much better.
- If you have a tan, show it off – don't cover it up. Short shorts and a bra top in a flowered print are perfect for the Body Beautiful look.

- Never, ever wear a slogan T-shirt.
- Never, ever wear the same outfit you wore to work to the disco.
- The shine in your disco dressing should come from your accessories and make-up only – never wear glitter or day-glo clothes.
- Black on black is a classy combination no matter what.

Ostentatious jewellery was no good on the disco floor – swinging medallions caused too many accidents – but earrings, toe-rings and masses of bracelets were in. As for make-up, disco lights were harsh, so the natural look was a mistake. To avoid looking washed-out or pasty-faced, women were advised to pile on the mascara (very necessary under strobe-lights), define their lips with crayon, and reconstruct their faces with a darker base than normal. It was Hollywood, it was Joan Crawford, and make-up always had to be applied under the harshest light in the bathroom to look effective in the disco glare. And if you couldn't be bothered making the effort, a turban and sunglasses was a viable alternative. Rich disco chicks had other ultraglamorous options available to them at the time. Disco Lashes were synthetic false eyelashes incorporating gold, silver, purple, turquoise and pink glitter, and gold and diamond fingernails (at £20 and £300 each respectively) also became a rage.

But despite all the admonitions to create your own image, consider looks you'd never usually go for and never follow any accepted fashion, the disco sheep did exactly the opposite. The cliché look for her was hot pants, a short feathery jacket, gold lurex tights, silver platform sandals and loads of black eyeliner, with body glitter on any remaining exposed part of the anatomy. For him it was high-waisted flared trousers, skin-tight at the crotch, a shirt with a round, flowing collar, wide-lapelled blue jacket and cream snakeskin platform boots. Hair for women was modelled on *Charlie's Angels* star Farrah Fawcett-Majors, for men on footballer Kevin Keegan. And her fragrance was Charlie, while his aftershave was Brut.

DISCO FACT!
Sharon Lee, deejay at Miami's Scaramouche disco, was picked by *Billboard* magazine as the top female deejay in the Unitd States in 1977.

DISCO FACT!
Disco owners offered rewards to anyone who ensured a major celebrity would turn up at their establishment. Cher and Sylvester Stallone were worth $100 cash-in-hand.

Do or Die

CELEBRITIES ABOARD THE FUNK TRAIN

One of the most extraordinary side-effects of the *Saturday Night Fever*-crazed summer of 1978 was how many completely unexpected – and unlikely – artists decided to jump aboard the disco bandwagon. Suddenly, after three years of slagging off the growing genre, they decided that if it was okay for The Bee Gees, it was okay for them. The result of this rush into recording studios to prop up questionable material with floods of beats-per-minute provided some truly unique listening experiences from both ends of the taste spectrum.

Occasionally a minor gem was cut by accident by producers who didn't know their A&Rs from their elbow tambourines. All disco music sounded the same, they thought, so how hard could it be to copy? They soon learned that it took a lot of expertise to craft a dance classic and one or two would rise to the challenge. Some, indeed, achieved much-loved cult status. Others, however, were absolutely hopeless farragoes and led directly to the 'Disco Sucks' backlash. When high-profile rock stars like Elton John, Rod Stewart and The Rolling Stones entered the fray, you knew something had to give.

Most of the songs listed below were released in limited edition extended 12-inch disco mixes or for promo purposes only. Exceptional efforts are starred or commented on:

BRYAN ADAMS (Canadian rock star) – 'Let Me Take You Dancing'

PETER ALLEN (Broadway and cabaret artist/Liza Minnelli's ex-husband) – 'Don't Wish Too Hard', 'I Go To Rio'*

HERB ALPERT (A&M label owner, Tijuana Brass man and discoverer of The Carpenters) – 'Rise'

FRANKIE AVALON ('60s teen idol/*Beach Party* movie star) – 'You're A Miracle', 'Venus'*. Producer Billy Terrell brilliantly updated Frankie's 1959 chart topper 'Venus' with taste and imagination and provided the singer with a major disco cult smash.

BURT BACHARACH (king of easy-listening) – 'When You Bring Your Sweet Love To Me'

SHIRLEY BASSEY (gay icon/*Goldfinger chanteuse*) – 'This Is My Life (La Vita)'*, 'Copacabana (At The Copa)'

BAY CITY ROLLERS ('70s Scottish teen idols) – 'Don't Stop The Music'

THE BEACH BOYS ('60s surf superstars) – 'Here Comes The Night'

JANE BIRKIN (actress/*chanteuse* muse of Serge Gainsbourg) – 'Lolita Go Home'

BLONDIE (punk new-wavers) – 'Heart Of Glass'

MIGUEL BOSE (Spanish singer and movie star – *Suspiria, High Heels*) – 'Omni Padme Um'* and 'Super Superman' from the *Chicas* album. The latter has Miguel asking a sexy guy to follow him to Studio 54.

CLAUDIA CARDINALE (*Once Upon A Time In The West* Italian actress) – 'Sun, I Love You'*. Sexy Eurodisco par excellence

ADRIANO CELENTANO (The Elvis of Italy) – 'When Love . . .'

MARILYN CHAMBERS ('70s porno actress, star of *Behind The Green Door* and the cult horror flick *Rabid*) – 'Benihana'

CHICAGO ('70s Super Group/'If You Leave Me Now') – 'Streetplayer'

VLADIMIR COSMA (French film composer) – '*L'Animal*'*. The bouncy theme tune to the 1977 action adventure film

L'Animal starring Raquel Welch and Jean-Paul Belmondo.

CREEDENCE CLEARWATER REVIVAL (John Fogerty/'Bad Moon Rising') – 'I Heard It Through The Grapevine'

NEIL DIAMOND (*Jonathan Livingstone Seagull* composer, *The Jazz Singer* remake star and pop legend) – 'The Dancing Bumblebee/Bumblebee Boogie'*

DOOBIE BROTHERS (Michael McDonald and Co) – 'What A Fool Believes'

BRITT EKLAND (Celebutante Bond Girl/*The Man With The Golden Gun*) – 'Do It To Me (Once More With Feeling)'

DAVID ESSEX ('70s British rocker/ *That'll Be The Day* film actor) – 'Oh What A Circus'*. Disco funeral rite from *Evita*

SERGE GAINSBOURG (Late French icon, sexual harrasser of Whitney Houston on prime-time television chat show) – 'Sex, Sea and Sun' from the film *Les Bronzés*

THE GLITTER BAND (Gary's glam rock gang) – 'Makes You Blind'

BOB GUILLAUME (Benson in the cult TV sitcom *Soap*) – 'I, Who Have Nothing'

BOBBY HEBB (US vocalist) –'Sunny 76' (an update of his own 1966 hit)

ELTON JOHN (singer at Princess Diana's funeral) – 'Victim Of Love'*

TOM JONES (Welsh Tiger) – 'Don't Cry For Me Argentina'. Forcefully bellowed, fully orchestrated cabaret disco.

KISS (heavy metal band in outlandish make-up) – 'I Was Made For Loving You'*

CHERYL LADD (Kris Monroe in *Charlie's Angels*) – 'Missing You'

LULU (singer of 'Shout', guest in *Absolutely Fabulous*) – 'I Love To Boogie'

HERBIE MANN (jazz great) – 'Superman', 'Yellow Fever', 'Hi-Jack'

ANN-MARGRET (Las Vegas songstress/star of *Bye Bye Birdie*, *The Swinger*, *Carnal Knowledge*) – 'Love Rush'*

242

AL MARTINO ('Spanish Eyes') – 'Volare'

JOHNNY MATHIS (international crooner) – 'Begin The Beguine'*

MAUREEN McGOVERN (singer of the theme song from *The Poseidon Adventure*) – 'I'm Happy Just To Dance With You'

ROD McKUEN (poet) – *'Amor Amor'*, *'Mon Amour Mon Ami'*

ETHEL MERMAN (Broadway and movie musical star) – 'There's No Business Like Show Business', 'Everything's Coming Up Roses', 'I Get A Kick Out Of You', 'Something For The Boys', 'Some People', 'Alexander's Ragtime Band', 'I Got Rhythm'. The nadir of the disco era sung by an 80-year-old movie diva. What should have been a marvellous concept was the worst release of 1979. La Merman murdered her best-loved standards and *Gypsy* show tunes, and the arrangements by Peter Matz missed the disco mark by miles. Absolutely dreadful and not even enjoyable on a kitsch level.

BETTE MIDLER (actress and gay diva) – 'My Knight In Black Leather'*, 'Married Men', 'Strangers In The Night'

LIZA MINNELLI (*Cabaret* star/Judy Garland's daughter) – 'Tropical Nights'

RITA MORENO (*West Side Story/The Ritz* movie, dancer and stage actress) – 'Have A Good Time' (sung with D.C. LaRue)

ENNIO MORRICONE (*A Fistful Of Dollars* film composer) – 'Come Maddalena'*. Souped-up version of Morricone's theme from the 1971 movie *Maddalena*.

MICKEY MOUSE (Walt Disney superstar) – 'Disco Mickey Mouse', 'Welcome To Rio', 'The Greatest Dancer', 'Zip-A-Dee-Doo-Dah', 'Macho Duck', 'Mousetrap', 'Watch Out For Goofy', 'It's A Small World', 'Chim Chim Chere-ee'*. Trust the Mouse House to cash in on the disco craze! But arranger Dennis Burnside did a great job with this mix of pop hits, Disney favourites and original tunes. 'Welcome To Rio' is especially notable. The *Mickey Mouse Disco* album was also turned into a half-hour animated TV special.

DAVID NAUGHTON (American sitcom actor/star of *An*

American Werewolf In London) – 'Makin' It' (the theme from his sitcom of the same name)

YOKO ONO (Conceptual artist) –'Walking On Thin Ice'

TONY ORLANDO (Dawn/'Bless You') – 'Don't Let Go'

DONNY OSMOND ('Love Me For A Reason' Osmond family member) – 'I Follow The Music'

DOLLY PARTON (larger-than-life Country and Western singer) – 'Baby I'm Burnin''

CLIFF RICHARD (perennial teen idol) – 'We Don't Talk Anymore'

THE ROLLING STONES (British super group) – 'Miss You'

DEMIS ROUSSOS (caftanned Greek star/'Forever and Ever') – 'L.O.VE.'

CAROLE BAYER SAGER (composer/lyricist of 'A Groovy Kind Of Love' and the musical *They're Playing Our Song*) – 'I Don't Wanna Dance No More'

MONGO SANTAMAR1A (Latin percussionist) – 'Watermelon Man'

SANTANA (Woodstock survivors) – 'One Chain'

FRANK SINATRA (father of Nancy) – 'Night And Day'

SPARKS (Ron and Russell Mael/'This Town Ain't Big Enough For The Both Of Us') – 'Beat The Clock'*

DUSTY SPRINGFIELD (legendary '60s diva) – 'That's The Kinda Love I've Got For You'

ILONA STALLER aka LA CICCIOLINA (Ex-member of the Italian Parliament, porn star, ex-wife of artist Jeff Koons) – 'Save The Last Dance For Me'

STEELY DAN (the 'Do It Again' band) – 'Glamour Profession' from the *Gaucho* album

ROD STEWART ('Maggie May') – 'Do Ya Think I'm Sexy?'

SLY STONE ('60s funkster) – 'Dance To The Music'

BONNIE TYLER (Welsh singer/'Holding Out For A Hero') – 'Married Men'

RICK WAKEMAN ('70s keyboard artist) – 'Rhapsody In Blue'. Down there with Ethel Merman as one of the worst disco records in history.

ANDY WILLIAMS (TV personality and MOR singer) – 'Love Story (Where Do I Begin?)'*. The theme from the popular film romance *Love Story*

WINGS (Paul McCartney etc.) – 'Goodnight Tonight'

FRANK ZAPPA (hippie iconoclast) – 'Sheik Yerbouti'*

Queen of Clubs

STUDIO 54

It was the Eighth Wonder of the World. A mecca of madness, mayhem and magic. Camelot for both the glitterati and the paparazzi. It was a Manhattan discothèque situated at 254 West 54th Street, between Seventh and Eighth Avenues, and for three years it was the most talked-about, written-about and shocked-about venue in the universe. Everyone wanted to go to Studio 54. They read about it in the tabloids and saw photos of the endless stream of celebrities parading through its burgundy-carpeted lobby lined with twenty-foot-tall fig trees. They heard about the bacchanalian drug-fuelled orgies in the dark off-limits areas and the outrageous no-expense-spared theme parties. And the icing on the cake? it was all being done to the hypnotic, thrilling and soothing throb of the loudest, proudest disco music.

If *Saturday Night Fever* was the film that epitomised the disco era, Studio 54 was its nightclub equivalent. In truth, despite expert mixing by resident deejay Richie Kaczor, there were far better places for the avid disco dancer to go and twirl the night away under state-of-the-art light shows – 12 West, Infinity and the Ice Palace, for example. But Studio 54 was Shangri-La for the crème de la crème, the terminal hipster, star-spotter, voyeur and poser. Never before, and never again, would the superstar famous mix with the general public in such harmonious accord at the altar of disco. Because, once past the notorious velvet ropes and through those imposing entrance doors, time stood still. You were forever young and, despite that old Scarlett O'Hara adage, tomorrow was *not* another day, it was always the perpetual fabulous present.

It all began with Steve Rubell, the son of a Brooklyn postal worker who doubled as a tennis pro when his post office shift finished at four o'clock in the afternoon. Although the dark-skinned, brown-eyed Rubell did become a ranked tennis player to please his father, he was never really enamoured with the game — or with the business courses he took at Syracuse University which he always said taught him absolutely nothing. In 1971 Rubell. took his first job running a Wall Street brokerage office, but didn't like it and quit. He borrowed $13,000 from his flummoxed parents and opened up a Steak Loft Restaurant in Rockville Centre, Long Island.

His partner in the venture was real-estate agent Ian Schrager whom Rubell had met at university and was surprised to learn had been raised in the same Brooklyn area. By 1974 the dynamic duo had four of the family-style restaurants, but it wasn't enough for Rubell who wanted bigger and better things out of life. As part of this burning desire for self-improvement and social acceptability, he turned one of the Steak Lofts in Douglaston, Queens, into a discothèque called the Enchanted Garden to cash in on the burgeoning disco vogue. Noisy customers and annoyed locals soon forced the venue to close its doors, but it was too late — Rubell had been bitten and smitten by the disco bug.

Over in Manhattan events were taking place that would have an amazing effect on the direction of Rubell's life. Hamburg-born socialite Uva Harden had always wanted to open a nightclub that would stop the world dead. The male model, once married to actress Barbara Carrera, found an empty building on West 54th Street and thought it would be perfect for the job. Built in 1927 and opened in the early days of the Depression as the San Carlo Opera House, it was converted into the Casino de Paris theatre restaurant in the '30s and finally turned into a CBS TV studio the following decade. The toprated shows *What's My Line?*, *The $64,000 Question* and *Captain Kangaroo* were all made at what was then dubbed Studio 53 because of an entrance on West 53rd Street.

When CBS relocated to Hollywood, the building was left derelict until Harden took out a lease on the property in 1976 and set about transforming it into a lavish discothèque. He suddenly lost his financial backing for the project, however, and in a panic turned to his friend, party promoter Carmen D'Alessio. When informed of the alarming cash situation, D'Alessio introduced Harden to Rubell and Schrager whom she had befriended after they had hired her to throw a theme party at the Enchanted Garden. In the ensuing negotiations, Harden was eventually paid off as Rubell and Schrager raised the $400,000 capital investment by splitting it three ways with their silent partner, discount retail businessman Jack Dushey.

248

Studio 54 was then conceived and designed within six weeks by gay Rubell. and straight Schrager to be the most exclusive and glamorous nightclub in history. The baroque fittings of the original interior were saved, restored and embellished. The 5,400 square-foot dance floor was blitzed with an array of 54 different lighting effects ranging from fluttering fabric flames, floating aluminium strips, neon wheels, strobes and towers of flickering multi-coloured lights that would rise and descend onto the thousand-plus dancers who would eventually fill the floor to bursting point. Blizzards of plastic snow would be blown through the entire area and balloons would fall at certain times too. Most notorious of all was the Man in the Moon figure which would be lowered at various key junctures during the nightly frenzy to sniff up the flashing white contents of a silver spoon. This was the perfect example of how Rubell would continually flout convention and display the club's illegal peccadillos for all the world to see. This daring strategy would eventually lead to his downfall, but in the beginning it was deliciously confrontational risk-taking.

The disco opened on the chilly evening of 26 April 1977 and immediately took the nightclub world by storm. It may only have been a club but the incandescent aura and pop culture craziness surrounding Studio 54 stamped it as beyond special. It also marked the first time ever that celebrity photos would appear on the front page of the tabloids for no other reason than that they were there. Bianca Jagger galloping through the club on a white stallion at her exclusive birthday party was just the first of many eye-opening photo opportunities mere mortals lapped up while making plans to infiltrate the hallowed halls of the disco shrine ourselves.

It wasn't easy. Studio 54 was the first disco to instigate the much-hated selective door policy just because you turned up with your $10 entrance fee didn't automatically mean you would get in. You had to stand behind the intimidating velvet ropes while doorman supremo Marc Benecke, or his substitute AI Corley (future *Dynasty* soap star and HI-NRG singer of 'Square Rooms'), decided whether you were beautiful enough, outrageous enough or famous enough to actually get in. Rubell called it 'tossing the salad'. He didn't want any one particular group to dominate the dance floor and would instruct his door staff to limit the blacks, the drag queens, the celebrities, the straights, the models, the bridge-and-tunnel brigade, the weirdos and the elderly accordingly.

If you were Andy Warhol, Liza Minnelli, Truman Capote, Halston, Calvin Klein or Diana Ross, entrance would be automatic. The velvet ropes would also part like the Red Sea for Moses if you were one of the self-styled fantasy folk who counted in their ranks Disco Sally, the 78-year-old former lawyer and accomplished hustle dancer, Spanish catwalk transvestite Potassa or skating starlet Rollerina. Everyone else, 'the grey people' as Rubell. described them, would have to queue up and take their chances. Unshaven? Forget it! Wearing a polyester twin set? Leave now and never return! Even Cher was refused entrance one historic night. Rubell knew that the more exclusive he made the club, the more desperate people would become to get in. He also knew that the crowd milling about outside the club was as much a part of the disco theatre as the élite show inside. The whole nightmare scenario was neatly summed up in 'Dario, Can You Get Me Into Studio 54?' sung by Kid Creole and the Coconuts and later covered by Dana and Gene.

Couples were known to have split up in their desperation to get into Studio 54. There's the famous story about the Just Marrieds who arrived and Benecke said he would only let the man in. And the groom instantly left his new wife out in the cold! Even worse, she waited for him to come back out. Some of the doormen would use their quite fascist power to mean extremes, like the time two girls were forced to strip off in the middle of winter and had to be taken to hospital with frost-bitten nipples. Lawsuits were served against the doormen by disgruntled Wall Street bankers who had been turned away. People climbed down the walls of the neighbouring building to sneak in through open skylights. Someone even tried to crawl through an air duct, got stuck, and was found dead weeks later after the smell of his decomposing body wafted through the building. Disco plebs were literally dying to get in. The whole phenomenon was turned into a cool joke when the club entered the clothing market and advertised their denim jeans line with the blurb 'Now everyone can get into Studio 54 . . . jeans'.

But once inside Studio 54's inner sanctum, you took your place in the most exclusive party in the world. You were past the embarrassing Guardian of the Gate/velvet rope initiation test and you were going to let everyone in the disco circus know it. And if you weren't in the proper Roman Orgy mood, Rubell was on hand with the party favours to make sure the night went with a bang. Whatever your vice, the disco maître

250

d' would supply it. Drugs? Take your pick from quaaludes, joints, Angel Dust, heroin and cocaine. Try the coke – in 1977 people told you it was proven to be non-addictive.

Sex? Either pick up a stoned date on the dance floor (just saying 'Hi' would get you into their pants), or ask one of the gay, straight and bisexual stripped-to-the-waist bar staff to accompany you to the darkened balcony area where you could get it on while surveying the seething spectacle below. Not intimate enough? Follow the celebrities into the securely monitored basement where you wouldn't be bothered by prying eyes or the undercover photographer. Rubell knew sex was as much a part of the design of Studio 54 as the lighting, and did everything to encourage it. Even in the bathroom cubicles where you either shot up or got fucked over the toilet.

Studio 54 also became famous for its theme parties. There was no limit on how much Rubell and Schrager would spend to transform their club into a totally different environment. There was a *Folies Bergère* Night complete with jock-strapped motorcyclists and semi-nude trapeze artists. There was the time when successful entrants were greeted by twenty violin players serenading them as they walked through the inviting corridor. Then there was the time the entire place was turned into a Shanghai street for the birthday bash of Tina Chow, wife of restaurateur Michael Chow. Not to mention the gala evenings where Grace Jones, drag queen Angel Jack or the gay ballet would perform. Or the *Grease* premiere party. No one ever knew what Rubell would get up to next or the lengths he would go to in providing escapist entertainment for his members. Would it be a Rio carnival, a Hawaiian luau or an African safari? And that was part of the cool charm of the place, as Studio 54 became a Fellini-esque fantasy-land where you escaped the confusing and exhausting '70s landscape outside its swing doors.

Everyone knew it couldn't last. it was far too wonderful, far too much and far too illegal. The first inkling of impending disaster came with the puzzling knowledge that Studio 54 didn't have a permanent liquor licence. Every single day Rubell had to apply for a twenty-four-hour cabaret licence in order to serve alcohol, which was a flagrant abuse of the law in itself. Then, one day, Rubell simply forgot to get it and was immediately barred from serving alcohol, much to the horror of the club clientèle. After a celebrity support rally, Rubell's well-connected and feisty lawyer Roy Cohn found a judge to overturn the ruling. But the authorities would put the place under the closest scrutiny from then on.

They didn't have to wait too long for Rubell's next gigantically arrogant gaffe. He gave an interview to *New York Magazine* and was quoted as saying that 'The [club's] profits are astronomical. Only the Mafia does better!' That caught the attention of Frank Trattolillio of the IRS criminal division, and when an anonymous tip-off was received from a vengeful ex-employee who revealed Rubell and company were skimming money, a search warrant was issued by federal prosecutor Peter Sudler.

The raid on Studio 54 took place at 9.30 a.m. on 14 December 1978. Forty agents ransacked the place under the bewildered gaze of the assembled staff who were waiting for their paychecks. Double sets of accounts books were found, as were sackloads of money secretly stashed all over the place. Then Schrager turned up with an envelope of cocaine in his briefcase and both his and Rubell's fate were sealed. Not even the demonically clever Cohn could save them when it was revealed that they had skimmed off a third of all the takings while only paying $8,000 in income tax for the entire 1977 period.

After plea-bargaining to income tax evasion on two counts, Schrager's cocaine charge was dismissed, and both men were given three-and-a-half-year prison sentences. The authorities felt they had to make an example of the disco upstarts to the rest of the profession. On 1 February 1980 Rubell and Schrager were jailed at the Metropolitan Correctional Centre – after, naturally, a fabulous Going-Away-To-Prison party at Studio 54 the night before.

Despite the fact that the owners were behind bars it was business as usual at Studio 54 – at least for a short time. By 28 February 1980, when the club's licence expired, it closed down for fifteen months. In desperate financial straits, Rubell needed to sell the club, and from prison negotiated a deal with hotel owner Mark Fleischman. For $5 million, and after agreeing to pay off the club's back taxes, Fleischman became the new owner of Studio 54 with both Rubell and Schrager retained as consultants. Transferred to Alabama's Maxwell Airforce Base to complete their sentences, Rubell and Schrager were eventually released on 21 January 1981, after being incarcerated for less than a year. This was because they co-operated with the authorities and informed on other members of the disco trade, particularly Maurice Brahms, the owner of rival club New York New York.

Life back in the disco hustle for the once-cosmic-couple-turned-hired-hands was hard. They were shunned by everyone in case they too became tainted by their bad reputations. In addition, the 'Disco is Dead' movement was gaining ground, punk was *the* happening thing downtown, the first warning signs of Aids were appearing, exhausted 24/7 revellers were staying at home and there was a clear shift in popular culture away from the devil-may-care hedonism of the '70s. Initially, crowds still came to Studio 54 out of curiosity and, because it was now a business and not a lifestyle, everyone was let in. Soon the magic faded, the stars stopped coming and the '80s dulled its lustre. Mounting lawsuits meant the club really couldn't stay open anyway, and it closed down for good after Fleischman sold the lease to a consortium convinced they could still sell the name. Three months after that transaction, Studio 54 was no more.

Rubell and Schrager tried to recreate the Studio 54

atmosphere and mystique with the Palladium, which opened its doors in 1985. But it never caught on and, for the mainstream clubber, the disco era was well and truly over. Rubell and Schrager moved on to make mountains of legal money in the niche-market hotel business. With Fleischman's help and know-how they opened a host of up-market, hip hostelries like Morgans and The Royalton in New York. Rubell died of Aids complications on 25 July 1989, at the age of forty-five. His gravestone has 'The Quintessential New Yorker' carved on it and everyone who attended his funeral had to pass through carefully placed velvet ropes. Schrager is still active in the hotel industry.

Studio 54 was the roof of the disco world, a mega firework that lit up the Manhattan skies with an incandescent sparkle before spectacularly fizzling out in the hypocritical glare of the media spotlight which had done so much to create it. Its epitaph is the theme disco of the same name in Las Vegas, scattered lyrics in popular songs of the era ('Fashion Pack' by Amanda Lear, 'Le Freak' by Chic), Anthony Haden-Guest's book *The Last Party*, and the movie *54*. But for those who danced, gasped, gawped, snorted and had sex there, Studio 54 was an experience that will never be forgotten and the progenitor of an abundance of urban disco legends.

DISCO FACT!
The porn industry cashed in on the disco craze with *Saturday Night Beaver* starring top stud John Holmes, Angel and Vanessa D'Oro.

DISCO FACT!
In 1978 there were over 1,500 registered mobile deejays working in America who charged up to $300 to bring the disco environment into your home.

* That's Where the Happy People Go

THE BEST CLUBS IN THE WORLD

What was it exactly that made a particular discothèque popular? Was it the fact that it was almost impossible to find? Or that it was hard to get in? Or that it played the most up-to-date imports? Or for the price of admission it laid on snacks, candy and fruit salads on vast trestle tables lined up against the walls? Manhattan's 12 West and London's Embassy were big on that particular trend.

It's often said that disco was more suited to New York, primarily because the phenomenon required the combination of energy, people, music and fashion then present in happening Manhattan to produce what became a social necessity in the '70s. But other cultures were also inspired by the dance-hall memories of earlier years and discos around the world became the modern version of a central location for socialising and forgetting the cares of the day. Designed to relieve the pressure of life and produce a mental high through lights and music, discos created a fantasy land where each individual was the entertainer.

Everybody had their own favourite disco, and for many different reasons: it was the easiest place to score; the light show was amazing; the drinks were a reasonable price; it had a friendly atmosphere; you were dating the barman; it stayed open until the early hours of the morning; it was the hot-spot *du jour*. Whatever the reason, as long as you could dance in conducive surroundings to music with a powerful beat pounding at you from a state-of-the-art speaker system, most discophiles, disco sluts and disco queens were happy. But dancing in the following discos was the cherry on the icing on the top of the cream cake.

THE CITY
Along with Italian restaurants, where gesticulations and dialects fly faster than the pizza dough, and with strip joints and funky cafès dating back to the Beatnik era, the North Beach area of San Francisco wowed the disco crowds with two popular venues. The larger Dance Your Ass off on Columbus Avenue, near Washington Square Park, is gone now and a furniture store stands in its place. But people still boogie on down at 1031 Kearny Street where The City club used to lure in the trendier contingent.

Back in those days, poseurs, spike-haired scene-makers in punk regalia and potential Armistead Maupin characters swarmed around the huge oval bar (made of illuminated glass tiles) looking out for celebrities. The dance floor jumped with mainly straight couples having riotous fun, doing the hustle any which way they could. Straight clubs like The City, or Disco International in nearby Oakland, were looser and less concerned with the very latest New York moves than their Los Angeles competition – and much more racially integrated. In 1978 Grace Jones's 'Do Or Die' could easily be followed by either Love and Kisses tracks or 'You And l' by Rick James. The City's mega-relaxed atmosphere was one of the best things about it.

THE EMBASSY
Immortalised on film in the video for Sylvester's 'You Make Me Feel (Mighty Real)', The Embassy's appeal stretched so far

across the board it was incredible. Aristos who couldn't face Annabel's up the road in Berkeley Square, low-rent starlets thrown out of Tramp around the corner, gays on the lookout for something a bit less posy than Maunk-berrys across the Dilly in Jermyn Street or Napoleon's a few streets away, and horsy Sloane Rangers all mingled together in happy harmony in this fondly remembered venue.

This was especially so on a Sunday afternoon for the all-day, all-night tea dances. For an entrance fee of £4 you could stay as long as you wanted, drink what you liked, eat as much from the buffet table as you could and dance yourself dizzy to the music – and then start all over again! The best position to be in was hunched around a table perched on the mini-balcony (where the Palm Court orchestra used to play back when the ritzy place was a supper club) so you could survey everyone on the dance floor. And make sure they saw you there, too, of course.

Situated at the bottom of Old Bond Street, the entrance to The Embassy was quite a way back from the main road and many people trying to find it would walk past it in a perplexed daze. But once through the discreet doors, the medium-sized ballroom offered a warm invitation. Its nearest equivalent today would be the Café de Paris in Coventry Street. The Embassy had one of the greatest club atmospheres in London during the disco heyday. You could walk in alone and know everybody there. That was its greatest attribute. Everyone was friendly, there was no attitude and people gathered there because they were genuinely in love with the music. This was where you came to share secret conspiratorial nods with complete strangers when a favourite track like 'Baby Love' by USA-European Connection began to play.

You had to step down to get onto the dance floor (that's how you could tell if someone was too stoned to pick up!) and the drinks were Up West expensive (the barmen were the first in London to wear skimpy shorts and practically nothing else). But while it was originated by fashion guru Michael Fish (the

Carnaby Street designer who made the kipper tie popular), manager Stephen Hayter eventually ran the Embassy in the manner of an old-fashioned members' club, complete with quirky affectations and fun privileges. It was always the first stop for any visiting American celebrities with nightlife on the agenda.

THE EMPIRE BALLROOM ROLLER-DISCO

Despite the fact that there was the Electric Ballroom in Camden Town, and the pre-Heaven roller-disco under the arches at Charing Cross Road, the most dedicated London skaters preferred the Empire Ballroom in Leicester Square to practically any other venue. The deluxe establishment only opened its doors on Sundays for the roller maniac. But from noon until six everybody in the roller world turned up to strut their stuff on the medium-sized dance floor. Menswear designer Paul Smith was a regular, as were many West End actors and pop stars. You had to be a member to get in (though joining was free) and the bar closed at two o'clock, but the superior lighting and comfortable surroundings made this the place to be every Sunday.

Amateurs were frowned upon as the deejay was good at picking good skating records and made sure the dance floor was constantly packed. The management went out of their way to encourage a club feel, with bottles of champagne for members' birthdays, spot speedskating prizes and other events – this was the club that premiered The Carmen Rollers' epic Christmas pantomime *Cinderoller* on 8 December 1979. Unlike the Electric Ballroom, though, where you could hire skates, you had to bring your own to the Empire.

FUNKY MARUSCHA

Studio 54 might have had all the effects money could buy plus Liz, Liza and other luminaries to look at, but Funky Maruscha had something else few clubs could offer. This old wooden fire station a good two-hour drive north of Helsinki, Finland, was situated right by a scenic lake in the middle of absolutely nowhere. You would arrive well before opening time in a car jammed with friends and nod coolly to the other devotees there weekend after weekend. Once inside, you would hit the dark, cavernous dance floor as if it was your last night on earth. Then, after hours of sweating to the hottest tracks of the summer, you would suddenly dash out into the midnight sun, rip off your clothes, run buck naked along the pier and plunge into the water. And you wouldn't be the only one. For the rest of the white night, it would be a joining of the tribes far away from civilization, rules and any inhibitions.

HEAVEN

London's premier gay disco opened on 6 December 1979 under the arches below Charing Cross station. It's still there today and remains as famous as ever. Built on the site of the former Global Village club which also contained a cinema and a performance art theatre, the site had become the Glades gay club in the mid-'70s and had then turned into a mixed roller-disco in 1978. Although roller-disco fans flocked to the place because it was open more often than the Empire in Leicester Square, it was a hopeless place to skate because the small-tiled floor made every manoeuvre a very bumpy ride indeed.

Inspired by the success of Studio 54 in New York, gay entrepreneur Jeremy Norman decided to import the grand-scale disco concept to London; he hired designer David Frost to bring his ideas of a 'Cruise Bar', 'Devil's Diner' and 'Gaming Area' up to standard. He also employed Stephen Hayter of the Embassy club in Bond Street to organise things, and the new recruit's first action was to sign up former Northern Soul deejay Ian Levine to play the hardcore American disco sounds in the cavernous dance arena.

The lighting in the dance area (surrounded by raised metallic walkways leading to three floors of smaller chill-out rooms) was created by Illusion Lighting using 600 square feet of lighting grid and featuring Atomic Balls, crystal creations that revolved inside each other and sported neon Saturn rings that chased from ball to ball. A new kind of ultra-violet light was installed which made people look attractive and so was a high-power colour floodlight system that shot brilliant single colours over the entire area. Worm Lights, a popular feature in Studio 54, were added to the overall lighting design as were lasers and spirals of light that squiggled around the dancers' feet as they moved. Upstairs in the 'Cruise Bar', a huge star pulsing with neon shone down like the light from a cathedral window over the entire area.

The sound system was by Harwell Instruments and was based on one developed for Elton John's concert tours. It was a flown system with bass horns built into the floor, and tweeter arrays overhead – hanging almost down to the dancer's head. Over £40,000 worth of air-conditioning was installed too to make sure the place was as comfortable as possible.

Hayter left soon after and in his place came David Inches who launched Heaven one cold December midnight with Dan Hartman's 'Relight My Fire'. Heaven made a huge and immediate impact on London's gay culture. At the time, the capital's gay scene was a thriving underground of cabaret camp, backroom bars (The Gigolo on the King's Road), lesbian basements (Gateways off the Kings Road) and clubs like Rod's (World's End, which became the cabaret venue Country Cousin), The Sombrero (Kensington High Street), Adams (Leicester Square) and, Heaven's biggest rival, Bang, at the corner of Tottenham Court Road and Oxford Street. Heaven gave gays their biggest meeting place in Europe and helped usher in the new era of Pink Pound confidence that was already seething under the capital's surface. The 3,500 initial members of Heaven, who paid £15 for the privilege and then £2 on the door (including two drinks), also had automatic membership of Studio One in Los Angeles and Bonds in New York.

Heaven's First Disco Top 10
1. 'Deputy of Love'/Don Armando's 2nd Avenue Rhumba Band
2. 'Danger'/Gregg Diamond
3. 'I'll Be The Music'/Bonnie Boyer
4. 'Night Dancer'/Jeanne Shy
5. 'Dance Until You Drop'/Ritz
6. 'More To Me Than Meets The Eye'/James Wells
7. 'Love Rush'/Ann-Margret
8. 'You're The One'/Rory Block
9. 'On The Run'/Colleen Heather
10. 'Go Dance'/Billy Moore

HOTEL BULKOVSKAYA

Leningrad, USSR, 1986. Heading back to the monolithic Hotel Bulkovskaya after an evening on the Nevsky Prospect, stuffed with beluga and blinis and reeling with vodka, it comes as no shock to find the basement nightclub is still playing the same twenty mid-'70s disco cuts they have been spinning for the last decade. The place has been suspended in time. The vaguely nightmarish sense of déjà vu and disorientation created by the dark-brown ambience and heightened by pungent four-in-the-morning cigarette smoke soon gives way to weird euphoria as the music takes hold. Not an eyebrow is raised by the bored hookers on the barstools or the men silently staring at melting ice in their glasses as you jump alone to such classic cuts as 'What A Difference A Day Makes' by Esther Phillips.

THE ICE PALACE

Unlike its notorious Fire Island sister establishment, the Ice Palace on the corner of Manhattan's 57th Street and the Avenue of the Americas was a discothèque first and foremost. Free of more aggressive heavyduty revellers and obtrusive door policies, the young mixed crowd came here to bop to the most lightweight of Eurodisco and New York sounds fired up by top deejays.

The centrally situated clean and classy premises attracted the committed and the curious alike, and the romantic disco dramas like Madleen Kane's 'Rough Diamond' that were played here compelled visitors who had never been interested in the music to stare dreamily into the mirror ball, suddenly yearning for a spin across the floor with an imaginary Rogers or Astaire.

Love was in the air as Fifth Avenue debutantes in Biagotti dresses exchanged dance steps with street hustlers and cute Puerto Ricans while sugar daddies eyed their tricks from the bar. The 'Ice' of the palace consisted of floor-to-ceiling mirrors, reflecting and multiplying the strobes *ad infinitum* and making the apparent size and layout of the club difficult to fathom.

At five in the morning the place would seem to have dematerialised and be constructed only of floating forms, recessed planes and unexpected fissures, and as the lights filtered and funnelled in disorientating ways, finding your way out and up the street would prove a major task in itself.

262 INFINITY

At 633 Broadway, between Third and Bleecker Streets, was an enormous disco which packed in more dancers than any other New York venue. A former factory, Infinity was a mind-blowing experience, a *Metropolis* fantasy where the sweaty bodies weren't working for future man, they were dancing to present disco hits. People danced on the ledges of the huge mirrored arches, on the pedestals of the Gothic pillars rising up to the pitch-black ceiling, in the vast lounges, at the bar — anywhere and everywhere there was a flat surface, there would be dancers on it. The crowd stretched off into infinity and that's where the name came from.

Infinity was open only on Friday and Saturday nights from 11 p.m. onwards, but Manhattanites flocked to the hot-spot to hear deejay Jim Burgess play the best sounds around. Considered one of the best in the business, Burgess insisted Infinity be the first disco ever to be lit with neon and have a light show synchronised with the music. Robert Lobi, the president of Design Circuit Inc., was the man employed for the job. The former rock guitarist who used to pick up extra cash by working the lights for other acts on his concert tour designed the Infinity 'harmony trip' and made sure the solid lights flashed, whirled and plunged down ceilings, across walls, around pillars and up arches, causing the dancers to howl joyously every time they were set in motion.

Free snacks were available for dance energy refuelling and the crowd was young, free, mostly single, middle class and ready for anything. Celebrities did pop in from time to time but dancing was the main business at Infinity, not relentless star-spotting, and that was why there was still a queue outside the place at five in the morning.

LE JARDIN

You had to take the elevator to get to Le Jardin because it was in the penthouse of The Diplomat, a dilapidated hostel for the homeless on Manhattan's West 43rd Street. But once past the uninviting entrance which stank of urine, you paid your $8 entrance fee ($2 less on week nights) and entered its art deco-designed confines where jaded New Yorkers came to spice up their life to hot and heavy disco played by Bobby DJ.

The crowd at Le Jardin consisted of fashion queens, fag hags and cool scene-makers like Hollywood Di Russo, public relations officer for the New York branch of Mary Quant. Other dance floor stars snaking and schmoozing around the place would include Rudolph Nureyev, New York Dolls singer David Johansen, gay activist writer Arthur Bell and top model Appolonia Von Ravenstein shrieking the trendy exclamation of the day 'Vous Etes!' at anyone who came within five yards of her new Halston ensemble. Drinks were available at the big white leather bar behind which muscular guys in basketball uniforms bounced back and forward filling orders for tequila sunrises and apple schnapps.

Le Jardin began life as an exclusively gay club when it was first opened in the '60s by John Addison, a Briton whom some dub 'The Father of Disco'. But when Steve Ostrow turned his Continental Baths sauna club over to women as well, other gay venues rapidly followed suit and went omni-sexual. The result was instant celebrity for Le Jardin, the one disco where you had a good chance of being discovered for whatever talents you wished to flaunt in the Hollywood Babylon establishment. Le Jardin was also the first disco to tentatively play the Door Game as stockbrokers and other uninteresting night owls were actively discouraged from entering its hallowed halls. In the weird and wonderful world of disco, it was no surprise that when Le Jardin closed down, Xenon opened up right next door to what was once a mecca for the hipper-than-thou.

THE LOFT

To get into The Loft you had to be personally invited by deejay David Mancuso himself. Liquor wasn't served although juices and food – often barbecued – were in plentiful supply And you had to really be in the dancing mood. Every Saturday night since the late-'60s, Mancuso had been throwing open his own home to five hundred guests for an all-night house party. He started doing it at his first abode on Manhattan's Lower Broadway and continued it from the early-'70s at 99 Prince Street in Soho's art gallery district. In fact, his residence did look like an art gallery from the outside thanks to the hundreds of multi-coloured helium balloons covering the ceiling.

One of the progenitors of the disco scene, Mancuso wrote the charter for the first deejay record pool (the consortium responsible for providing deejays with white-label 12-inch promos), brought the Barrabas Eurodisco album back from Spain and sold the American rights to it in The Loft, and aggressively promoted Eddy Grant's music to the hardcore clubber. One of the major differences between the music at The Loft compared to other in clubs was that Mancuso didn't overlay or remix the records, he simply let them follow on after each other as rhythmically as possible. He wanted what was in the vinyl groove to be transmitted through the speakers in the purest way possible to uphold the artist's original intention. The Loft was the hippest, coolest club in the world. If you were invited, you had made the disco A-list.

LOUISE'S

Louise's was a club of stark contrasts. It turned into the hippest hangout in 1977 mainly because The Sex Pistols and their ripped-and-torn punk acolytes used it to escape the relentless hounding they faced from rabid fans if they went to the Roxy or the 100 Club. The mainly lesbian disco was run by Louise herself, a fifty-year-old matriarchal bull-dyke with a platinum rinse and loads of eyeliner that looked like it had been applied months before. She was the one you'd have to convince to let you in as she stood guard at the door in Lower Poland Street, Soho.

Once inside, you could relax in the jet-black street-level bar run by Tony, the head waiter with the Twix fetish. (No, he didn't put the chocolate fingers in his mouth. Guess where he ate them out of!) This is where The Sex Pistols would lounge around: Sid Vicious with a condom pinned to his leather trousers, Vivian from The Slits, his girlfriend at the time, draped on his arm; Siouxsie of the Banshees would be glowering at everyone who walked by; and Seditionaries shop assistant extraordinaire Jordan would be chatting away as usual. The lesbian regulars wouldn't take a blind bit of notice of them in their Vivienne Westwood fashions, and that's why it became such a punk palace.

The dance floor was down a spiral staircase and was a pretty poor relation in the light-show and glitter-ball stakes. But no one cared because the deejay, whom everyone thought was a dead ringer for Prince Charles, still played the hottest disco sounds and kept the speed freaks and Tuinal two-steppers happy. it was very rare to see any punk dancing the light fantastic, though.

No one ever really picked anybody up in Louise's, there was scarcely any toilet activity, and it was really nothing special. But between 1977 and 1978 it was the Saturday-night Holy Grail for the hardcore punk and uptown dyke brigade.

NEW YORK NEW YORK

Is that Warren Beatty? I'm sure I passed Gregory Peck at the cloakroom. Wow! There's novelist Norman Mailer talking to Robert Duvall, star of the hottest movie of the season, *Apocalypse Now*.

New York New York at 33 West 52nd Street, home of the famous Toots Shor restaurant, was Disco Apocalypso Past, Present and Future to the discerning Manhattan clubber. It was often called the most beautiful disco in the world thanks to designer Angelo Donghia's grey flannel walls, Chinese red lacquer surfaces, glass art and polished metal fittings. New York New York was one super-cool venue.

You lined up along the mirrored bar with lilac neon light sculptures that seemed to float over the heads of the bartenders. There was an elegant outer lounge for rest and recuperation with banquettes around the floor where you could sip the unusual cocktails (remember the crème de menthe-based Snake in the Grass?) and watch the disco action – not that you'd be watching for long thanks to the pounding music and the amazing light show.

Fitted by Design Circuit Inc., the top disco lighting designers of the day, New York New York had laser beams, neon bolts and revolving spotlights. But the most spectacular special effect dancers would wait all night for was the dry-ice mist that rose from the floor as fountains of smoke poured out from the ceiling enveloping everyone in a shroud of musical mystery. Owned by Maurice Brahms, who admitted non-members only when there was space, New York New York was less famous than Studio 54 but a far better club for actually dancing in.

LE PALACE

A huge mob caused traffic chaos at the crossing of Rue Montmartre and the Boulevard Poissonnière every weekend night in Paris. On one side hungry tourists and locals alike lined up to gorge on the cheap and robust fare at the Restaurant Chartier. The pavement opposite was jammed with screaming people of all ages, desperate to squeeze into Le Palace, the Gallic version of Studio 54. In the spirit of *égalité* there was no door policy as such – the problem was more the immense popularity of the venue. Just about everybody in Paris had caught *Le Fievre du Samedi Soir* and Le Palace had taken off like no other club before it.

A rococo and ornate forty-year-old former musical theatre like its New York model, the club attracted the crème de la crème of the elegant Paris party brigade who champagned the night away in the exclusive basement restaurant. That's where you'd see the Yves Saint Laurents and Loulous checking out the cute nobodies, Isabelle Adjani lookalikes and wannabe Alain Delons.

But, unlike Studio 54, most joined the stampede to Le Palace doors just to dance the night away. The whole place was one huge dance floor – including the steep balcony in the four-level fun house. Music was the central focus and the programming was geared to follow the *Billboard* disco charts with a larger ratio of Cerrone and home-grown talent thrown in. The mixing was technically as precise as at most Manhattan clubs, with careful blends and rising energy reflecting and accelerating the mass hysteria on the dance floor. Le Palace is the Catherine Deneuve of French discos – ageless, sophisticated and just as beautiful as ever – even though it was put up for sale in 1998 for £1 million as a going concern.

PARADISE GARAGE

For a decade, the boosted bass kick of the hottest, blackest disco records boomed out in a vast concrete truck garage at 84 King Street in New York. Paradise Garage remains a place of club legend and dancing there was a deeply religious experience for its devotees — everybody called it Saturday Mass.

Entry was restricted to members and their guests only but a handful of outsiders would always be selected from the crowd of hopefuls milling at the door. The look was ready-to-sweat; uptown celebrities or rich kids slumming it had no chance. As you ascended the steep, dark ramp to reach the dance floor, intense heat would steam towards you, generated by a thousand glistening half-naked bodies. Here the black and the Latin gay underground, the wildest dancers in New York, would congregate every weekend to worship the awesome sound system.

Presiding over the floor would be Larry Levan, one of the most influential deejays of the disco era, whose dance-mix style had been termed 'a dialogue with individuals in the room'. The deejay who started his career at the Continental Baths, a sauna-cum-cabaret-club (home of Bette Midler and Barry Manilow), would work the crowd with three turntables, a Bozak mixer and a custom-built Richard Long sound system, creating astonishing waves of textured sound. Moody bass-lines would lead into a Loleatta Holloway screamer or 'Weekend' by Phreek, followed by Kraftwerk techno prototypes or a mean future classic like 'I Got My Mind Made Up' by Instant Funk. Familiar five-minute vocal tracks were transformed live into percussive fifteen-minute dub monsters, reshaped by electronic effects and melted down with Latin or new-wave elements.

From the disco heyday, the Paradise Garage party would continue throughout the early-'80s as tracks like 'Walking On Sunshine' by Rocker's Revenge would start to ignite the dancers to 'jack' their bodies to the new emerging house sounds. The powerful sound system – for the longest time the finest in the world – was transported to London after the club's drug-induced decline and eventual demise in 1986. It was installed in the Ministry of Sound in the capital's Elephant and Castle district. But when Larry Levan died there was no way anybody anywhere could hope to recreate the singular atmosphere of the Garage at its spiritual peak.

REGINE'S

When former brassiere pedlar Regina (Rachel) Zylberberg opened her first Chez Regine's club on the Rue du Four in Paris she didn't let anyone in for an entire month. As the doors opened on the first night, she posted a 'Disco Full' sign on the entrance and politely rebuffed all-comers while inside the music blared and the bar staff sat around playing cards and drinking. When she did finally let people into her park-themed club (decorated with trees and benches stolen from the Bois de Boulogne), she was besieged by a crowd hyped up with glamour gossip and celebrity rumour.

She didn't have to go to such lengths when she opened her New York watering-hole designed by Alberto Pinto in her favourite art deco theme. Here, sophistodisco types sat in the circular banquettes surrounding the plexi-glass disco floor pulsating with four built-in heart-shaped neon tubes, she in her Halston original from Macy's munching imported Portuguese olives, he toasting her with Cristal champagne in his Giorgio Armani dinner suit.

Regine's was outrageously chic, impossibly expensive and situated at 502 Park Avenue in New York. You needed reservations, a commitment to 'evening elegance' (jackets *always* required) and absolutely loads of money to party at this establishment boasting a $500,000 design refit and a $20,000 sound system. At this twinkling disco for the rich and famous, dinner cost you $100 and three glasses of Perrier and a Drambuie would set you back $32. And that was after you had paid the admission price of $12 – and these are 1978 prices. You had to be Paloma Picasso, Jackie Onassis or Andy Warhol to afford even to step into the Queen of Disco's mirrored Hall of Fame populated with all the big names from Wall Street, Washington and Hollywood. The glittering fantasy palace reflected its reserved clientèle's tastes with a mix of mellow disco music – Ultimate's '*Ritmo De Brazil*' would softly segue into 'Café' by D.D. Sound. Nothing too hard or funky was played within these ornamental surroundings, or at any of the disco entrepreneur's numerous other dance franchises in London (on the Roof Garden of the Biba department store in Kensington), Montreal (in the Hyatt Regency Hotel), Monte Carlo, Rio de Janeiro and Bahia.

Dancing was not the point of Regine's. Rubbing shoulders with the *fashionista* was what this refinery was all about. But you had to go at least once just to be able to say you had, even though getting through the door in last season's Fiorucci was no easy task. Extra brownie points could be scored when Regine herself was in residence, too. Whenever she was hostessing (always in high heels – 'I dance better when my feet hurt,' she once said), the place zinged with further fabulousness you'd be talking excitedly about for weeks afterwards.

ROSELAND

Low on technology but high on energy, New York's legendary Roseland Ballroom on 52nd Street between Eighth Avenue and Broadway went disco on weekends after the stroke of midnight. This aircraft-hangar-sized relic from the big-band era positively reeked of kitschy nostalgia, with ornate balustrades, staircases straight out of *Snow White*, vast lounging areas and hysterically frilly restrooms. You can see what it looked like in the 1977 movie *Roseland* directed by James Ivory.

With no alterations to the outré decor, the space was discofied with huge stadium-strength lighting consoles that blinded you on arrival and rotated menacingly in the air, washing over the thousands of kids from the boroughs who'd be jamming the biggest dance floor in town. Parents would lounge on red vinyl banquettes inspecting the action and looking out for any sign of improper conduct. They needn't have worried. Here, dancing was a serious business, meaning five hours of strenuous non-stop activity. If any dance move was new, you saw it being done here first. One end of the dance floor was reserved for the best hustle-dancing couples competing fiercely with athletic drops and spins, surrounded by a tightly packed ring of onlookers.

The crowd at the Roseland was one that lived for music. Every record mixed in was welcomed like the Second Coming with ecstatic screams. The biggest summer hit in 1979 was Anita Ward's 'Ring My Bell' and it would cause the masses to break into the Freak, whooping with wild simulated 'OOO-OOO' syndrum sounds. Famous deejay names would often drop in for a special session at the turntables while live performances by top disco combos Chic and Ashford and Simpson would pack the place further. The ballroom would also attract refugees from the often ugly Studio 54 or Xenon queues in the same vicinity, a plethora of stunned tourists and disco accidentals from all walks of life.

THE SAINT

People travelled from all over the world to go to The Saint which was based at the old Fillmore East Theatre at Second Avenue and 10th Street in New York. No alcohol was served, just soft drinks and juices. Yet it was known as the ultimate disco – and reunion parties are still held acknowledging that fact – because it had such an unusual design and created such a party atmosphere.

You walked into the converted cinema foyer and through the corridor to a huge sunken bar at the bottom of a Hollywood-style staircase. At the end of that massive bar was another metallic staircase which led you up into the Dome. And that's what separated The Saint from all the competition. The Fillmore had been turned into a planetarium at one stage and the perforated aluminium dome was still in place over the large dance floor. In the middle of the floor was a central console which projected stars all over the inner dome, while a light system behind it shone laser lights through the perforations as you danced to the best gay disco sounds played by deejays Robbie Leslie and Sean Buchanan.

The Saint was exclusively gay, although certain favoured fag hags could get in on a Saturday night if they were persistent enough. They wouldn't dare venture into the balcony orgy area, though, where disco queens, T-shirted clones and leather guys openly had rough sex while looking down on the dancing throng. Those looking for 'Ack Shon' certainly found it here! Most members had been poached from The Flamingo's list and, indeed, The Saint also copied that gay venue's most popular stunt by throwing theme parties. It cost $30 to enter the hallowed hall when the Black or White parties were in full swing, but it was worth it. Expect a hushed, reverential tone from anyone who was either a member of The Saint, or who attended one of their legendary party nights, as they describe the entire evening in painstaking detail.

STUDIO ONE

This was the club where Divine camped out by the cloakroom every time he was in Los Angeles. The transvestite star of John Waters' cult classic *Pink Flamingos* loved the attention he got whenever he was spotted by besotted movie queens. Then there was the cloakroom attendant who would do anything, *anything*, for Marilyn Monroe memorabilia. But that kind of starry-eyed curiosity and rabid fanaticism is what fuelled Studio One and made it the longest-lasting Hollywood hot-spot. You never knew which top name was going to be there with their girlfriend, boyfriend or both.

Formerly known as The Factory, Studio One opened its doors at Santa Monica Boulevard and Robertson Boulevard for the first time in January 1974 and rode the crest of the disco wave along with 'Love's Theme' by the Love Unlimited Orchestra. The football-pitch-sized dance floor would be packed with a typical mix of straights, gays and women and the ambience was *Day Of The Locust* frenetic tempered with *There's No Business Like Show Business* glitz.

Unusually, Studio One was one of the few clubs where the balance between dancing and cruising was almost equal. In a town notorious for moving on to the Next Big Thing, the club saw off competition from all sides, including Scandells (just around the corner from the A&M Records offices), Dillon's (four floors in Westwood Village popular with a young crowd), Osko's (made famous as The Zoo in *Thank God It's Friday*), The Odyssey and the New Penny Club. Incidentally, Californians never danced alone. They always had to have a partner. if you tried to go solo, you were stared at unmercifully, as if you were from another planet.

12 WEST

If you were choosing the best disco in the world, Manhattan's 12 West would pop up in numerous categories. It could garner votes for the most relaxed and friendly party atmosphere or rnor the best music. It could also be cited as the best reason for straight men to act as gay as they could at the door in order to gain entry to this, the New York disco experience personified.

Tattoos and leather outfits or not, you walked down Christopher Street at midnight, past the cafés and the Badlands bar where the talk was all boys, politics and weightlifting tips. A turn right and a few blocks up at 491 West Street, the party would already be in full swing. The air was thick with scented oxygen and fine mist, illuminated by giant mirror balls that sprinkled golden and purple lights across the room with enough seductive power to get the coolest clubber all hot and bothered.

The sound was a raunchy, seamless 130bpm meat-rack beat with no variety whatsoever, but all the more exciting for it. On the floor it was a fantasy trip. Mustachioed college professors dressed as construction workers and shirtless gym boys in all shapes, sizes and jockstraps shook and shivered. This is where producer Jacques Morali was inspired to form The Village People. A few women and straight men arrived every night for the incredible energy the place generated, and they blended right in. An early-morning buffet was stacked with fresh fruit and juices. As you laid back after the marathon boogie session, they tasted better than any Dom Perignon.

XENON

Every club tried to lure people away from Studio 54 and Xenon was one of the many that attempted to usurp its position in the late-'70s. The $2 million club didn't have a very auspicious start, though. Not quite ready, it closed after its launch in June 1978 only to reopen a few weeks later in a much more finished state. Owned by actor-turned-rock-promoter Howard Stein ('I speak Gucci fluently,' he quipped) and Peppo Vanini, Xenon was hyped as a disco that 'combined the craziness of Studio 54 with the comfort of Regine's'.

Located in the former Henry Miller Theatre porn cinema at 124 West 43rd Street, Xenon was more of a playground than the place for an ego-trip and boasted a sophisticated sixteen-channel state-of-the-art stereophonic sound system – the most expensive ever installed in any New York nightclub. It also featured a startling twenty-four-foot-wide suspended Mothership weighing 7,000 pounds which acted as a whirling space-age mirror ball as it descended to a point just above the revellers' heads.

On the balcony were seven playpens fitted out with video machines and electronic toys, including guns that shot rays of

274

light towards the stage – whenever the target was hit, neon sculptures lit up. Other light shows could also be manipulated. In the restaurant, behind the glass-enclosed top balcony, you could watch such famous acts as Eartha Kitt as they interrupted the flow of the top-flight hardcore disco sounds which were the place's trademark.

DISCO FACT!
More people danced in the mid-'70s than at any other time since the Great Depression in the '30s.

DISCO FACT!
The trend to feature live performers in discos began in January 1977 when gay icon Bette Midler appeared at the Copacabana in New York, and Manhattan's Starship Discovery 1 featured Crown Heights Affair and The Andrea True Connection. The Chicago club Happy Medium swelled its attandance with shows by BT Express, and San Francisco's The City showcased Tuxedo Junction and Silver Convention. London's Maunkberry's had Grace Jones carried in on a leopardskin couch by lionclothed musclemen.

Great Expectations

THE LOWDOWN ON 'GOT TU GO DISCO'

A remarkable sidebar to disco's darkest hours, the *Got Tu Go Disco* story is an outstanding one. It began with producer Jerry Brandt, a denim-jeans-entrepreneur-turned-rock-promoter, who owned the Electric Circus club, discovered Patti LaBelle and (unsuccessfully) tried to hype an American David Bowie clone named Jobriath during the glam rock era. Like movie producer Allan Carr and his *Can't Stop The Music* débâcle, Brandt thought the world was ready for the first Broadway disco musical just as the general public was beginning to tire of the genre. His brainchild was *Got Tu Go Disco*, a disco Cinderella story, conceived and created by noted costume designer Joe Eula.

Originally entitled *Gotta Dance*, and with seed money supplied by Spring Records, his neighbours on West 54th Street, Brandt's folly was ostensibly about Studio 54 and what made such a place tick. First-time writer Steven Gaines was hired to write the musical because he had a novel, *The Club*, ready to be published about a Studio 54 type of establishment.

Capitalised at $2 million, and set to open at the Minskoff Theatre on 25 June 1979, the problems encountered during rehearsals became the stuff of Broadway legend. It was Joe Eula who introduced Brandt to Studio 54 regular Alan Finkelstein,

276

the major investor in the show. Although Finkelstein was the owner of Insports, an upmarket sportswear store on Madison Avenue, his main source of income came from marijuana smuggling. Arrested on 24 April for illegally importing $200 million worth of pot through Kennedy airport, it soon became an open secret, thanks to newspaper leaks, how Brandt could afford to stage *Got Tu Go Disco*.

As cast and script changes occurred almost on a daily basis, Gaines only learned he had been fired from the production by reading about it in the *New York Times*. Then Eula and Brandt had a falling-out and the director was finally banned from the premises as the production staggered on to meet its premiere date. Of the eleven composers listed as songwriters, only three had any real disco credibility (John Davis, Ashford and Simpson) and the show is mainly remembered today for starring Irene Cara as the shop girl-turned-disco personality before she hit the rocky road to *Fame* and 'Flashdance . . . What A Feeling'.

Brandt. had changed the 'To' in the title to 'Tu' on the advice of his astrologist who assured him it was a money spelling. Some more cynical observers said it was just a shameless tie-in with the local radio station WKTU who were co-promoting the show. (WKTU, along with WBLS, were the two most significant disco radio stations in the New York area.) Unfortunately, when the show finally did open on schedule (but over-budget by $1 million), that heavenly sign made not one iota of difference. Got Tu Go Disco was mauled by the critics. 'Will it catch on?' asked one reviewer. 'Well, German measles periodically does!'

Apart from the opening sequence (where clips of New York-based movies like *On The Town* were shown on several big screens which descended from the ceiling) and a few fleeting flashes of élan in the 'Dress You Up' scene (where two ropes hanging with club clothes suddenly swooshed out from the wings), *Got Tu Go Disco* was unimaginatively staged. There was nothing on display worth the expensive $20 ticket and you saw more on show in any disco around the corner from the Broadway theatre itself. That way you certainly didn't have to pay to see the sorry spectacle of Studio 54 doorman-turned-bad-actor/singer Marc Benecke pressganged into making an appearance to give the show some much-needed hip pizzazz.

Benecke explained his ill-advised career move as 'Everything has been going well for you. You think, sure! Why not? There's a certain naïveté . . .' There sure was! Those clubbers Benecke hadn't let through the Studio 54 velvet ropes finally had the last laugh when he croaked the show-stopper 'In or Out'. Although audiences wished it had indeed stopped the show for good, they still had to endure the not-so-grand finale where the entire cast disco danced on a very basic, and not very well-constructed, multi-level platformed stage.

The morning after the premiere Brandt went on television with John Simon, one of the show's most vitriolic critics. As Simon laid into Brandt and ripped the show apart, the producer staged a desperate publicity stunt. He stood up in front of the cameras and told the viewing nation that anybody who came along to the next evening's performance would be let in free. Although he had to buy out the entire theatre using his American Express card, Brandt felt it was important that the public rather than the critics had the final say over whether the show was any good or not.

Unfortunately the free audience didn't see Irene Cara in action. The star had been so freaked out by the devastating critical notices that she didn't turn up. And, when Cara's understudy accidentally fell into the orchestra pit, Brandt knew it was all over. He closed *Got Tu Go Disco* a week later, after only eight performances. As he watched them tear down the marquee at the Minskoff, Brandt had exactly sixty-four cents to his name. He ceremoniously threw the money into the Broadway gutter, moved on, and six months later opened The Ritz club.

Now the only reminder of the *Got Tu Go Disco* fiasco is the title song by Pattie Brooks. That it received any airplay and got any dance-floor outings at all was entirely due to Brooks punching over the inane lyrics with her trademark forcefulness beyond the call of duty – which took on a rather grim patina as Manhattan clubbers walked past the deserted Minskoff Theatre advertising the live-on-stage disco fête worse than death.

DISCO FACT!
On 21 January 1977, at the Hollywood Palladium, 415 dancers tripped the light fantastic in the first 24-hour disco marathon. It netted $70,000 for the Los Angeles County Easter Seals Society.

DISCO FACT!
Part-time deejay and community medicine student Jill Carty caused a storm when she warned that loud disco music could cause permanent hearing loss. A test was carried out in July 1977 on assorted Big Apple deejays by the New York League for the Hard of Hearing; ten of the twenty-five deejays tested showed hearing loss. The results prompted Norton Safety Products of California to develop a special filter to be worn in the ear, allowing users to hear the music clearly but eliminating the pain of high volume.

Number One Deejay

TURNING THE BEAT AROUND

Of course, the pioneering deejay auteurs we bow down to today did not begin their careers at superclubs like Studio 54 or Xenon and other places equipped with state-of-the-art turntable stations, multilevel dance floors, cabaret bars, posing PRs and gleaming metal toilets. Like so many unsung heroes and heroines all around the world, they lured the crowds to walk down grim back alleys and got the groove going at decidedly lo-fi basement clubs, with two record players, a primitive microphone board and no pitch controls to adjust the tempo of the seven-inch singles and the R&B album cuts. What they possessed was innovation and talent. Icons such as Francis Grasso, the first priest to members of a new urban secret society devoted to music, drugs and hedonistic rituals at New York's Sanctuary club, started to develop techniques like 'slip-cueing'. This meant holding a record still with your thumb and a forefinger while a protective slipmat and the steel platter of the turntable revolved underneath. He then released the vinyl at the exact moment he wanted to come in with the new song, creating a sudden segue from the previous track, similar in the beats-per-minute range and orchestration. Grasso also invented the playing of two records simultaneously for long stretches of time for a spaced-out phased effect. He made a hybrid of familiar musical forms, elevating his audiences to new spiritual planes with soul songs elongated by wild drum breaks discovered from rock tracks such as 'Whole Lotta Love' by Led Zeppelin.

That same weekend in 1970, across the town in Manhattan's Soho district, a guru-like David Mancuso would be hosting his Loft party for selected guests only in his private residence, programming his sounds by a narrative flow rather than a rhythmic overlaying of beats. In this compound that echoed semi-mythical names like Grasso, Mancuso, Ray Caviano, David Rodriquez and Steve D'Aquisto, a new breed of deejays grew, secure in the knowledge that they could infiltrate the crowds with their love of music. A Brooklyn-born 16 year old called Nicky Siano heard David Mancuso spin at the Loft and with his brother proceeded to open his own venue, The Gallery, in 1972. An instant cause célèbre, the club attracted New Yorkers eager to get engulfed in the communal club lifestyle. They were treated to Siano's mixing and matching of musical elements that he personally found exciting and they were the first audience to dance to now established classics like 'Love's Theme' and 'Love Is The Message'. It was during these early years that Siano was befriended by two future notables, Larry Levan and Frankie Knuckles, both of whom he taught the art of precise beat-mixing. In tune with the more soulful dance material later made famous by Levan and Knuckles, Siano was clearly not inspired by the poppier sound scenarios he was expected to orchestrate during his later drafting to Studio 54 by Steven Rubell and Ian Schrager. After a six-month commission he was unceremoniously sacked. Siano duly moved on to follow his calling by entering the recording business, producing and creating sounds he truly loved.

Coming to the scene with all credentials required were Wayne Scott, who played at the notorious New York gay clubs Flamingo and The Saint, and Jim Burgess, who worked the equally hardcore 12 West and Infinity. The Thursdays club in

Manhattan and Metro 700 on Long Island reverberated to the sounds fired up by Jenny Costa, one of the influential female deejays of the pioneer years. On the West Coast Bobby Viteretti created his own mixes of the current hits by using two reel tape decks, then letting the echoing, electronically twanging and often amazing results loose at San Francisco's Trocadero Transfer club. Figures like Viteretti were an inspiration for bedroom studio remixers – fans wanting to put their own personal stamp on their favourite tunes. By utilising the pause button of a cassette player and recording portions of the songs out of the original order or slipping in instrumental bits they were able to break up the tracks for their house parties – 'No, it's not Walter Gibbons, it's me, the No. 1 Deejay!'

Though some of the hits actually did sound richer in their original and un-remixed form, like Bebu Silvetti's 'Spring Rain', for example, the need to spin unusual and different versions of known songs along with the new ones fast became a craving. Already in 1975 David Mancuso had invented the first 'record pool', a service delivering promotional vinyl products from various companies to subscribers. The reactions to these were varied, and sometimes the customers of a particular pool were left with songs long past their dance-by dates. The harmony group Fantastic Four addressed this problem with the 1977 *Billboard* chart hit 'Disco Pool Blues', a classy Philly-style number chronicling the ups and downs of a deejay at the mercy of a particularly slow operation. New York-based Disconet, one of the best known and reliable companies that emerged later on, also distributed ready-made 18-minute-long medleys on special 12-inch records ready for club play. A typical example from 1979, mixed by Bobby 'DJ' Guttadaro, begins at 128bpm with an extended and speeded-up 'Feed The Flame' by Lorraine Johnson. This segues into 'Tahitian Orgy', a reconstructed and renamed 'ethnic' cut from the second *Voyage* album. The tempo quickens with '(I Lost My Heart To A) Starship Trooper' by Sarah Brightman and Hot Gossip, and remains at 136bpm for Rosebud's minor hit 'Have A Cigar'. For the discerning deejay, the lifespan of this kind of recording was limited, as fans would not be fooled hearing the same segue twice.

In Europe, where many deejays followed the US *Billboard* charts, the Disconet pressings were a hot commodity. Those catering for the more soulful end of the spectrum expanded their perimeters by seeking out obscure jazz or funk-based records favoured by fêted British maestros such as Paul 'Trouble' Anderson. Others programmed sounds that they knew would really work for their café society audiences, who wanted to sing along to the refrains of 'Rain' by The Goombay Dance Band or to The African Magic Combo's 'Magic Combo', with its relaxed rhythms and delicious violins in perfect sync with luxury life on the Riviera.

Realising the importance of the deejay in the breaking of a song, trendier record companies started to utilise more and more jockey talent to lend club and street credibility to their output. This generally happened only in America, where François Kevorkian was hired to contribute adventurous studio blends to popular tracks like 'In The Bush' by Musique. A 'Mix By Savarese' on the sticker came to mean an obscure sounding 12-incher like 'Fire' by Lizzy Mercier-Descloux would definitely be worth a listen to deejays and fans alike. While most 12-inchers continued being released in limited pressings only, an increasing number of clearly specialist cuts started to get distributed in album form even outside large metropolitan areas. To attract buyers, most were illustrated with more or less unrelated sexy imagery, as was the case with the brilliant Tom Savarese-mixed 'Let Me Be Your Fantasy' by Love Symphony Orchestra, a consistently building bass groove out on Bob Cuccione's Penthouse label. Incidentally, Cuccione's next attempt at attracting the loners, wife-swappers or swingers in need of softcore aural stimulation was a soundtrack album of his legendary $15 million porno production *Caligula*.

This contained a mid-tempo dance version of the main title theme 'We Are One', but the tune derived from the adagio of Khachaturian's *Spartacus* ballet had none of the earlier effort's mesmerising qualities.

By 1979 a number of large commercial record companies, such as RSO, had begun to experiment on the deejay-turned-remixer as a marketing force for their mainstream product. Linda Clifford's big budget *Let Me Be Your Woman,* a double album designed to elevate the singer to the heights of a Donna Summer-like status, employed several known names such as Jim Burgess and Jimmy Thompson to add energy to the cuts on offer. Instead of being mentioned like an afterthought near the bottom end of the album jacket, the remixers were now credited in big, bold letters right below the track title. The roles of the singer or the band and the remixer-cum-deejay began thus to merge, signalling a new era for DJ culture – just as disco was starting to retreat back to the underground where its most fervent fans thought it had belonged all along.

Hell on Wheels

ROLLER-DISCO

It all began with Rollerina, one of the most celebrated of the disco fantasy folk to grace the dance floor of Studio 54 and put on an ego show. On Hallowe'en night, 1977, the terminally eccentric male clubber (who insisted on being called a cross-dresser rather than a drag queen) debuted at Manhattan's top night spot wearing a chiffon ballgown, school-marm glasses and a flowered hat. In his hand he waved a glittering fairy wand and on his feet he wore roller-skates. The way the lawyer-by-day/fairy-godmother-by-night glided, spun and manoeuvred around the floor stopped trendsetters dead in their tracks – and roller-disco was born.

Soon everyone was doing it in America. Skates (or 'quads' as the four-wheelers are called in today's roller-blade terminology) cost $30 (£20) a pair, and new technology meant their polyurethane wheels lasted for ages. New York's Central Park was the place to be. It was packed with amateur skaters learning how to keep their balance and with the more proficient practising nifty moves they were desperate to dazzle the crowds with later that night at venues eager to cash in on the craze.

Brooklyn's Empire Roller Rink turned Rollerdrome disco to attract hip customers. Bonds and the Roxy opened in

Manhattan soon afterwards to mop up the roller masses. The Roxy was the poshest place in the world to skate. Located at 515 West 18th Street, it had an enormous 60,000-square-foot rink and a raised dining/relaxing area with spotlighted red roses on each table. The red brick walls were covered in neon artwork and the place just oozed style. 'Relax!' said the fun in-house flyers, 'Stretch your leg muscles . . . keep your knees bent . . . centre your body weight, lean slightly forward . . . if you feel you are going to fall forward, sign up for lessons!'

In California, Venice Beach fulfilled much the same purpose as Central Park, as did Battersea Park in south London and the Trocadéro in Paris. Disco producer extraordinaire Alec R. Costandinos immortalised the latter area situated close to the Eiffel Tower in the dance soundtrack to the French documentary film *Trocadéro Bleu Citron*.

Then the stars got in on the act. Diana Ross had twelve pairs of roller-skates custom-made to match different outfits. Joan Collins and Leonard Rossiter wore skates in one of their famous Campari commercials. 10 cc's rock video for '125 Beats to the Minute' featured skaters in Carnaby Street. Even the character of Mrs Slocombe kept mentioning it on the popular BBC TV sitcom *Are You Being Served?*. The reason for the latter? Gordon EIsbury, one of the producers of the show, ran central London's best roller-disco, the Electric Ballroom, and couldn't resist the opportunity to plug the dance sport. Everybody was willing to have a go, from Prince Andrew to Barbra Streisand, Robert Redford to President Jimmy Carter, Jack Nicholson to Christopher Reeve and, most importantly, Cher.

The former Mrs Sonny Bono was so enamoured of the craze she not only added the track 'Hell On Wheels' to her *Prisoner* dance album in 1979, she also opened up one of the most popular roller-discos in West Hollywood – Flippers at La Cienega and Santa Monica Boulevard.

Unfortunately, very few other records aimed specifically at the exploding market were as good as 'Hell On Wheels' with its rocking riff, hard drive and clever lyrics. Martha Reeves badly updated 'Dancing In The Street', her '60s Motown hit with the Vandellas, to 'Skating In The Street'. 'Let's Rollerskate' by Poussez (singers of the classic disco erotica 'Come On And Do It'), Citi's 'Roller Disco' and Al Di Meola's 'Roller Jubilee' weren't much better either. Poppy Eurodisco roller cash-ins included Arabesque's 'Roller Star' and Champagne's 'Rollerball'. The disco labels realised pretty quickly that roller-discophiles didn't want gimmick records, they just wanted the same tracks they would normally dance to. Some cuts, however, such as Kat Mandu`s 'The Break', suggested speed skating by their fast rhythms anyway, so deejays had no problem catering to the ardent roller-disco enthusiasts and keeping them happily gyrating.

There were five major reasons why roller-disco took off like lightning:

(1) The never-ending search for something new in any subculture.
(2) It hit the newly expanding fitness craze, especially amongst body conscious gay groups, because roller-skating burned up 350 calories an hour under sweaty, bright lights.
(3) Expressing your artistry and proficiency was the greatest fun.
(4) You could save a fortune on transport by simply skating home from the clubs (the disco whistle accessory neatly transforming into a safety device).
(5) Sony launched the first portable stereo cassette player on the market in 1979.

This last was the most important reason of all. The Stowaway, as the first Walkman was called, gave roller-disco the total freedom it needed to blossom and engage new disciples. If you could afford the original hefty price for a Stowaway (£99 was a lot of money in the late-'70s), you could listen to your favourite dance-mix tapes while gliding in the park and on the streets as well as over the speakers at the roller-disco *du jour*.

Three things you couldn't really do on skates were drink alcohol, take drugs and have sex in the club toilets. Not many adhered to those hard-and-fast roller rules but everyone found out the hard way that each did impair balance and technique and invariably led to minor accidents. Roller-disco managers in America were quick to ban the use of poppers because skaters were dropping crushed amyl nitrate capsules and bottles on the floor, creating hazardous conditions for other revellers.

Fashion-wise, everyone wore satin shorts, skimpy T-shirts, rainbow-striped leather knee and elbow pads (a safety must!) and specially designed wallets which slipped around the leg at sock level. Comfort and manoeuvrability were the absolute keys to roller-disco etiquette, and amateurs were soon spotted via their inappropriate attire of Gloria Vanderbilt jeans and denim shirts.

The one area you did go berserk was with your skates. They came in a variety of leathers, plastics and colours and could easily be customised with glow-in-the-dark decals, glitter laces, strap-on silver wings for that Achilles-heeled Greek God look, and day-glo plastic toe protectors. Flashing wheel lights were an expensive option and winged baseball caps to match the similar footwear were in vogue for a while. So too were wraparound disco glasses, usually red-framed, containing distorting prisms which produced a kaleidoscopic hallucinatory effect when you stared at the lights for any length of time. You had to be a very good skater to wear these with any conviction.

And there were some very good skaters who took their flashy dance-floor routines to the next level and turned into professional entertainers. April Allen, Jack Cortney, C. C. Boots and Stephanie Starr became stateside roller celebrities, as did The Body Gliders group. The Roxy Rollers, their British equivalent, comprised George Campbell, Dennis Fuller, Aden Ephrain and his sister Ann. They practised for eight hours a day and soon featured on TV variety shows and commercials and made personal appearances all over Europe, billed as a roller-style Hot Gossip. They made two records, 'I Need a Holiday' and 'Rollin', Rollin', Roller Skatin'', but both went absolutely nowhere. Yet their singing style would lead two of the group to eventual worldwide fame. Aden and Dennis settled in Germany where they became The London Boys and packed global dance floors in 1988 with the HI-NRG anthem 'Requiem'.

Roller-disco filtered into every area of life during its 1979-80 peak. The movies *Can't Stop The Music*, *Xanadu*, *Roller Boogie*, *Skatetown USA* and *Fame* and the three documentaries *Get Rollin'*, *Stepping Out* and *Roller Mania* all prominently featured the craze. So did *Heavens Gate* in its retro way. Even the horror flicks *Monster* and *Scared to Death* had roller victims dying gory deaths. Then there was the porno cash-in *Roller Babies*. Top-rated TV shows *Dallas*, *C.H.i.Ps* and *Charlie's Angels* staged scenes on wheels and the magazines *Rinksider*, *Hot Roller*, *Roller Skate Express* and *The Roller Skate Rag* hit the news-stands to inform the eight-wheeled fanatic what was hot and what was not. In Britain, The Carmen Rollers staged their much-publicised disco-pantomime *Cinderoller* at selected venues, and the world-famous gay club Heaven put on a roller fashion show. Practically every club turned into a roller-disco for one night a week during early-1980.

Then, just as suddenly as it had started, the fad fizzled out. It was an exhausting lifestyle to keep up, after all. Roller-skating through the parks during the day, swirling in the clubs at night, constantly oiling and cleaning the wheels for tip-top performance levels and all the heavy-duty essential foot-care finally took their toll. In California, skating moved out of the discos and back on to the streets. If you were an avid roller-skater you wanted to be out in the fresh air, not cooped up in cinemas watching people doing badly what you could be doing so much better instead, or bumping into amateurs in cramped clubs. More sophisticated personal stereos meant you literally could go where the music took you, and that's exactly what people did.

Britain's roller-disco mania was dictated by the weather. Summer in the city was fabulous, but winter was a rusty-wheel nightmare. By the time the sun shone again, the inclination to strap on the roller-boots was often at a low ebb. Yet there was always the die-hard skater who could be seen in the park gliding along to Andy Williams' disco version of the theme from *Love Story*, 'Where Do I Begin?', the thinking roller fan's favourite because, if you got it exactly right, you could twirl on each soaring violin beat with precision without exhausting yourself in the process.

Roller-disco was the apotheosis of the dance-floor fantasy. You could be Jane Torvill or Christopher Dean – often both! – and pirouette yourself to ecstasy enclosed in your own musical universe. It was also the ultimate in image redefinition because all skaters looked graceful and fluid while on the move, even if they were awkwardly self-conscious in a normal disco environment. That was the real key to it becoming an overnight sensation and success.

290

DISCO NARCISSISM AND SOCIETY

'The mania which is becoming the cultural phenomenon of the 1970s is rooted in narcissism. Separated by walls of deafening music and swept up in a frenzy of bright lights, dancers do their own thing, seldom touching, never looking at each other or even speaking. It's a lot like standing in front of a mirror shouting, 'Me, me, me . . .' endlessly. This pure self-indulgence reflects a dangerously deep-rooted philosophy in our society. It preaches that anything an individual feels like doing is 100 per cent right – no matter how it affects anyone else. The attitude shows up in our soaring divorce rate, our legions of broken families and in countless books and movements keyed to self-gratification and self-esteem. There is too little room for love in the philosophy that permeates the disco world. And that is a pity, for those who have forgotten – or never known – the joys of giving and sharing are missing the richest part of life.'

New York Daily News editorial on the danger of disco

And the Beat Goes On

Most musical trends just fade away and fizzle out at the end of their natural cycle. Unlike any other genre, however, disco was driven out of American towns like Frankenstein's monster – only this time the villagers weren't brandishing burning torches but flaming copies of Amii Stewart's 'Knock On Wood'! Chicago's Steve Dahl was only the most vocal of the 'Disco Sucks' deejays when he hosted the 'Death of Disco' record-burning party at his local Cominskey Park in front of a load of jerks wearing 'Shoot the Bee Gees' T-shirts. While America was fast becoming the most anti-disco nation, others across the world had also had enough of the trend, fuelled by the stance of practically the entire music press that the music couldn't possibly be taken seriously on any social, cultural or academic level. If you did, you were either a drugged-out dance casualty, gay or a moron.

Lifestyles were rapidly changing, too. Going out every single night, or even on a regular basis, was very time-consuming and costly. Leisure time was limited, after all. People had other things to do and had probably met their boyfriend/girlfriend at the disco and therefore saw less point in going out any more. The young disco tearaway had matured, settled down, raised a family, shopped at the local supermarket every Saturday and now had different priorities.

Or maybe the drugs were finally taking their toll and the disco fan was checking into a rehab clinic. Gays were starting to fall ill with a mystery virus that would have a profound effect on an entire generation used to the disco/backroom/Continental Baths weekend recipe. The generosity of spirit and camaraderie that was part and parcel of the disco era were being replaced by a more venal, money-grabbing, self-obsessed Yuppie ethic. Nor could disco music be explained as radical or political in the way pretentious rock critics loved to write about post-punk bands. Then Studio 54 closed down. And along with the unofficial disco headquarters that symbolised everything excessive and fabulous about the era, the general public's interest quickly waned too.

Yet all through this downturn in popular consciousness, the music continued to galvanise the die-hard devotee. Canada suddenly became a major force in the disco market with the globe-trotting 'Take Off' by Harlow, 'Angel Eyes' by Lime (from Denis Lepage, producer of Kat Mandu's 'The Break'), 'Dancin' The Night Away' by Voggue, 'Feel Your Way Around' and 'Love Dance' by Ann Joy, 'Underwater' by Harry Thumann, 'Melting Pot' by Soundblast and 'Super Queen' by Beckie Bell.

San Francisco producer Patrick Cowley was on the verge of becoming a composer/songwriter superstar with 'Menergy', 'Mind Warp' and 'Megatron Man'. Cowley would eventually form the Megatone label and produce hits for Paul Parker, his 'Lift Off' vocalist, before tragically succumbing to the Aids virus as one of its earliest famous victims. Viola Wills released her classic 'If You Could Read My Mind' and 'Gonna Get Along Without You Now', and Lipps, Inc. their superb 'Funkytown' and 'All Night Dancing'. The former was the big summer hit of 1980 and if any obituaries were being written for disco around this time, Lipps, Inc. certainly put the funeral on hold.

But when the bottom did suddenly fall out of the popular disco market in America, dance culture quickly and silently disappeared into the gay, black and Hispanic ghettos from where it had started before being turned into the nightmare urban polyester phenomenon. Producers Ian Levine and Fiachra Trench in Britain transformed gay disco into HI-NRG with their '60s/Northern Soul artists Evelyn Thomas and Miquel Brown. For Afro-Americans, disco was reborn as rap in New York, pioneered by Run DMC. Eurodisco moved to Spain and especially Italy where the Italodisco trend took off with such artists as Ken Laszlo and Den Harrow taking control of the insanely romantic and melodic hooklines. Disco was never seen as a negative word in those countries anyway and is still freely used today. Fans of Brazilian music didn't have too long to wait for the lambada either!

Has any part of pop culture been so lavishly enjoyed to the maximum or as sharply reviled and vilified as disco? It's doubtful. You either embraced it or you hated it. Those into disco just carried on dancing to whatever music was around. HI-NRG, rap, house, acid house, garage, handbag, hardbag, NU-NRG, speed garage, hip hop, trip hop, jungle, drum and bass, techno, rave, nuyorica, electroclash, yoga house – call it what you want.

And the legacy lives on. From large metropolitan areas to small provincial towns, fans of all ages seek out specialist vinyl stores such as A1 on 6th street in New York or Demonfuzz Records in the city of Rotterdam to find that elusive 12-incher from 1977. Some of these stores have become legends all over the globe and ensure that regardless of laptops and next month's new gadget, vinyl will remain the format of choice for both the hip deejay and the serious collector of dance music. Established names like Danny Krivit and Dimitri of Paris continue to re-edit classic as well as obscure disco tracks, bringing the rhythms to new generations of dancers. Sometimes their edits present a favourite like Salsoul Rainbow in a woefully abridged form, on occasion they come up with results that would make the original composer proud. The spirit of pure Eurodisco has never let go of clubbers either, who all over the world keep swooning to the glittery tracks of Kylie Minoque, Alcazar and whatever new ultra-glamorous chart sensation the coming season in the sun will bring. But it is still the original, acoustically played, ecstatically sung, exuberant seventies disco records that will always be hailed as the ultimate soundtracks to Good Times past, present and future.

'I Will Survive' by Gloria Gaynor lives on today like the vast majority of equally magnificent disco records because it's an anthem of triumph, of personal strength, with a good solid sound. The song's powerful message, attention-grabbing opening words, strong bass-line and melodic violin break keeps it locked in the memory forever. Unlike the Swinging '60s — which in reality was roughly 150 Beautiful People moving from one pop star party to another — the disco '70s could be enjoyed by everyone. It's said that if you remember the '60s, you weren't there. But if you remember the '70s, you were here, there and everywhere a mirror ball was in evidence.

Disco is *not* dead.

Long live disco!

DISCO FACT!
Deejay Francis Grosso, of The Haven fame, was the first to achieve icon status because he invented the technique of 'slip-cueing' — splicing two records together precisely on the beat by using his thumb and earphones.

DISCO FACT!
The BBC co-produced the 75-minute variety show *Disco In The Snow* in 1979. Featured artistes included Leif Garrett, Amii Stewart, Boney M, the Jacksons and Patrick Juvet — in leather!

✳ Extra! Extra! (Read All About It!)

AN APPENDIX OF DISCO ESSENTIALS

CLAUDIA BARRY

Cruising effortlessly from slow-burn ballads and classic Munich sound stompers to HI-NRG hits and beyond, the glamorous Jamaican-born Barry was the reigning diva of producer Jurgen Korduletsch's Lollipop Records. While she was backed by Donna Summer's session musicians and did retain the bass-heavy rhythmic components and violin essence of that sound in her early songs 'Sweet Dynamite', 'Why Must A Girl Like Me' and 'Dancing Fever', she made them distinctly her own with a vocal range cannily alternating between sensuous and powerful. 'Boogie Woogie Dancin' Shoes' was a more straightforward offering in the 1979 New York style and was a hit in clubs everywhere.

LINDA CLIFFORD

A Miss New York State in 1966, Brooklyn-born Linda Clifford still looked stunning on her album covers. Her image perfectly matched her music – a sophisticated lady with a Gucci bag of attitude – and her first disco smash was 'From Now On' taken from the *Linda* album in late-1977. It set a record for being played twice every hour on every major radio station in the New York area. But it was the 1978 breakthrough hit 'If My

Friends Could See Me Now' (taken from the Broadway musical *Sweet Charity*) and the fierce 'Red Light' groin-grinder (featured in the movie *Fame*) of 1980 which proved beyond a doubt that Clifford was no fool for love. Each portrayed a financially and emotionally secure woman in complete control of her life. To maintain this diversity she included themes of strong feminine independence on all of her sets, and the cut 'Runaway Love', from the *If My Friends Could See Me Now* album, became a huge radio hit as well as a dance-floor favourite. Pre-dating 'I Will Survive', 'Runaway Love' (written by her producer Gil Askey, a former Tamla Motown employee) begins with a bitter Linda telling her man to stop doing her wrong and causing her any more heartache. It then gradually loosens up with a self-redeeming rap and ends with a defiant shout-out where all the Sinner Man's belongings are flung out of the door along with his whining dog. The Gloria Gaynor perennial and the Patrick Adams production 'Weekend', forcefully sung by Christine Wiltshire, together with 'Runaway Love' form the definitive disco torch song trilogy.

CRISTINA

Checking the latest 12-inch import arrivals, you were always on the lookout for yellow sleeves with a cab door pictured on them. For these would contain the esoteric releases of the Ze label, founded by Michael Zilkha from Britain and originally an outlet for punk bands like The Jerks and Teenage Jesus. The most famous Ze releases were 'Deputy Of Love' by Don Armando's 2nd Avenue Rhumba Band and a sax-heavy dance experiment by rockers Contortions, now calling themselves James White and the Blacks. But it was for two scintillating solo releases by Cristina Monet-Pilaci that most discophiles fondly recall Ze. Cristina was the high-heeled, drop-dead gorgeous wife of Zilkha and she had a definite penchant for the bizarre, much like Dr Buzzard's August Darnell whom she arranged to produce and write for her. The inner sleeve of

Cristina brazenly displayed her in a white bra on satin sheets while the music continued Darnell's recurring themes of depravation, sexual unfulfilment and interracial lust. The hipstress was at her cooing best on a surrealist version of '*Une Poupée Qui Fait Non*' and the extravagantly suggestive 'Jungle Love'. The latter had the blonde Venus bound between two giant stakes in Darkest Africa while wild sax players lurked in the mix and restless natives drummed and chanted to summon the hairy and horny god Kong. In her other release, the now much-sought-after 12-incher 'Disco Clone', Cristina invaded a discothèque with an army of sex-crazed girl replicants and led them through several steamy Latin-tinged passages. The voice of the male protagonist in this very un-PC fantasy affair belonged to actor Kevin Kline. Cristina also found herself in legal hot water with veteran songwriters Jerry Leiber and Mike Stoller when she sexed-up the lyrics in her version of the Peggy Lee classic 'Is That All There Is?'.

298   CROWN HEIGHTS AFFAIR
They stepped out in 1975 with the soulful harmonies and easyflowing melodies of 'Dreaming A Dream'. They moved on to the extended Shaft-styled wah-wah moods of 'Dancin''. And they hit paydirt with the chart-busting pop funk of their 1978 offering 'Galaxy Of Love'. Crown Heights Affair were an eight-man troupe from Bedford-Stuyvesant, New York, and they always seemed to tap into a commercial vein reaching a wide cross-section of dancers and record-buyers alike. Their highly danceable output had the ability to shift tempos with the times up till 1980 when they enjoyed yet another huge seller with 'You Gave Me Love', a highly regarded and perfectly formed slice of commercial bop with a contagious hook and a luscious chorus line.

DISCO TEX AND HIS SEX-O-LETTES REVIEW

The singer's voice seemed familiar. But nobody expected the strong 'Dancing Kid' number from the album Manhattan Millionaire to turn out to be credited to Disco Tex, alias Sir Monti Rock III, who fluttered about club stages like a Puerto Rican Liberace decked out in white feather boas, a white cape and matching fedora. The flamboyant former hairdresser of Johnny Carson and numerous other Hollywood celebrities also flouted his own traditions with the driving salsa-influenced 'Hot Lava'. It was all a far cry from the bubblegum bounce of his fondly remembered camp hits 'Get Dancin'' and 'I Wanna Dance Wit' Choo' of 1974. After several well-received world tours Disco Tex released a 7-inch single 'Hot City Streets' in 1978 backed by another hot Latin jiggler, 'In Havana'. Both the record and the artist sank without a trace.

CAROL DOUGLAS

Were you tickled by the delicious 'Doctor's Orders' heard during the opening montage of The Last Days Of Disco? While that classic update of the Sunny original from The Carol Douglas Album may remain the New Yorker's finest five minutes, there is more of one-time Broadway actress Douglas worth seeking out. Her next album contained the wonderful 'Midnight Love Affair' suite, a tuneful course through the smoochier side of dance, accentuated by classy production values by the dependable John Davis. But 'In The Morning', will you still be there? If you are, and can't wait to leave, 'Lie To Me' and tell me you really do care. 'Midnight Love Affair' was the perfect pick-up dilemma of the '70s complete with schmaltz, sentiment, strings and cynicism. Douglas also gave a pleasing new twist to Abba's 'Dancing Queen' in 1977 and the following year glowed in the dark far brighter than The Bee Gees with her up-tempo rendition of 'Night Fever'. Check out 'Baby Don't Let This Good Love Die', too. Just follow 'Doctor's Orders'!

ANDRE GAGNON

Among the first Canadian orchestral boogie merchants was Andre Gagnon. Dramatically building from the essential drumbeat and galloping upfront congas, his 1975 'Wow' whipped dancers into instant frenzy with lashings of striking piano chords and a rising and falling symphonic backing. Blasted full volume, the record is electrifying and one of the most memorable three-minute masterpieces of early disco. The flipside, 'Ta Samba', is a flirty and well-dressed Latinate shuffler and is equally addictive. Gagnon further refined his formula with 'Smash', adding a female chorus and alternating sensuous, floating passages with familiar pianoforte crescendos.

TAANA GARDNER

Restoring digital vigour by applying drum machines or by pumping up the bpm count can sometimes work with a lesser cut, but, generally, tampering with club anthems only robs the recordings of much of their original power – take the Atmosphere, Giorgio Moroder or Amanda Lear updates, or indeed the British 'Stomp' project by Chocolate Fudge for sorry examples of pointless remixing. One of the mutations on the latter EP is a version of Taana Gardner's West End label classic 'Work That Body', transformed into a mechanical series of sampled phrases, earthquake house beats and abridged bass lines.

The original Kenton Nix production of 'Work That Body', which exploded onto the scene in 1979, remains fresh, and swiftly takes you back to the heart of the Paradise Garage sound experience with relentlessly churning bass lines and huge upfront percussion jams. Ultimately, though, it is the extraordinary wide-eyed yet commanding voice of Taana Gardner that makes the record an enduring classic. Her cult status nourished and grew with the equally acclaimed 'Heartbeat' and 'When You Touch Me', 12-inchers that epitomise the latter Garage era with Larry Levan's liquified beats and slowed-down expressions of rhythmic disorientation.

DAN HARTMAN

'Instant Replay' . . . We all screamed at the countdown, we all danced to it and we never got bored with it. Hailed on its arrival as Utmost Disco Dynamite, the eight-minute track still compels everyone to move their feet whenever it's revived. The saxophone solo on the track came courtesy of long-haired '70s rocker Edgar Winter. He had been brought along to the studio because singer/writer/arranger Dan Hartman had been an integral member of Winter's highly respected progressive band. Hartman himself played most of the remaining instruments. So what we all danced to was basically a worldwide disco smash by The Edgar Winter Group! That would have been a major shock to the system for most clubbers at the time.

Despite featuring Hartman's somewhat teenybopperish vocals, his next hit was also a truly massive foot-stomper thanks to a far tighter tune and its legendary guest star voice. Getting into gear with 'Vertigo', a spiralling instrumental intro section with a jazzy vibraphone solo, 'Relight My Fire' throbbed along with attractively syncopated piano chords until it exploded halfway through with a sudden, instantly recognisable, floor-shaking scream from Salsoul belter supremo Loleatta Holloway. Measured against the following display of vocal acrobatics, Lulu, on the '90s update by Take That, did not disgrace herself completely, but reassured us of the magnificence of the original.

FRANCE JOLI

Canada's tastiest contribution to disco society was France Joli, a ravishing nymphette who scored her first US album chart hit in 1979 when all of sixteen years of age. Not one in the league of lisping Euro kittens, like Luise Fernandez or Sandy (of 'I'm So in Love With John Travolta' infamy), this girl could really sing. Joli's torch song 'Come To Me' stood out of the solid selection on her debut album and sold enormous quantities as a single. It secured Joli No. 1 positions in dance charts the world over. Her Quebec-based producer Tony Green had earlier been the man behind Carolyne Bernier ('Secret Agent Love') and another teenage singer, Freddie James ('Hollywood'). Green continued to work with Joli and, two decades and numerous hits later, the diva is still delighting her fans in much-loved live appearances in Canadian clubs and across the USA.

RAY MARTINEZ
Writer/producer Ray Martinez was one of disco's foremost stylists, having refined the classy semi-instrumental New York disco to perfection. This meant sweeping, romantic melodies being treated like gradually evolving symphonic themes over a sparsely thudding 130bpm base, lengthy percussion breaks leading into unobtrusive male vocals and very high production values. Martinez knew how to make it all click and among his best works are 'If There's Love' by Amant and 'In New York' by Passion – two beautifully pitched evocations of the disco heyday.

WILL MORRISON AND IAN GUNTHER
The 1977 excursion into aural soft porn, 'Two Hot For Love', was the first worldwide success for Three Hats Productions, the brainchild of Toronto producers Will Morrison and Ian Gunther. They collaborated on two more THP Orchestra albums that packed a disco-sexual punch, several one-off projects like 'Sticky Fingers' and 'Going South', and recorded a hard-hitting solo project in 1979 for their main vocalists Phyllis and Helen Duncan. The Three Hats sound had its roots in Eurodisco and was sumptuously arranged and orchestrated, on occasion begging favourable comparison with the more melodic moments of Voyage. The 1977 *Grand Tour* album is the best example of their magic manipulation.

ODYSSEY

The two vocally talented Lopez sisters, Louise and Lillian, had already served a long apprenticeship in cabarets and bars by the time they met established songwriter Sandy Linzer in 1976 through their prolific session work. Linzer envisioned the duo as sophisticated and musically diverse performers, added Manila-born Tony Reynolds, and put them in the studio as the Odyssey trio. This business association proved to be extremely fruitful as the group struck platinum with record number one, a romantic paean to the subways, checker cabs and street smart denizens of the Big Apple. Sung with cool elegance by Lillian Lopez, and featuring a hot sax break, 'Native New Yorker' was a tough act to follow. Their second album moved no mountains, but the third one, *Hang Together* of 1981, contained a smash hit far surpassing their first one in Great Britain. 'Use It Up And Wear It Out' was a rattling, whistle-blowing party popper – much like the ultrapercussive 'In The Forest' by Baby O which it was often mixed out of by sussed deejays.

PINK LADY

Pink Lady was the one Japanese disco act to make an impression on the West. The duo's two young vocalists, Mie and Kei, were already superstars in their own country when they were assigned by Elektra/Asylum Records to record an album in Tokyo for the international market in 1979. All the tracks were sung in English, but the intonation remained distinctly and engagingly Japanese. Remixed in New York, the *Pink Lady* album contained the only known dance version of the Tom Jones hit 'Love Me Tonight' as well as 'Deeply', the theme from the home-grown motion picture hit *Happy*. The pink album cover featured the leggy girls posing in skimpy schoolgirl outfits. A Baccara-esque curio for arcane disco collectors.

VICKI SUE ROBINSON

A sassy-voiced *chanteuse* hailing from the Broadway show world (she played parts in *Hair* and *Jesus Christ Superstar*), Vicki Sue Robinson became a well-known name thanks to producer Warren Schatz and a demo given to the singer by a friend. The tune was 'Turn The Beat Around', a peak-hour energy rush and one of the most joyous celebrations of the dance-floor lifestyle right up there with 'Boogie Wonderland', Gino Soccio's 'Dancer' and Karen Young's 'Hot Shot'. Although Gloria Estefan covered the song in the '90s, the Miami Sound Machine couldn't match the sheer ecstasy of the original. Vicki Sue's second album offered more great eight-track music to pound your steering wheel to – a wonderfully exuberant rendition of Bobby Womack's 'Daylight' and a marvellous mood medley 'Should I Stay/I Won't Let You Go' performed with The New York Community Choir. The singer wreaked more havoc on the dance floor with 'Hold Tight' and 'Nighttime Fantasy' (a great song from the dreadful film *Nocturna*) and then paid her respects to her roots with a discofication of 'Hair' on which she was joined by Evelyn 'Champagne' King of 'Shame' fame.

SESSOMATTO

Held in God-like esteem by Shake Beat freaks and collectors of Italian B-movie soundtracks, composer Armando Trovajoli coloured lurid thrillers and sexy comedies with psychedelic bossa novas topped with jazzily abstract female vocals. His most-wanted cut is the theme of the 1973 comedy hit *Sessomatto* ('Mad Sex'), a groovy instrumental with a giggling lady repeating the title over and over again. Recently subjected to a CD full of remixes, the original 1977 disco version under the title 'How Funny Sex Can Be' still remains the best and is one of the most sought-after 12-inch discs.

STAINLESS STEAL

Amii Stewart managed to make The Doors' bombastic 'Light My Fire' presentable. But most disco acts striving to upgrade tired rock material failed miserably. Witness the dysfunctional Rosebud record with its brick wall medley of Pink Floyd songs or Wonder Band's creaking 'Stairway To Heaven'. Light classical themes fared little better. There were a few exceptions such as The Salsoul Orchestra's 'Magic Bird Of Fire' based on Igor Stravinsky's *The Firebird*. There was also 'Can Can' by the German studio project Stainless Steal. After an abysmal earlier attempt by Red Miller, a reinterpretation of the irritatingly jolly Offenbach wig-out sounded like a bad idea. However, the prolific Pete Bellotte, one of the Munich Machine engineers, made it work. Naturally, with no pretence at capturing actual musicological accuracy, the fourteen-minute permutation twisted the over-familiar tune into interesting new shapes and made it bubble with enthusiastically fiddling string sections, whooping girls, fan-faring woodwinds and lots of Parisian gaiety.

TAVARES

It took more than a minute for the five close-knit Tavares brothers from the Portuguese-speaking Cape Verde Islands to get to see their name high up on a huge billboard on Hollywood Boulevard. The boys had toured the supper-club circuit for ten years before landing a deal with Capitol in 1974. From this moment on it was success all the way as Tavares spread their distinctive brand of uplifting pop disco and chart-busting ballads to universal audiences. 'It Only Takes A Minute' and 'She's Gone' were followed by the rocketing 1976 album *Sky High* giving the group clubland credibility with the monster hits 'Don't Take Away The Music' and 'Heaven Must Be Missing An Angel'. The next year Tavares scored with the shuffling 'Whodunnit' and harmonised 'More Than A Woman' for Karen Lynn Gorney and John Travolta as the couple did the tango hustle into pop culture history. A few more best-selling albums later, Tavares retired but their special reunion concerts have been filling venues like the New York Palladium to capacity ever since.

JOE THOMAS

What possessed Joe Thomas, a seasoned flautist and alto sax player, to dedicate a dance tune to 'Plato's Retreat' is anybody's guess. In this establishment situated on New York's posh Upper East Side, you were handed a private locker key on arrival. While it was not permissible to shed your towel in this heterosexual bath house and cavort stark naked on the dance floor, you could jump on anything that moved in either the saunas, steam-rooms or fully mattressed orgy chambers seething with sweaty male and female flesh. However, the record 'Plato's Retreat' is a very classy affair indeed with Jocelyn Brown, Diva Gray and Gwen Guthrie singing the vocals over a superlush backing and a thrilling poly-rhythmic tribal chant break. Thomas's follow-up was 'Make Your Move', another chiselled slice of sleek New York disco at its peak.

VIOLA WILLS

Suffused with campy grandeur, Gordon Lightfoot's 'If You Could Read My Mind' was choice material for any disco diva hoping to milk for all it was worth the tale of broken movie goddesses and haunted wishing wells. As delivered by Viola Wills, a gospel-trained cabaret professional and one-time Joe Cocker backing singer, it conveyed a high sense of style as well and became one of the most played club cuts during the summer of 1980. Her album on the German Hansa label also contained another reworking of an old standard, the less distraught 'Up On The Roof', plus a short version of Wills's earlier Euro hit 'Gonna Get Along Without You Now'. She reached her high notes again with '(There's) Always Something There To Remind Me' in 1981, and played the keyboards on a

1982 HI-NRG rendition of 'Stormy Weather'. 'If You Could Read My Mind' returned, retuned by the Stars on 54 (Ultra Nate, Amber and Jocelyn Enriquez), as the theme for the movie *54*.

WING AND A PRAYER FIFE AND DRUM CORPS

Slipping occasionally off the dance floor and wavering into easy-listening territory with Walt Disney classics and other loony tunes like 'Popeye The Sailor Man', the two Wing and a Prayer Fife and Drum Corps albums are much loved by the discognoscenti. They were fun, expertly manufactured with the best session musicians around, and produced high musical camp of the most outré kind. The first album, identifiable by its cover picture of a blonde model wearing a pink plastic nose *à la* Groucho Marx, actually spawned a sizeable US singles chart hit in 1976. This rendition of the Harry Akst standard 'Baby Face' caused much radio-play offence, while the full six-minute album version pleased students of disco esoterica with a kicking arrangement lifted straight out of the MFSB classic 'TSOP'. The album also showed experimental flair with the chugging funk rhythms, mournful strings and girlie vocals given to a bizarre version of 'Eleanor Rigby'. The second album, *Baby Face Strikes Back*, took on 'Rhapsody In Blue' and the schmaltzy showbiz of 'Yes! We Have No Bananas' in an equally successful way while the group's trademark plastic nose graced the face of King Kong atop the Empire State Building.

STEVIE WONDER

Stevie Wonder a disco star? The one-man music factory was fêted in clubland with an extremely strong cut that spelt jazz disco heaven through the 1976 Christmas season. 'Another Star' was taken from the Grammy-winning *Songs In The Key Of Life* double album produced by Wonder at the height of his creative powers and featuring his emotional vocals over an eight-minute piano-driven Latin groove. While this was the sole cut with a disco structure, the *Key Of Life* package also included three shorter tracks for party purposes. 'Sir Duke' was a brassy, swinging tribute to Duke Ellington, 'I Wish' was booty-shaking funk and 'Isn't She Lovely' was a mellow, harmonica-laden celebration of the birth of Wonder's baby. The latter cut was limply covered by David Parton for the British market, while 'Another Star' received an expertly handled instrumental 1977 makeover in the States from the Joe Bataan-led Laso Players, complemented by sizzling sax and extra Latin percussion.

Further Essential Disco Records
PRE-1975
'Enter The Dragon' – Percy Faith
'Ode To Linda' – Montevideo
'*Se A Cabo*' – James Last
'Arabian Melody' – Pop Concerto Orchestra
'Kung Fu's Back Again' – Roberta Kelly
'Guilty' – First Choice
'Burning Spear' – Joe Pass
'*La Fine Di Cobb*' – Stelvio Cipriani
'Corazon' – Ltg Exchange
'Theme From *Bullitt* ' – Lalo Schifrin
'Shaft' – Joe Bataan
'Jesus Christ Superstar' – Armando Sciascia
'Make Me Believe In You' – Patti Jo
'Africa' – Mat 3
'Moulinex' – Gerd Wilden
'Piacere Sequence' – Teo Usuelli
'OK Chicago' – Resonance
'Violet Lips' – Barigozzi Group
'*Nues Dans L'eau*' – Georges Garvarentz
'The Girls From Maracaribo' – Berry Lipman
'Coco' – The Sweet

1975

'One Man Ain't Enough' – Paul Jabara
'Shaft And Karate' – Karateka
'Shake Me, Wake Me (When It's Over)' – Barbra Streisand
'Papaya' – Ursula Dudziak
'Lady Lady Lady' – The Boogie Man Orchestra
'As Long As You Know Who You Are' – Dooley Silverspoon
'Chinese Kung-Fu' – Banzaii
'Sunny' – Bobby Hebb
'Honey Trippin'' – The Mystic Moods
'Porto Rico' – Tropical Band
'Bandolero' – Juan Carlos Calderon
'Band Of Gold' – Armada Orchestra
'Tornado' – The Original Cast Of The Wiz
'*Foi A Madame*' – Maracana
'Sea Lion' – Grover Washington Jr
'Lover's Concerto' (Instrumental) – Jo Bisso
'Extra! Extra! (Read All About It!)' – Ralph Carter
'Crystal World' – Crystal Grass
'That Old Black Magic' – Softones
'Overture' – The Miracles
'Foot Stomping Music' – Gil Ventura
'Viva America' – Banzaii featuring Les Glodettes
'I Just Can't Give You Up' – Floyd Smith And The Salsoul
    Orchestra
'Escape From Tomorrow' – Lalo Schifrin

1976

'Volo Az 505 (*Les Oiseaux De Thailande*)' – Albatros
'American Symphony' – Steve Nichols
'*La Bagarre*' – Amanda Lear
'Cumba-Cumba' – Monstars
'Disco Lucy (I Love Lucy Theme)' – Wilton Place Street Band
'*Le Chat*' – Weyman Corporation
'Feel Africa' – Box-O-Lettes

'Street Talk' – B.C.G (Bob Crewe Generation)
'The Caves' – Family Tree
'Land Of Make Believe' – Champs Boys
'I Got Your Love' – Stratavarious
'New York City' – Miroslav Vitous
'Peter Gunn' – Deodato
'Strangers In The Night' – Bette Midler
'. . . Like Her!' – Gentlemen And Their Lady
'*Volare*' – Al Martino
'You've Got The Power' – Stu Kramer
'Touch And Go' – Ecstasy, Passion & Pain
'Whachersign' – Pratt & McClain
'Emanuelle In America Theme' – Nico Fidenco
'Taj Mahal' – Jorge Ben
'Brothers Theme' – Brothers
'*La Vita*' – Fussy Cussy
'Going Up In Smoke' – Eddie Kendricks
'Inside America' – Juggy Jones

'Harem' – Les Allumettes
'You Don't Have To Go' – The Chi-Lites
'Troublemaker' – Roberta Kelly
'Theme' – Webster Lewis
'Turn On To Love' – Jumbo '76
'Keep On Rolling (Disco Train)' – Ujima
'I Wanna See You Dance' – Jerry Rix
'Pretty Maid' – Pretty Maid Company
'Moving Like A Superstar'– Jackie Robinson
'Calypso Breakdown' – Ralph McDonald
'Love In Motion' – George McCrae
'Lunaris' – Daniel Sentacruz Ensemble
'Salsa' – Louie Ramirez
'Fantasy Girl' – Steven Schlaks
'*El Velero*' – Lucio Battisti
'I'm Gonna Let My Heart Do The Walking' – The Supremes
'Auringonmaa'– Anneli Pasanen

'Joe Cuba's Latin Hustle' – Joe Cuba
'Summertime' – MFSB
'Un Largo Weekend' – Saldisco Band
'You + Me = Love' – Undisputed Truth
'Blue Circuit' – Jacky Giordano
'Zone' – Rhythm Makers
'Bandolero' – Viva
'Dragging My Heels' – Hollies
'Love Bite' – Richard Hewson Orchestra
'Spaced Out' – Atmosfere

1977
'Hail To The Teeth' – District Of Columbia
'Love In The American Express' – Hollywood Brown
'I Got You, You Got Me' – Theo Vaness
'Back To America' – Paradise Birds
'Burning Love' – D.D. Sound
'Come Maddalena' – Ennio Morricone
'This Will Be A Night To Remember' – Eddie Holman
'Moebius' – Zanov
'Disco Panther' – Cassandra
'We Got Our Own Thing' – C.J. & Co.
'It's Ecstasy When You Lay Down Next To Me' – Barry White
'Stick Together' – Minnie Riperton
'There's Fire Down Below' – Fantastic Four
'Funky Flamenco' – Soul Iberica Band
'Rhapsody In Blue' – Walter Murphy
'Bee Sting' – Camouflage
'Charlie's Angels' – Donna Lynton
'Watch Out For The Boogie Man' – Trax
'Disco Spaceship' – Laurie Marshall
'Laso Square' – Laso
'Do You Speak French?' – Nite School
'Erotic Soul' – The Larry Page Orchestra
'Lalabye' – D-R-U-M

311

'Benihana' – Marilyn Chambers
'Magic Love' – Michele
'Sweet Beginnings' – Marlena Shaw
'Dream Express' – Dream Express
'Donna' – Andre Gagnon
'I Don't Love You Anymore' – Teddy Pendergrass
'Stone To The Bone' – Timmy Thomas
'Down By The Docks' – Sailor
'5 O'Clock In The Morning' – La Guapa
'Answer Me My Love'/'Chase!' – MBT Soul
'Don't Turn Away' – Midnite Flite
'24 Hours A Day' – Barbara Pennington
'Love Magnet' – Freda Payne
'Macumba' – Marboo
'Theme For A Dream' – Dino Solera and Giorgio Moroder
'Hopscotch' – Eli's Second Coming
'Easy Come Easy Go' – Odyssey
'Mefisto' – Diabolic Soul Invention

'Let Yourself Go' – The Supremes
'Voltaire Pier' – Chocolat's
'Sun . . . Sun . . . Sun' – Ja Kki

1978
'*Si Si – No No*' – Nino Velasquez
'Loco-Motive' – Passport
'Elle Et Moi' – Max Berlins
'Oriental Tango' – Magic Carpet
'Love Concert' – Cocktail Naif
'Workin' & Slavin'' – Midnight Rhythm
'Spanish Fever' – Fania All-Stars
'The Evidence' – Evidence
'Spanish Harlem' – Jorge Dalto
'Stubborn Kinda Fella (Remix)' – Buffalo Smoke
'Sinner Man' – Sarah Dash
'Perfect Love Affair' – Constellation Orchestra

'The Robots' – Kraftwerk
'Nobody But You' – Theo Vaness
'Super Queen' – Cellophane
'Plug Me To Death' – Erotic Drum Band
'Fais-Moi Danser' – Jane Manson
'Ite Missa Est' – Martin Circus
'My Baby's Baby' – Liquid Gold
'Romantic Lover'/'Paradis Samba' – Pierre Bachelet
'Passion Flower' – Cannonball
'Baby You Ain't Nothing Without Me' – Karen Young
'Groove Time' – Motown Sounds
'Moon-Boots' – Orlando Riva Sound
'Dance To Dance' – Gino Soccio
'Ain't Nothing Gonna Keep Me From You' – Teri De Sario
'The More I Get The More I Want' – Lorraine Johnson
'The Girl From Ipanema'/'All I've Got' – Astrud Gilberto
'Shoot Me' – Tasha Thomas
'Café'/'She's Not A Disco Lady' – D.D. Sound
'Fantasia'/'Carnival' – Fantasia featuring Peggy Santiglia
'I Just Keep Thinking About You Baby' – Tata Vega
'Weekend' – Phreek
'Love Theme From *Love Boat* ' – Key-Hano
'Dance The Night Away' (Spanish Version) – Viva
'Jungle DJ' – Kikrokos
'Don't You Want My Love' – Debbie Jacobs
'Rio De Janeiro' – Gary Criss
'Classical Love' – Flower
'Pow Wow' – Cory Daye
'Don't Turn Around' – The Raes
'Mary Hartman Mary Hartman' – Sounds Of Inner City
'Dancing In My Feet' – Laura Taylor
'Copacabana' – Shirley Bassey
'Copacabana' – Line Renaud
'En El Copa' – Barry Manilow
'La Nuit Blanche' – Munich Machine

'Lonely In Time' – Edna Bejarano
'Theme From Roots' – Chocolat's
'Lady In Black' – Hans Edler
'A Symphony Of Love' – Miquel Brown
'The Beat Goes On And On' – Ripple
'Play Me' – Jo Bisso
'*Nessun Dolore*' – Lucio Battisti
'Love Dance' – Playmate
'I Got My Mind Made Up' – Instant Funk
'My Claim To Fame' – James Wells
'Takes Me Higher' – Canymed
'Pick Me Up, I'll Dance' – Melba Moore
'Mellow Lovin'' – Judy Cheeks
'Disco Magic Concorde' – Michel Legrand
'Strip Tease' – Cerrone

1979
'*Puente De Colores*' – Pedro Marín

'Freak Le Boom-Boom' – Gretchen
'USA Disco People' – New Paradise
'Problemorama' – Dalida
'Sing Sing Sing' – Charlie Calello Orchestra
'Disco Choo Choo' – Nightlife Unlimited
'Don't Fall In Love' – Alma Faye
'Could It Be Magic' – Dante's Inferno
'Boogie In The Bush' – Max Berlins
'Super Sweet' – Wardell Piper
'Love Suite' – Romance
'New York's On Fire' – Seventh Avenue
'New York' – Nuggets
'Dance Do Dia' – Banda Black Rio
'Queen Of Fools' – Jessica Williams
'The Beat Of The Night' – Fever
'Lovin' Tears Suite' – French Kiss
'I'm OK, You're OK' – American Gypsy

'Tonight' – Gloria Gaynor
'Savage Lover' – The Ring
'Hold Your Horses' – First Choice
'I Close My Eyes And Count To Ten' – The Simon Orchestra
'Amityville Frenzy' – Lalo Schifrin
'This Is Hot' – Pamala Stanley
'*Vamos A Bailar*' – John Ozila
'Dance Fantasy' – Free Life
'Ain't No Stoppin' Us Now' – McFadden & Whitehead
'No-One Gets The Prize' – Diana Ross
'*La Bamba*' – Antonia Rodriguez
'Hideki Disco Special' – Hideki
'Love Insurance' – Front Page
'Midnight Dream' – Dream Express
'Phantasm' – Captain Zorro / Biddu
'Crazy Chat' – Rosa Fumetto
'An Evening In Paris (Decadancing)' – Clabbe
'(Everybody) Get Dancin'' – The Bombers
'Sentimentally It's You' – Theo Vaness
'Honeymoon In Puerto Rico' – Paul Jabara
'Walk The Night' – Skatt Bros
'Can't Live Without Your Love' – Tamiko Jones
'Jingo' – Candido
'Love Me Tonight' – D.D. Sound

1980 AND AFTER
'*Maracaibo*' – Luisa Colombo
'Take Off'/'Road To Mandalay' – Harlow
'He's Speedy Like Gonzalez' – Passengers
'Earth Can Be Just Like Heaven' – Two Tons O' Fun
'In The Forest' – Baby O
'Brazilian Dancer' – Kasso
'Don't Stop The Train' – Phyllis Nelson
'*El Bandido*' – Goombay Dance Band
'Dance It's My Life' – Midnight Powers

'*Magnifique*' – Magnifique
'Unexpected Lovers' – Lime
'A Night In New York' – Elbow Bones And The Racketeers
'A Child Is Born' – Black Russian
'*C'est Magnifique*' – Santa Esmeralda
'Follow The Brightest Star' – Voyage
'Cycles Woman'/'Trippin' On The Moon' – Cerrone
'Dance Madame' – Madame
'Hot Wax' – Mother F
'Maybe This Time' – Norma Lewis
'Self Control' – Laura Branigan
'Puerto Rico' – Decoupage
'A Cha Cha At The Opera' – Cha Cha At The Opera
'Assassino' – Amanda Lear
'Marcia Baila' – Les Rita Mitsouko
'*Ocho Rios*' – Paul Jabara
'Jacky' – Marc Almond
'So Cold The Night' – Communards

'Paris Paris' – Catherine Deneuve & Malcolm McLaren
'*La Passione*' – Shirley Bassey
'Plans & Designs' – Faze Action
'The Hip Sheik' – The Karminsky Experience
'K-Jee' – Satoshi Tomiie presents Shellshock
'New York City Boy' – Pet Shop Boys
'Your Disco Needs You' – Kylie Minogue
'Paiste' – G-Litter
'Alcastar' – Alcazar
'Until The End Of Time' – Joey Negro presents
    The Sunburst Band

From Here to Eternity

THE AUTHORS' TOP 20 DISCO FAVOURITES

ALAN JONES
1. *Evita* /Festival
2. 'How Much, How Much I Love You'/Love and Kisses
3. 'Follow Me'/Amanda Lear
4. *From Here To Eternity*/Giorgio Moroder
5. 'Star Wars'/Meco
6. *Make That Feeling Come Again!*/Beautiful Bend
7. 'Doctor's Orders'/Carol Douglas
8. 'Another Cha Cha/Cha Cha Suite'/Santa Esmeralda
9. 'Love Story (Where Do I Begin?)'/Andy Williams
10. 'Love Love Love/Still Not Over/On and On/Using You Medley'/The Michael Zager Band
11. *'Ritmo Do Brazil'*/Ultimate
12. 'Soul/Heaven Above Me'/Frankie Valli
13. 'Lady Night'/Patrick Juvet
14. 'Forbidden Love Suite'/Madleen Kane
15. *Pinocchio*/Masquerade
16. 'Turn The Beat Around'/Vicki Sue Robinson
17. 'Dance A Little Bit Closer'/Charo and the Salsoul Orchestra
18. 'This Time Baby'/Jackie Moore
19. 'Suite Seventeen'/Marlena Shaw
20. *Companion*/Boris Midney

JUSSI KANTONEN

1. 'Come Into My Heart/Good Loving'/USA-European Connection
2. 'Love In C Minor'/Cerrone
3. 'Follow Me' (Wally McDonald mix)/Amanda Lear
4. 'Quiet Village'/The Ritchie Family
5. 'To Be With You'/Jimmy Sabater
6. 'O Ba Ba'/D.C. LaRue
7. 'Don't Leave Me This Way' (Tom Moulton. Mix)/Harold Melvin and the Blue Notes
8. *Cosmic Wind*/The Mike Theodore orchestra
9. 'Begin the Beguine'/Johnny Mathis
10. 'Peanut Vendor/Frenesi/Brazil Medley'/The Ritchie Family
11. *Make That Feeling Come Again!*/Beautiful Bend
12. 'Manhattan Love Song'/King Errisson
13. 'Down To Love Town'/The Originals
14. 'My Sweet Summer Suite'/The Love Unlimited Orchestra
15. 'Salsoul Rainbow'/The Salsoul Orchestra
16. 'Gigi In Paradisco' (13-minute version)/Dalida
17. 'Breathless'/Trax
18. 'Good Times'/Chic
19. *Romeo And Juliet*/Alec R. Costandinos and the Syncophonic Orchestra
20. 'Pretty Maid'/Pretty Maid Company

PUTTIN' ON THE HITS: THE TOP 20 DISCO SONGS THAT STILL PACK THE DANCE FLOORS

1. 'I Will Survive'/Gloria Gaynor
2. 'YMCA/Village People
3. 'Stayin' Alive'/The Bee Gees
4. 'That's The Way I Like It'/KC and The Sunshine Band
5. 'Le Freak/Chic
6. 'The Hustle'/Van McCoy
7. 'Don't Leave Me This Way'/Thelma Houston
8. 'I Feel Love'/Donna Summer

9. 'You Make Me Feel (Mighty Real)'/Sylvester
10. 'We Are Family'/Sister Sledge
11. 'Got To Be Real'/Cheryl Lynn
12. 'Born To Be Alive'/Patrick Hernandez
13. 'Disco Inferno'/The Trammps
14. 'Boogie Wonderland'/Earth Wind and Fire
15. 'Funkytown'/Lipps, Inc.
16. 'Turn The Beat Around'/Vicki Sue Robinson
17. 'Best Of My Love'/The Emotions
18. 'Don't Stop `Til You Get Enough'/Michael Jackson
19. 'Boogie Oogie Oogie'/A Taste of Honey
20. 'I Love the Nightlife (Disco Round)'/Alicia Bridges